HUMANOLOGY

HUMANOLOGY

—

A SCIENTIST'S GUIDE TO
OUR AMAZING EXISTENCE

—

PROFESSOR
LUKE O'NEILL

GILL BOOKS
Hume Avenue
Park West
Dublin 12
www.gillbooks.ie
Gill Books is an imprint of M.H. Gill and Co.
© Luke O'Neill 2018
978 07171 8015 8
Designed by www.grahamthew.com
Edited by Neil Burkey
Proofread by Jane Rogers
Illustrations by Sally Caulwell

For permission to reproduce photographs, the author and publisher gratefully
acknowledge the following:

© Alamy: 10, 32, 42, 85, 99, 101, 117, 134, 137, 141, 142, 153, 187, 201, 208, 212, 215, 284; Image
courtesy of NIAID / Flickr: 196; Image courtesy of Oak Ridge National Laboratory / Flickr: 285;
Image courtesy of Allison Meier / Flickr: 316; © Getty Images: 95, 136, 207, 259, 292, 330; © iStock
/ Getty Premium: 9, 14, 24, 53, 57, 69, 89, 96, 102, 122, 131, 151, 155, 159, 173, 181, 184, 194, 231,
248, 252, 260, 265, 268, 275, 296, 299, 300, 308, 310, 324, 342; © NASA: 223, 227, 313; © U.S. NLM:
177, 219, 291; © Smithsonian Institution Archives: 63; Photograph courtesy Department of Geology,
Trinity College Dublin: 11; © Wellcome Collection: 239, 250; WikiCommons: 67, 80, 110, 114, 115,
161, 179, 199, 240, 247, 264, 278; Image courtesy of MRC Laboratory of Molecular Biology (From
the personal collection of Jenifer Glynn) / WikiCommons: 33; Image courtesy of National Library of
Wales / WikiCommons: 47; Image courtesy of Hans Bernhard / WikiCommons: 50; Image courtesy
of Harold Heaton / WikiCommons: 82; Image courtesy of Mark Coggins / WikiCommons: 109;
Image courtesy of Scewing / WikiCommons: 121; Image courtesy of Keith Schengili-Roberts (original
photo) and Liberal Freemason (reworking) / WikiCommons: 129; Image courtesy of Hyacinth
/ WikiCommons: 147; Image courtesy of Chris Collins of the Margaret Thatcher Foundation /
WikiCommons: 164; Image courtesy of Lucas Taylor /CERN / WikiCommons: 234; Image courtesy
of Einsamer Schütze / WikiCommons: 244; Image courtesy of the National Museum of Health and
Medicine/WikiCommons: 314; Image courtesy of Jost Amman / WikiCommons: 323; Image courtesy
of UK Department for International Development / WikiCommons: 327.

The author and publisher have made every effort to trace all copyright holders, but if any
have been inadvertently overlooked we would be pleased to make the necessary arrangement
at the first opportunity.

Printed by BZ Graf, Poland
This book is typeset in Walbaum MT Std, 11.5 on 16 pt.
The paper used in this book comes from the wood pulp of managed forests. For
every tree felled, at least one tree is planted, thereby renewing natural resources.
A CIP catalogue record for this book is available from the British Library.
5 4 3 2 1

ACKNOWLEDGEMENTS

Many thanks to the following people. Pat Kenny for inviting me to contribute regularly to his Newstalk show where we have great conversations on science which directly inspired these chapters – many thanks Pat. George Hook for giving me 'the start' to have the temerity to talk on science topics outside my own specialty. Sarah Liddy (Gill Books) for asking me to consider writing a book and for her encouragement, and Sheila Armstrong for excellent editing. Jess Kelly of the excellent TechTalk on Newstalk for helping me get started with the writing and asking for progress reports to keep me writing. Andy Gearing for reading the entire manuscript (it was a wet weekend in January) and allowing me to plagiarise some of his witty, mildly offensive phrases. The following people for reading various chapters to help with content and fact-checking (any errors are theirs): Andrew Bowie (fellow innate immunologist), Dan Bradley (geneticist), Annie Curtis (circadian biologist), Dave Fahy (good egghead), Caroline Collins (communications guru), Ken Mealy (surgeon), Mike Murphy (chemical mitochondriologist and all round know-all), Brian Murray (day job: neurology, main job: Metabollick), Ciaran O'Byrne (the brother ... in-law who is a 'funny guy'), Claire O'Connell (science communicator and Wings nerd (rare indeed)), Colm O'Donnell (day job: neonatology, main job: another Metabollick), Cliona O'Farrelly (immunologist), Sam O'Neill (bass guitarist who needs to go to the barbershop and get that hair cut off his head), Stevie O'Neill (surfing barman), Stephen O'Rahilly (physician scientist), Tomás Ryan (neuroscientist), Fred Sheedy (yet another immunologist) and Margaret Worrall (a real biochemist). Thank you all for being encouraging and giving up your time for free (you'll pay the full price for this book like everyone else).

As you read *Humanology* and ponder the enormity of the question of what it is to be human, remember one thing: we're all together now.

For Marg, Stevie and Sam, who are the answer ...
and I don't even know what the question is.

CONTENTS

INTRODUCTION

THE ARTS AND SCIENCES are often seen as different activities, with different kinds of people engaged in them. The arty-farty type has floppy hair, a cool, detached look, and in the good old days before science ruined it, smoked French cigarettes. The science nerd has buckteeth and glasses and is great at hard sums. They often run in different cliques and hold mutual disregard.

And yet, if we look more closely, both artists and scientists are actually at the same game. Why would someone pick up a paintbrush and daub colours onto paper? Equally, why would someone try to understand the inner workings of our brains or immune systems? Well, first off, it might be fun! But more important, these are all attempts to answer the very question that unites the arts and the sciences: What does it mean to be human?

Erwin Schrödinger was someone who spanned the divide. He won the Nobel Prize for physics in 1933 for his work on quantum mechanics, but he also wrote poetry. On a cold February night in 1943 in Dublin, as World War II raged, he gave a public lecture in Trinity College Dublin entitled 'What is Life?' – and changed the world for the better. What was he doing there and why was he asking that particular question? He was obliged to give this public lecture in his capacity as Professor in the Dublin Institute for Advanced Studies. The then Taoiseach, Éamon de Valera, had coaxed him to come to Dublin in what was effectively Ireland's first attempt since independence to engage in scientific research. Schrödinger was curious about the basis for life and what it is to be human (being all too human himself), and brought a physicist's mind to bear on the topic. When he gave his lecture, our knowledge of what life is was very limited. For example, his lectures predated the discovery of DNA as the material that genes are made of. And we humans, like all life on Earth (that we know of – scientists must always be open-minded), have DNA as the key ingredient. A recipe and ingredient in one. The book that resulted from Schrödinger's lectures was hugely influential and directly inspired many scientists to embrace the big scientific questions in life, not least Watson and Crick, the co-discoverers of the structure of DNA. This is widely felt to be the biggest scientific advance-ment of the 20th century, since it helped explain the basis of life itself – the passing of information to the next generation in the form of the double helix. This was mind-blowing when it was discovered and still mind-blowing today.

If we fast forward 75 years to today, our understanding of what life is has advanced hugely, and, given our narcissism as a species, we can also better comprehend what humans are. Schrödinger lit the touch-paper to launch a rocket that continues to soar. That understanding is a testament to the commitment of scientists, whose restless curiosity has driven all this fabulous knowledge forward.

In this book I will tell you all about these advances, starting with the origin of life (we're coming close to understanding this event that occurred at least 4.2 billion years ago); how we as a species evolved on the plains of Africa some 200,000 years ago, and how we populated the planet; how we find a mate, and how sperm and egg get it on; what makes us straight or gay; what and why we believe; what makes us interesting as a species (our love of humour and music); why we sleep and have a roughly 24-hour rhythm; our unending efforts to find new ways to stop disease; whether we will create superhumans and the huge machines we've already built; how and why we age; how we die and possibly can escape death; and our eventual extinc-tion as a species (which, cheerily enough, is inevitable). I will also discuss how the process of discovery is now being enhanced and accelerated by our own inventions – computing, robotics and artificial intelligence, which are bringing many benefits but also concerns.

My goal is to introduce you to how great science can be as a way of understanding life and what it is to be human. This pursuit is the pinnacle of evolution, involving individual and collective analysis and action by humans working for the greater good. Whether you're arty-farty, nerdy or a mixture of both, embrace your inner scientist and join me on this exciting journey into the origin of life to us and beyond, the biggest mystery of all – humanology.

CHAPTER 1

WELCOME O LIFE! HOW LIFE GOT STARTED

F OR SOME PEOPLE it began with two hippies and a talking snake. For others a giant cosmic egg – or a rainbow serpent shaking the world into life. Some of these *might* be true, and certainly many millions of people still believe in some of these so-called creation myths. But if you're scientifically inclined you are compelled to follow the motto of the world's oldest scientific society, the Royal Society in London, founded by Isaac Newton, Robert Boyle and other scientific luminaries in 1660: '*Nullius in Verba*', or 'Take Nobody's Word for it'. In other words, show me the evidence; otherwise, stop talking. At scientific gatherings, you're only truly listened to if you have the data to back up what you're saying. So what does science tell us about that most narcissistic and fundamental of questions – the selfie of all questions: How did life begin on Earth?

To try to answer that question we need everything that science has to throw at a problem – from chemistry to biology to geology and even astrophysics. But we also need modesty. It is a devilishly difficult question to answer. It's a great puzzle, and science at its best is about solving puzzles. And the truth is there's an awful lot of science still to be done about everything. We know a lot about a lot of things, but there's an awful lot still to be found out.

As to how life began, scientists still have no definitive answer to the puzzle of how inanimate matter, effectively rocks and minerals, somehow formed

a living organism. How could a lump of clay turn into a living organism? And don't mention God; that's for a different kind of book. But there has been great progress and we now have a reasonable

A RAINBOW SERPENT, PART OF THE CREATION STORY OF SOME ABORIGINAL PEOPLE OF AUSTRALIA.

understanding of how life began, and of how that life led to us.

Careful dating of rocks tells us that the Earth formed around 4.54 billion years ago[1], and the evidence for the first living creature on Earth is from 4.28 billion years ago[2]. So a vast amount of time separates us from the first cell to arise on Earth: our most important ancestor. Imagine that amount of time for a moment. Imagine how we perceive one year passing. We can grasp 10 years passing. But how about 1,000 years? A hundred thousand years? A million years? Or 4.28 thousand million years? Such time spans are well beyond our comprehension. If humans had appeared at that time (and they didn't) there would have been around 55,000 generations of us since then.

BISHOP JAMES USSHER (1581–1656), ARCHBISHOP OF ARMAGH AND PRIMATE OF ALL IRELAND. USING MAINLY THE BIBLE FOR EVIDENCE, HE ESTABLISHED THE TIME AND DATE OF CREATION AS 6 P.M. ON 22 OCTOBER 4004 BC. NOT A BAD ATTEMPT FOR THE TIME – BUT WRONG.

This gives us an indication of how long ago it was – there have been 15 generations of humans since the year 1000 AD. This is probably why we were more comfortable with the notion that the Earth is only 6,000 or so years old.

An Irish bishop, James Ussher, gets credit for the first systematic attempt to age the Earth. In 1650 he went to the library (in those far-off days people used to go to places called libraries to read books), and using the main book he found there, the Bible, figured out that creation began at 6pm on 22 October 4004 BC, and was completed by midnight[3]. Remarkably fast, and for most people scarcely enough time to eat dinner and binge watch the latest season of *Game of Thrones*. This date for the creation of the Earth was put into the King James Bible and held to be true until well into the 1800s, because someone clever had figured it out using a book which people believed contained by definition only truth. This seems ludicrous now, but in 1650 this was a good attempt, given what he had at his disposal, his systematic approach to the question at hand, and the fact that science hadn't really been invented then.

When the idea was first suggested that the Earth was more than a few thousand years old, people were understandably confused and worried. In 1899, the Irish physicist John Joly, who was a pioneer in the effort to age the Earth, calculated that it was 80–100 million years old, based on how salty the oceans are, and assuming that the salt was caused by rocks being dissolved by rain at a certain rate[4]. Again, this was a reasonable attempt, and probably caused consternation in some circles. Finally, using a method called radiometry, the formation of the Earth was dated to 4.567 billion years ago. Radiometry involves measuring the radioactive state of elements such as lead, calcium and aluminium in minerals containing uranium. These are known to decay at a particular rate, and so how much they have decayed can be used to date rocks. So although impossible for us to grasp we can state with confidence that the Earth formed 4.567 billion years ago.

We can also tell from looking at the rocks that date from then that it was a very inhospitable place, where no life could exist. The atmosphere was full of toxic chemicals like hydrogen cyanide. We have to wait hundreds of millions of years for the first agreed evidence of a living organism to appear. No life on Earth for millions of years, just a vast bubbling cauldron, with random chemicals forming and being destroyed and reacting with other chemicals. And then, somehow, all these random chemical reactions, with energy in the form of heat, coming most probably from warm vents at the bottom of the sea, lead us to the first

JOHN JOLY (1857–1933), PROFESSOR OF GEOLOGY AT TRINITY COLLEGE DUBLIN, CALCULATED THAT THE OCEANS WERE 80–100 MILLION YEARS OLD, SUBSTANTIALLY PUSHING BACK THE AGE OF THE EARTH FROM WHAT WAS THEN KNOWN, CAUSING CONSTERNATION IN SOME CIRCLES.

living creature. What has been observed is not the actual creature, however, but a series of tube-like structures that scientists believe is good evidence for living creatures. These have been observed in rocks from Quebec in Canada. It's as if the Earth was like a giant test tube full of chemicals and gases, with a Bunsen burner in the form of heat coming from the sea floor. There was also electricity sparking in the form of lightning strikes. The lightning strikes and heat in the Earth provided the energy for the water in the 'tube' to boil and simmer and allowed the chemicals to hit off each other and react.

What with all the lightning, life therefore effectively began in bad weather, and we get to the first cell. Was the first cell Canadian or Australian, however? The matter isn't fully resolved, as there is a competing claim that the oldest evidence for life on Earth is seen in rocks in Western Australia which date from the more recent 4.1 billion years ago[5]. This evidence is in the form of what one of the scientists involved (Mark Harrison) called 'the gooey remains of biotic life'[6]. This whole area of science is very much a work in progress, and typifies the scientific process – produce evidence, evaluate and come to a conclusion. Whatever the outcome, the first cell was likely to have been not American (thankfully), but Canadian (who must love that) or Australian.

Whatever it was, it changed everything. If you had gone back in time to look at it you would need a microscope. It is in fact what we now call a bacterium, a single-celled creature. Not like us at all, as we are made up of lots of different types of cells, all of them working together. When looked at down a microscope our cells are quite different from a bacterium, which is actually pretty boring-looking. But 4 billion years ago, boring was good. The bacterium thrived, sucking up nutrients and dividing to make baby bacteria. This was the start of us. The first cell ever. There should have been some great blast of trumpets, or perhaps as Shakespeare wrote when describing the birth of the Welsh wizard Glendower, 'The front of heaven was full of fiery shapes … The frame and huge foundation of the Earth shaked like a coward … the goats ran from the mountains'. No goats ran from the mountains when the first cell arose, because goats (and possibly mountains) hadn't been invented.

We define a cell as the unit of life because all living things are made of cells, but another definition is a bag with chemicals inside it that can make copies of itself. So the 'origin of life' question then becomes, How did this first cell arise? A microscopic bag had to form, and in that bag there had to be a molecule that could copy itself to make more bags. How on Earth (literally) could this first bag have arisen?

We're not completely sure of the answer to this question, but we know it must lie in the realm of chemistry and must obey the laws of physics. What happened was that chemistry and physics gave us biology. There must have been chemicals around that would react with each other to form more complex chemicals that in turn would go on to form the first cell, which is after all composed of sets of biochemicals all contained within a bag we call a cell. The formation of the actual bag itself was probably an early event, as that allowed the chemicals to become concentrated inside, which in turn would allow them to react with each other. The bag must have been made of molecules that were insoluble in water, just like the bags that make our cells today are made of fat molecules (also called lipids).

Chemical reactions need proximity – the chemicals that react have to hit off each other and form a product, and this happens when each constituent chemical reaches a certain concentration and is near another chemical. They then react with each other to form a new chemical, usually with the help of catalysts. In the case of the first cell this would have meant a chemical being able to make a copy of itself, which, as we will see, is what DNA can do. Once that happened the new chemical that formed would become sealed inside its own fatty bag and we now have two bags – the first bag having copied itself. And so, off we go, life begins, with each bag dividing to make a new bag. One definition of life therefore is 'bags of chemicals that can make new bags of highly similar chemicals'. Or perhaps 'Papa's Got a Brand New Bag'?

To answer this question in more detail we need to know a little about the chemistry of life. What are living things made of? In the early days of biology, this was a straightforward question to answer, as biologists could break open cells and tissues from living things and, using chemical analysis, find out what they were made of. It starts out quite simply. There are four main types of chemicals that make up all living things. All are equally important for life because they work together and depend on each other, but we usually start with nucleic acids. These are the information molecules of life – DNA is the chemical recipe to make a cell. It can be copied and has the information that tells cells how to make proteins.

Proteins are the second class of life molecule. They are highly sophisticated biochemicals and are the grunts of life; they extract energy from food, catalyse the chemical reactions of life and copy the information in DNA to make another cell. It's as if life began with a photocopier that could copy documents (the DNA), and then office workers come along in the form of proteins to help this process along.

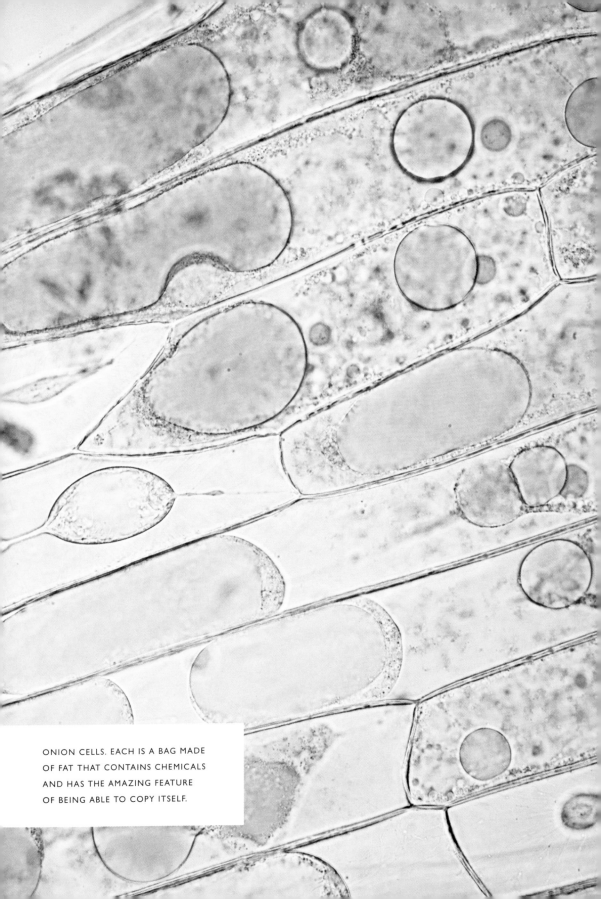

ONION CELLS. EACH IS A BAG MADE OF FAT THAT CONTAINS CHEMICALS AND HAS THE AMAZING FEATURE OF BEING ABLE TO COPY ITSELF.

The third family is called carbohydrates. Glucose is a typical carbohydrate. We burn these for energy (critical for any machine to do work), and they also go into structures like the collagen that holds our joints together. In our office analogy, the carbs are the lunch the workers eat.

Finally there are the fats – also known as lipids. These turn out to be absolutely crucial for life. They are insoluble in water, and make the membranes that form the little bags that contain everything else. Without these membranes, everything would be too dilute and nothing would happen. This is what defines the room that has the photocopier. The office workers can go there instead of wandering off in all directions – a much more efficient process. And so we get to our definition of life as being a bag full of complex chemicals that can make copies of itself. Or a room with a photocopier in it.

The photocopier for life has been running for at least 3.567 billion years, and has kept going relentlessly until it got to you and me – a very long string of DNA stretching back 3.567 billion years. The only rational purpose we can give to life therefore is the copying of DNA. Cells are the vessel in which this happens, and all of life that we see on Earth is still doing it. By this definition, then, it turns out that we humans are insignificant. We most likely contain only a tiny bit of the total DNA on Earth. And remember, all life on Earth is descended from that single Canadian (or Australian) cell that first copied its DNA. A recent study has shown that humans make up about 0.01% of all life on Earth[7]. Most of the rest is in plants with the next prominent group being bacteria, which are abundant and occur everywhere. So if that first cell that arose said to all subsequent cells of which it is the ancestor, 'Go forth and multiply', meaning 'Keep copying your DNA', we are making a tiny contribution. Even worse, we have caused the loss of 83% of wild animals and nearly half of all plants. We therefore shouldn't be so full of ourselves. This is especially the case when we consider how many other organisms we carry with us in the form of abundant bacteria in our bodies.

The first problem we run into in trying to explain how the first cell arose is that all these chemicals are very fragile. They don't like things like acid, or heat, or even oxygen. That last one will come as a surprise, as we normally think of oxygen as being essential for life. It is for us, as we use it to extract energy from food. But it's also very toxic, and cells had to come up with a way to use it. As for heat, look what happens when you boil an egg, which is mainly made of protein. Conditions to make these chemicals therefore had to be just right – not too hot, not too cold. Life had to be like the tale of Goldilocks, except we're not talking porridge here, we're talking nucleic acids, proteins, carbohydrates and fats.

A mere 3.567 billion years afterwards, humans performed the first experiment to try and recreate this Goldilocks world[8]. In the early 1950s, two scientists (Stanley Miller and Harold Urey), using the knowledge of what the early Earth might have been like, set up a piece of apparatus with a glass vessel that held water. They provided an atmosphere that contained ammonia, methane and hydrogen (which are all simple chemicals and would have been in the Earth's atmosphere at that time), and set up a storm by sending sparks through it with an electrode. They put the vessel over a flame for heat and let the vapour form and recirculate through a condenser to allow it to form water droplets and made sure the whole thing circulated. Their lab must have looked something like Dr Frankenstein's lab, all sparks and bubbling noises. They let this run for a few days and then came into the lab one morning and, to their amazement, saw a tiny creature crawl out of the vessel. Life had formed! Well, not quite – but what they did observe was almost as astonishing.

They took a sample and found in it amino acids, the building blocks that make up proteins. This said that those early chemical conditions on Earth, although seemingly unpromising, did indeed have the capacity to make organic building blocks for life. The experiment, dubbed the Miller–Urey experiment, became famous, and it was published in the same year as the more famous Watson and Crick paper on DNA being a double helix. The year 1953 can therefore be seen as something of an *Annus mirabilis* for explaining life. The Miller–Urey experiment established the principle that applying bad weather to a pond with simple gases dissolved in the water could make at least one life molecule. And it's been repeated using different combinations of chemicals and has become even more impressive.

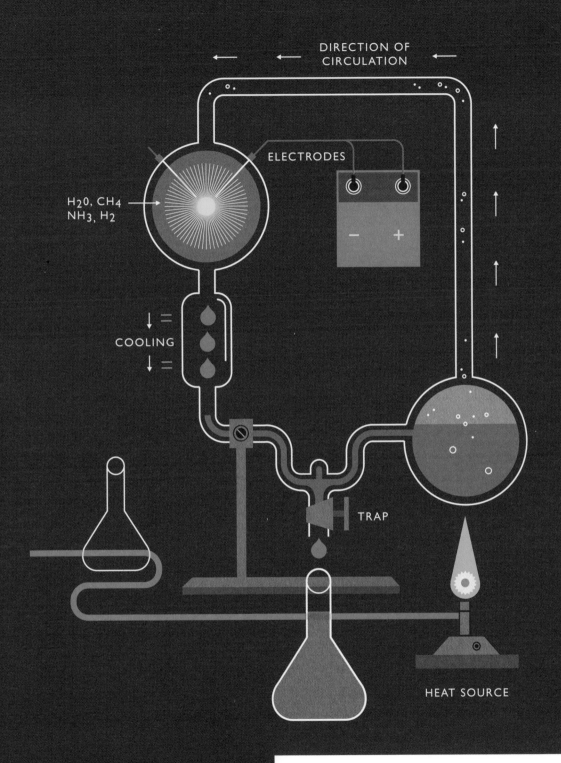

DIRECTION OF
CIRCULATION

ELECTRODES

H_2O, CH_4
NH_3, H_2

− +

COOLING

TRAP

HEAT SOURCE

THE ORIGIN OF LIFE. MILLER AND UREY RECREATED
CONDITIONS ON THE PRIMITIVE EARTH IN THE LAB.
A SIMPLE MIXTURE OF GAS AND WATER COMBINED WITH
HEAT AND ELECTRICAL DISCHARGE (BAD WEATHER) GAVE
RISE TO AMINO ACIDS, KEY BUILDING BLOCKS FOR LIFE.

Another important information molecule for life is called RNA. There is evidence that RNA might have come first, ahead of DNA, and this is because RNA holds information like DNA, but can also act like an enzyme to help everything along (think of a robotic office worker who is a photocopier). Researchers set up an experiment similar to that carried out by Miller and Urey[9], but this time all they had was hydrogen cyanide, hydrogen sulphide and UV light. That's it – two gases that were in the early atmosphere, and some sunlight, which was more than abundant. And this was enough. They saw building blocks for RNA molecules. And it got better. These conditions also led to the production of starting materials for proteins. Finally it got better again – they saw building blocks for lipids, the fats that can form the membranous bags to make a cell.

This suggests that a single set of reactions could give rise to most of life's building blocks simultaneously. So now even in good weather, and with fewer gases, a lot of life's basic units come together. Mother Earth has made the flour, sugar and eggs. Hydrogen cyanide might be especially important, as the evidence suggests that this was raining down on the Earth for millions of years. We can therefore now envisage that, over the course of millions of years, the conditions on Earth eventually give rise to the ingredients which then self-assemble into the first cell. This then copies DNA, and we now have the first offspring from that cell – thus life on Earth, which leads to us, begins.

This cell even has a name – we call it LUCA. This stands for Last Universal Common Ancestor. Sadly, given the name, LUCA isn't Italian (unless we find it in rocks in Italy and they predate the Canadian rocks). We need to put statues up to LUCA all over the world. LUCA and the cells that arise from LUCA are single – they didn't associate with other cells, and were happy to live alone. We still see that today in the form of bacteria. Sometimes, though, they form colonies, and clump together into filaments or mats, but each cell in the colony is identical and hasn't specialised.

The next big step towards us is for organisms to form that are colonies of cells but with cells showing specialisms. That is the type of organism we are: multicellular, but with cells having special roles. In your body you have cells called neurons in your brain, cells called macrophages in your blood that fight infection and cells in your liver called hepatocytes that help you detoxify alcohol. And remember, all these come from the cell made when a sperm fertilises an egg, which therefore has all the information needed to make all the cell types in your body. How did we get from single-celled life to complex multicellular life?

Well, again science has the answer. For it to happen, however, we need to be very patient. It takes another 2.5 billion years before we see complex multicellular life on Earth. Life that you don't need a microscope to see. This means it took a lot longer to arise than the time it took for the first cell to arise. The reason for this seems to be due to its being very unlikely. The chemical reactions that gave rise to LUCA are a bit like monkeys typing Shakespeare (also known as the 'infinite monkey theorem'). It is theoretically possible to put a huge numbers of monkeys in a room each with a typewriter for a certain amount of time and eventually one will type a line of Shakespeare. This appears to be the case with the random chemical reactions needed for the first cell to arise. For multicellular life to arise something very unusual happened: one bacteria went inside another and stayed there. When the host bacteria divided, it too divided. They formed a mutually beneficial alliance. The term for this is 'endosymbiosis', a symbiotic relationship that happens because one cell goes inside (hence 'endo') another[10]. This event, however, is likely to fail, because the cell that goes inside is likely to be eaten.

It turns out that a possible reason for this event was oxygen. Bacteria eventually evolved a way to capture the energy in sunlight. These became the first plants, which arose around 3 billion years ago. This in itself is a remarkable achievement. It meant that life on Earth could directly connect with the cosmos, harnessing sunlight, as opposed to depending on chemicals on Earth for energy. Plants also use the sunlight to make sugars, which can be further burned for energy. Life had come up with a way to make a battery. A way to store energy in the form of sugars which could be burnt when needed. A by-product of this process, however, is oxygen, and this is highly toxic, oxidising molecules it encounters and effectively turning Earth into a rust bucket.

However, what if you can use the oxygen to burn food and get even more energy from it? That is what happened, and one of the cells that could perform this clever piece of biochemistry climbed inside one that couldn't, forming an alliance. This new host cell had a way of creating an environment where oxygen levels are low, because the invader is utilising the oxygen to burn glucose. This provides the organism with energy. The host meanwhile provides a safe haven and nutrients. It's almost as if the photocopying room that we've used as our analogy of a cell is invaded by the generator for the whole factory, providing an abundant source of energy. This gives rise to a very successful arrangement.

We know it's successful because from then on, a huge number of species evolve that all have this arrangement. These cells are called eukaryotic cells, and we now call the cells that went inside 'mitochondria'. From this moment on, cell specialisation evolves. Different cells in the colony develop different roles, with some, say, absorbing food, and others digesting it. This division of labour makes for a very efficient creature indeed, which survives and evolves further. The office/factory analogy can again be used here. There are now different departments, each with their own photocopying room (the nucleus), which has the instructions to make a new department (which happens when a cell divides), with each department having a different function. Some are involved in packaging, others in receiving goods and so on. Evolution then continues to have its effect.

It's important to remember that evolution is a random process, driven by the fact that every time DNA is copied there are minor errors, giving you slightly different cells. The ones that are better suited to the prevailing environment survive – survival of the fittest in Darwinian terms, although the term was coined by Herbert Spencer after reading Darwin's book *On the Origin of Species*. In this way, different species begin to form, and we get the abundance of life on Earth emerging relatively quickly. In one remarkable period, only 541 million years ago, most types of animals on Earth appeared over the course

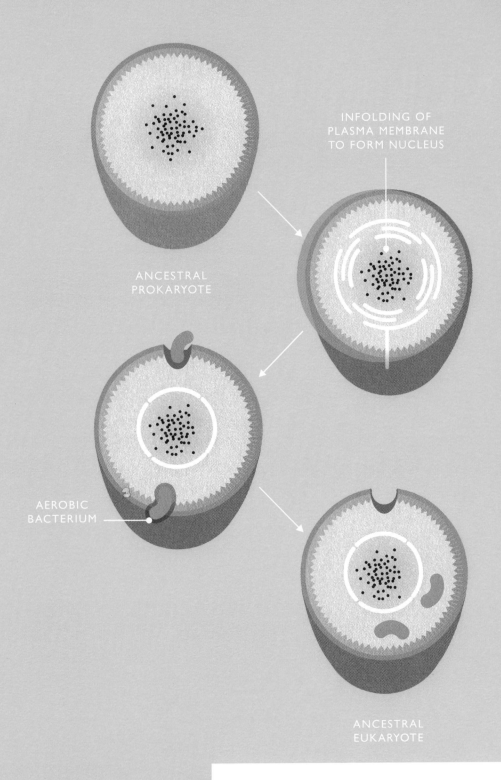

INFOLDING OF
PLASMA MEMBRANE
TO FORM NUCLEUS

ANCESTRAL
PROKARYOTE

AEROBIC
BACTERIUM

ANCESTRAL
EUKARYOTE

ENDOSYMBIOSIS: A KEY EVENT IN THE EVOLUTION OF COMPLEX
LIFE ON EARTH, WHEN ONE BACTERIUM CLIMBED INSIDE ANOTHER
MORE THAN 1.45 BILLION YEARS AGO AND STAYED THERE.

HISTORY OF LIFE ON EARTH

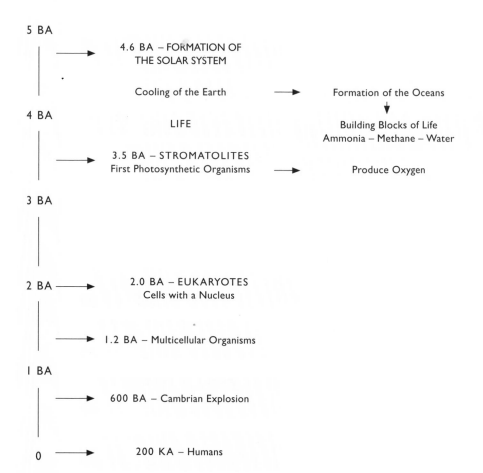

5 BA

4.6 BA – FORMATION OF
THE SOLAR SYSTEM

Cooling of the Earth ⟶ Formation of the Oceans

4 BA

LIFE   Building Blocks of Life
                        Ammonia – Methane – Water

3.5 BA – STROMATOLITES
First Photosynthetic Organisms ⟶ Produce Oxygen

3 BA

2 BA ⟶ 2.0 BA – EUKARYOTES
Cells with a Nucleus

1.2 BA – Multicellular Organisms

1 BA

600 BA – Cambrian Explosion

0 ⟶ 200 KA – Humans

BA = Billion years ago
KA = Thousand years ago

of 20–25 million years, in what is called the Cambrian explosion (after the period in which it happened).

What all of this means is that the explanation of how life went from LUCA to us involved energy. The generator climbed inside the photocopying room. It was the ability to use oxygen to burn food that allowed for lots of energy to be captured. As Nick Lane said in his book *The Vital Question*, 'it is high time energy joined DNA as the driver of evolution'[11]. In our case, efficient energy production stemming from endosymbiosis resulting from the presence of oxygen was needed for complex multicellular life to evolve, including us. All of this allows for a very pithy definition of life for us — we're here because of the copying of DNA and oxygen being used for energy. All of this was driven by the random chemical reactions on the early Earth that gave rise to the first cell, and then the bumping of a cell that could use oxygen to burn food into one that couldn't. The alliance allowed for highly efficient production and use of energy, and this new eukaryotic machine needed the energy to go on to form multicellular organisms that evolve and thrive and give rise to us.

A well-known way to illustrate this is to describe it in terms of a 24-hour day. If all this happened over the course of a single day, then we humans appear at 17 seconds to midnight. Multicellular organisms might have a high energy demand because they have to coordinate the activity of all the cells in the organism, which requires communication, which in most organisms comes in the form of neurons, which are big energy-users. It's a very far cry from two hippies and a talking snake. But the science behind this narrative is so well supported that it is almost universally accepted as the most likely answer to the question of how life arose on Earth and then got as far as us.

From all of these findings two important questions arise in the minds of scientists. First, Will we find life on other planets, or are we unique

ENCELADUS: ONE OF SATURN'S MOONS. DID ANOTHER GENESIS HAPPEN HERE?

in the universe? The former is becoming more and more likely. The amino acid glycine has been found in the cloud of gas surrounding the comet 67P/ Churyumov-Gerasimenko, along with other precursor organic molecules and phosphorus[12]. Planets are being found that are in the Goldilocks zone. At the last count there may be as many as 40 billion of these, all the right size and distance from their suns to allow for the chemistry of life to occur. Forty billion. Like monkeys and Shakespeare.

It is now almost certain that we are not alone. One recent candidate as a place where life might exist or have existed is the moon Enceladus, which orbits Saturn. In a combined NASA/European Space Agency mission, the probe Cassini went there. This spaceship left Earth in 1997 and travelled the 1.272 billion miles to Enceladus, arriving on 1 July 2004. This was a huge achievement. Enceladus is so far away that if you were to get into your car one night and drive upwards at 50 km per hour it would take 3,000 years to get there. You'd better bring a flask of coffee and some sandwiches. To get there as quickly as possible Cassini had to do four slingshots: two around Venus, one around Earth and one around Jupiter.

Astronomers had observed jets of steam breaking through the ice that covers Enceladus and wondered what was in them. Cassini found out, and, strikingly, detected free hydrogen. This is a great source of energy. The kind of energy plants make from sunlight in photosynthesis. The kind of energy mitochondria use to make the energy currency of all cells, a molecule called ATP. This caused a huge amount of excitement, as not only would the building blocks of life be possible, but free energy would also be present to drive everything forward. Free hydrogen is the missing piece to allow the sugar, flour and eggs to form together into a cake – energy. It is the heat for the oven to bake life.

Scientists are therefore more confident than ever that there may have been more than one Genesis, more than one situation where life arose. Yet again we humans are shown to be not particularly special, not the centre of the solar system or the universe, and not even special for being alive as opposed to being inanimate. We don't know whether we will find intelligent life, but scientists are confident that other living systems will be found which, who knows, might evolve into complex living systems like us, provided the conditions for endosymbiosis prevail.

The second question that arises is, What will happen next? Life will keep evolving on Earth as it has done since it started. That is, unless we destroy life on Earth, which sadly is not as unlikely as it sounds. If we wreck the Earth because of global warming or another kind of catastrophe, some life might survive and keep on evolving. For all life to be destroyed a cosmic event, like a huge asteroid or burst of gamma rays, would probably have to happen. But even then life in some nook or cranny might survive. We ourselves might evolve further if selective pressure for certain traits is evident. If, after all this struggling from the origin of life, life on Earth becomes extinct, it is likely to continue on some other planet in a galaxy far far away.

After all, life is just a bag of chemicals that can copy itself time after time, and if not on Earth then why not somewhere else?

CHAPTER 2

HOW WE GOT TO BE SO SMART AND WHY SEX WITH A CAVEMAN WAS A GOOD IDEA

S YOU SIT THERE reading this sentence you are living in a body and with a mind very similar to an ancestor that lived some 200,000 years ago. Our species, *Homo sapiens sapiens* (or 'wise wise human' — so wise they named us twice), then lived on the plains of Africa with no smartphones, no obesity, no nuclear weapons, no spaceships or large hadron colliders and no knowledge of DNA. If we took someone from that time to today, we could, with education, make them exactly like you and be well capable of all the things you can do. We could turn them into airline pilots or doctors or politicians. All that's happened since then is that we've used the cleverness that we evolved way back then in all kinds of interesting ways'.

To begin with, we used our special intelligence to anticipate drought, protect our children from dangers, work together to kill a large animal, try to deal with the death of a loved one, and figure out where we were in the pecking order with our fellow tribe members. The key scientific question is: How did we evolve from an ancestral ape akin to a chimpanzee, who couldn't do lots of the things I've listed (or at least not as well as we can) into us?

Of course if you're a scientologist you might believe that the alien Xenu brought humans to Earth 75 million years ago and put us in volcanoes to emerge later. But science tells us the ancestor of modern humans arose in

Africa at least 200,000 years ago and came to Europe 45,000 years ago, and finally to Ireland around 10,000 years ago. How did a species that would have been classified as a third species of chimp (the other two being chimpanzees themselves and the bonobo – the most closely related apes to us) some time before 200,000 years ago, go beyond their ape identity and become us? From bonobo to Bono in 200,000 years.

As ever with this kind of question we must start with DNA. Remember, DNA is the recipe to make all living things. It provides the instructions to make proteins, the grunts of every cell in your body that do all the heavy lifting, from digesting food to making your brain work to defending you from infection. This recipe is written in a chemical code that is made up of building blocks called nucleotides. These are akin to very tiny beads on a string, each nucleotide being a different bead. Somewhat mercifully, there are only four nucleotides, which go by their letter: A, T, C and G. These are strung together to make up your chromosomes – the structures that contain DNA.

Incredibly, the total number of beads strung out along the chromosomes in you is 3 billion. That's an awful lot of beads, and an awful lot of threading, and yet it's real. But it's even more wonderful, because DNA is actually made of two separate strings that wrap around each other, twisting into the iconic double helix. This arrangement makes it stable, a bit like a ladder, though twisted around its centre. When Watson and Crick first inferred that 3D shape, from a picture taken of DNA by Rosalind Franklin using something called X-ray crystallography, they couldn't believe it. Watson said they ran to their local pub (The Eagle in Cambridge) that lunchtime and exclaimed 'We've found the secret of life!' Why did they exclaim

WITH JAMES WATSON OUTSIDE THE EAGLE PUB, WHERE HE AND FRANCES CRICK ANNOUNCED THEY HAD DISCOVERED THE SECRET OF LIFE IN 1953.

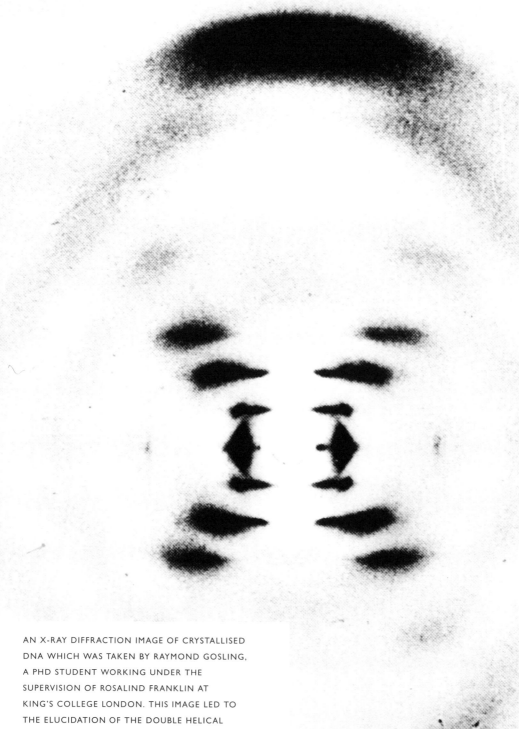

AN X-RAY DIFFRACTION IMAGE OF CRYSTALLISED
DNA WHICH WAS TAKEN BY RAYMOND GOSLING,
A PHD STUDENT WORKING UNDER THE
SUPERVISION OF ROSALIND FRANKLIN AT
KING'S COLLEGE LONDON. THIS IMAGE LED TO
THE ELUCIDATION OF THE DOUBLE HELICAL
STRUCTURE OF DNA, CREATING MODERN
MOLECULAR BIOLOGY.

that? Well, if we look at the two strings that wrap around one another we see something quite remarkable. We see that if there is an A bead on one string, it is always pairs with a T bead on the other. They click together a bit like Lego blocks. If there is a C bead on one string there is always a G bead on the other string. These are a bit like the rungs on the ladder that connect the two sides.

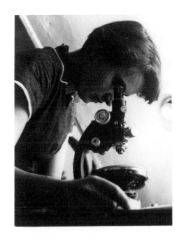

This suggested to Crick that the way we pass on information to make a new cell involves the two strings unravelling from each other and then a new string being made one bead at a time, each bead clicking into place by bonding with its corresponding bead on the single string. This process is termed DNA replication. Two strands link together into a

ROSALIND FRANKLIN, INSTRUMENTAL IN DISCOVERING THE MOLECULAR STRUCTURE OF DNA.

double helix, then separate when a cell divides. Each separate strand then gets copied – A bringing in T and C bringing in G – to form a new double helix. In a moment they had found the secret of life – how information is passed on to the next generation. The rule of A clicking into T and G clicking into C applies in all forms of life on Earth, and initially arose in the first cell, from which all other cells are descended.

Now once you have the sequence of the beads on the string – the DNA sequence that tells us the order of the A, T, C and G – you have the recipe

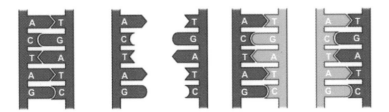

DNA REPLICATION: TWO STRANDS LINK TOGETHER INTO A DOUBLE HELIX, THEN SEPARATE WHEN A CELL DIVIDES. EACH SEPARATE STRAND THEN GETS COPIED – A BRINGING IN T AND C BRINGING IN G – TO FORM A NEW DOUBLE HELIX.

for life. The sequence instructs the cell to make proteins in a very complex process called translation. Runs of nucleotides make specific proteins – we call these runs genes. The proteins then make you the living creature that you are. The proteins might give you horns on your head or determine whether you're hairy or make you tall or short.

We can therefore compare different species for how similar they are to each other in terms of their DNA sequence. An Irish molecular biologist called Des Higgins and colleagues came up with a computer program to do just that: to align DNA sequences and compare how similar they are[2]. His publication on this is the world's most cited paper in computer science, which means it has been referred to by more scientists than any other publication in that field – no mean feat. It turns out that half of the beads on the string from a banana are in roughly the same sequence as half of the beads on the string from a human. We share half our recipe with bananas. Sadly some of my friends are probably slightly more banana than human. This makes overall sense as bananas have many of the same features we do: they have cells broadly made of the same things, and use similar enzymes to do lots of 'housekeeping', like taking out the trash or extracting energy from food.

When we compare ourselves to chimpanzees and bonobos, we are around 95 per cent identical in our DNA recipe, confirming our close shared ancestry[3]. We had a common ancestor some 2 million years ago, a creature that looked a lot like a chimpanzee. It had offspring and one of those became our ancestor and another became the ancestor of chimps or bonobos[4]. Gradually over time, a 5 per cent difference in the DNA sequence became apparent. The trouble is we don't know what is in that 5 per cent that makes us smartphone-using creatures and the chimp not. It might be a recipe for

```
HUMAN:   G   C   C   G   A   T   A   G   C   C
         |   |   |   |   |   |   |   |   |   |
CHIMP:   G   C   C   G   A   G   A   A   C   C
```

a special brain protein that makes our neurons work better. It might be a recipe to make our vocal cords better at speaking and for a wiring protein in the brain that allows us to process sounds better. We just don't know.

An interesting experiment (which could actually be done today because of a gene-editing technique called CRISPR) would be to replace the 5 per cent of DNA in a chimp with the 5 per cent of our DNA and see what happens. Would we make a human? Probably not, as what is also important is the amount of ingredients specified by the recipe (which is also built into the DNA sequence), not just the name of the ingredients, and that is also different between chimps and humans. If you make two cakes from the same recipe but put in different amounts of flour, you will end up with two cakes but they will be slightly different, a bit like how we are broadly like chimps but with clear differences. But still, it might give interesting insights. That 5 per cent difference is certainly a part of what makes us human.

It's easier to describe the actual differences between us and chimps. This is the work of anthropologists, who have studied other apes and compared their behaviour and abilities to ours. What is thought to have happened is that a trait called inventiveness arose in us humans, or at least we became much more inventive than chimps. We began to use tools in all kinds of interesting ways. We also used this inventiveness and capacity for observing and learning to make fire, which gave us a huge advantage, as we could use it to cook food. Cooking means partial digestion, which means more efficient extraction of energy from the food. It was also a way to preserve food (e.g. by smoking it), which would have been useful in times of food scarcity. A human who could do these things was more likely to survive and pass on that trait to his or her offspring, and that trait would then begin to dominate[5].

We also learnt to make elaborate tools for cutting or killing animals or defending ourselves. At some point we began to walk upright, and again that gave us an advantage, as it freed our hands to do other things, such as hunt efficiently, and allowed us to observe our environment more effectively[6]. We also became very social. Again this provided advantages (as it does in other organisms), but in our case it meant we had to figure out where we stood in the pecking order. We became status obsessed, because to get this wrong could be lethal. If you think you're the alpha male or female and you're not, the true alpha might kill you or harm you or exclude you. Equally, you had to lord it over a lesser mortal to get more resources. And so status anxiety became a feature which afflicts us to this very day, and explains much of our behaviour, from the type of car we drive to where we live and to the clothes we wear.

All of this happened on the savannahs of Africa. We then begin to move around, most likely in search of food or other resources. We evolve a hungry heart and a curiosity which drives us to move on in search of adventure. This trait of curiosity is why we eventually become so successful and dominant as a species on Earth. It's why we become scientists. And our inventiveness allows us to use what science discovers to make things that are useful to us, be it to provide power beyond muscle power to make machines to help us, or to find new medicines to treat diseases that ail us. The curiosity probably evolved to make sure we would move to a new place if resources became scarce, or perhaps to help us find a mate and pass on our DNA. Or it could be a consequence of our ability to anticipate what might happen next and to be curious about that, which would give a clear survival advantage.

Other animals display these traits too, but not to the same extent. Other animals will use tools elaborately, but nowhere near as elaborately as us. Chimpanzees, for example, will strip a twig of its leaves and use it as a tool to catch insects. They also use twigs to fish honey from beehives or to extract marrow from the bones of animals they have caught. Or they use bunches of leaves to soak up water for drinking. Gorillas use walking sticks to help them cross deep rivers. So we're not alone in using tools – it's just that we have taken their use to a much higher level, giving us a killer advantage over other species.

We're so clever that we eventually learn to paint pictures on cave walls. This may have first been a way to pass information on to others ('hunt these animals') but it was also the beginning of art, which is a way to express ourselves and give us satisfaction. Our smartness might have had artistic ability as a by-product. We paint the animals we hunt. We must see them and then notice that we can put marks on a wall that resemble them and perhaps that makes us feel we can control them. Or perhaps it just made us smile, our smart brains enjoying the pleasure of it.

We certainly begin to wonder about death. We see our children die, or friends die in a fight, or our old relative dies and we don't like it because we are so attached to them. Other animals grieve when a loved one dies. A male gorilla will wail beside the dead body of his mate. Dolphins will make keening noises after losing a baby dolphin. But we go one step further. We carefully look after our dead, probably for reasons of hygiene, but also because death disturbs us, and we try to control it somehow. Again, this might be a by-product of us being smart.

So the two traits that emerge that begin to define us — artistic activities and ritualistic burial of our dead — become evident. No other animal is as artistic as us, spending as much time as we do in creating or appreciating art. And no other animal goes to the trouble that we do to look after our dead loved ones, burying them with such ritual, marking where we bury them and visiting where their remains lie.

We take these traits with us as we move around the world. This begins around 90,000 years ago. We begin to get restless and we start to move out of Africa[7]. The evidence of this is very compelling, based on the dating of fossils from human bones. Maybe it happened because of overcrowding. Maybe it happened because of an accident — a tribe wandered over into the Middle East and couldn't get back. Evidence suggests that only a small number of our ancestors made this journey, and that all Europeans, Asians and Americans are descended from this intrepid group. And when we leave Africa, two interesting things happen. We move into a part of the world where plants are easy to grow: the so-called Fertile Crescent in the Middle East. We notice this initially perhaps when we drop seeds from a plant and see that the same plant grows there. And so we discover agriculture.

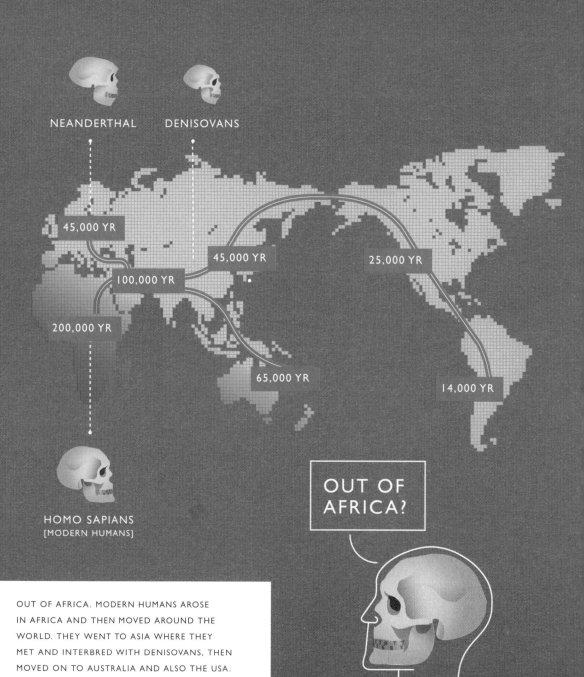

NEANDERTHAL   DENISOVANS

45,000 YR

45,000 YR

25,000 YR

100,000 YR

200,000 YR

65,000 YR

14,000 YR

HOMO SAPIANS
[MODERN HUMANS]

OUT OF
AFRICA?

OUT OF AFRICA. MODERN HUMANS AROSE
IN AFRICA AND THEN MOVED AROUND THE
WORLD. THEY WENT TO ASIA WHERE THEY
MET AND INTERBRED WITH DENISOVANS, THEN
MOVED ON TO AUSTRALIA AND ALSO THE USA.
THEY MOVED INTO EUROPE, WHERE THEY MET
AND INTERBRED WITH NEANDERTHALS.

Some scientists see this as a big mistake, as the invention of agriculture may have given rise to misery[8]. Misery in the form of a job that is hard physical work. Misery in the form having to get up early the next morning to work in the field for 'The Man'. We suddenly (about 10,000 years ago) go from being hunter-gatherers to being farmers. This also means having to live in bigger communities. We build the first towns and villages. And we get sick from infectious diseases, as bacteria and viruses spread more readily between our tired bodies and perhaps jump into us from the animals we have domesticated. They live happily in these animals and don't make them sick, but in us they wreak havoc.

Society also becomes more unequal. A more pronounced hierarchy is established – the haves (who might be slightly smarter such that they own the land or control the seeds) and the have-nots (who must work for them). An unequal society begins to emerge which we continue to endure to this very day. It may well be that when we start to cultivate crops and breed animals, instead of this being the Garden of Eden, we actually create a living hell for the masses. This is difficult to say for sure, as we don't have enough information on what life was actually like for humans before agriculture. For most of human history, however, a tiny minority have had a great life controlling and abusing the mass of humanity. Socialism changed this to some extent, but we still live in a very unequal world.

Today's equivalent is perhaps the masses working for Google or Facebook. The founders of these companies are ultra-rich, while all the workers earn a tiny multiple of their wealth. They won't revolt as long as they have what the Romans called bread and circuses (takeaway food and Netflix?), but we can't help but wonder that the reason for the opioid crisis in the USA, or why people binge drink at the weekend is because we should really be living free on the savannahs of Africa. Hard to know, because there are many reasons why people use drugs or alcohol, which include to ease anxiety, alleviate boredom or relieve stress. But perhaps if we were freer in our lives, living in an environment for which our evolution optimised us (as may have been the case before agriculture), we would need less chemical support.

The move out of Africa also leads to an encounter with a distant cousin: Neanderthals, in Europe some 40,000 years ago. They are another species of *Homo*, with whom we shared an ancestor about 600,000 years ago. Some of the descendants of that ancestor became us – the clever cousin who got 630 points in his Leaving Cert (or whatever the equivalent might have been all those years ago). The Neanderthals didn't do quite so well in terms of brain power (although recent work is challenging this notion), but they nonetheless thrived. At one point, scientists think there were as many as a million of them living in Europe. And then they encounter us, and within about 5,000 years they die out[9]. We probably wipe them out because we outsmart them, pushing them to the margins of Europe where they can't survive. Or maybe we gave them a nasty germ which they couldn't fight. Or we might simply have swamped them rather than slaughtered them, as our population grew.

A debate has raged for some time over whether we had sex with them. This seemed unlikely – it would almost be like having sex with a chimpanzee. But then the DNA evidence told us that we did[10]. Some of the genes we carry actually came from Neanderthals. There may have been numerous sexual encounters over time. Recent evidence also suggests that there might have been sex even earlier, with small amounts of *Homo sapiens* DNA being found in Neanderthal DNA. Whatever happened, we are all descended from the offspring of our matings with Neanderthals – the classic knuckle-dragging cavemen of movies, with their thick foreheads, and with limited evidence that they were in any way artistic like us or that they buried their dead. Evidence for these things may well still be uncovered, however, so we can't be certain. What we can be certain about is that humans and Neanderthals were very close neighbours indeed. We now know that around 1.8 per cent of our DNA came from Neanderthals. Some of my friends may have slightly more …

One of the genes (called *BCN2*) is a recipe for pale skin pigmentation. This means that Europeans owe their pale skin partly to Neanderthals (we were dark-skinned when we came out of Africa). The pale skin is likely to have given us an advantage in the northern hemisphere, where the sun is weaker. Our skin makes Vitamin D in response to sunlight, which is important for the health of our bones, among other things, and pale skin allows for maximum penetration of sunlight. So Neanderthal DNA might have helped us adapt to life outside Africa.

Not all of the Neanderthal DNA is beneficial, though. Some of it makes us more susceptible to certain diseases, such as type 2 diabetes and Crohn's disease, an inflammatory disease of the digestive system. Our lifestyle may have been different from that of the Neanderthals (for example our diet), and this, combined with these Neanderthal genes, might put us at more of a risk of these diseases, although we don't know.

Another interesting gene we got from Neanderthals makes us more likely to be addicted to nicotine. A gene associated with the inability to stop smoking from Neanderthals is a surprise. The scientists who found this are not of course suggesting that our evolutionary cousins were puffing away in their caves. This gene must have some other function, perhaps involving a craving for a foodstuff key to survival. Genes for keratin filaments – a fibrous protein that lends toughness to skin, hair and nails, also came from Neanderthals. This may have provided us with thicker insulation against the cold.

One gene that we have that they didn't is called *FOXP2*. This is a very interesting gene, as scientists think it provides us with the ability to make elaborate vocal sounds, making us much more linguistically versatile. When this gene was put into a mouse, the mouse could make all kinds of guttural noises that it was unable to make without it. Effectively the scientists had made a mouse that roared, although its brain was no different, so it couldn't understand what it was saying. This must have given rise to a very puzzled mouse, making noises it couldn't understand. As Neanderthals lacked this gene, their vocal repertoire was likely to be more limited. No wonder we often depict them as the strong, silent type.

Finally, we also got from Neanderthals genes that boosted our immune systems. Neanderthals probably evolved these genes to survive the harsher conditions in Europe, where injury may have been more common (possibly

COLUMBUS ENCOUNTERS
NATIVE AMERICANS, A
FAMILY REUNITED AFTER
40,000 YEARS.

because of violence between Neanderthals, although we don't know) and therefore infection more likely. Neanderthals with stronger immune systems survived, and passed those genes on to us.

We have, then, a picture of a post-coital hairy guy smoking a cigarette, who is an excellent conversationalist and whose immune system can fight off any germs he may have picked up during sex. That, my friends, is our ancestor. No wonder he outbred his more crude Neanderthal cousins.

If we move outside Europe to Asia, we find evidence that there was interbreeding with another *Homo* species, called Denisovans. These were closely related to Neanderthals (and us). Evidence suggests that Denisovans interbred with *Homo sapiens* too, and passed on genes which can be seen in Melanesians (who live in Papua New Guinea) and indigenous Australians[11]. The latter deserve a special mention, as they reached Australia around 65,000 years ago, long before their brothers and sisters went into Europe. They are like the family member who goes travelling, leaving the family behind, and the descendants of the family finally leave home after another 5,000 years and go to Europe. Then, many thousands of years later, in 1770, the long-lost descendants of this family are finally reunited when Captain Cook lands in Australia. This family reunion, however, doesn't go so well for the Aborigine cousins, who should have hidden behind the sofa when the relatives came knocking on the door. They are still paying the price of this reunion.

Our current view of these three branches of *Homo* are therefore that they are all descended from a species that lived between 300,000 and 400,000 years ago in Africa. One branch move into the Middle East and then split, with some of their descendants becoming Neanderthals who move into Europe and another branch becoming Denisovans who move into Asia. By 130,000 years ago, those who stayed in Africa eventually evolve into us – *Homo sapiens*. Some 75,000 years ago we ourselves move and go to Europe and Australasia, but we interbreed with our long-lost cousins the Neanderthals in Europe, and the Denisovans in Asia. The Asian branch around 20,000 years ago move on to the Americas and their descendants are the Native Americans.

Finally, in 1492, there is another reunion – this time of the European branch of the family with their cousins who had travelled through Asia to the Americas[12]. This is a family that had been separated for at least 40,000 years. Again, this doesn't end well for the Native Americans. The Americas, though, are perhaps the big melting pot, where all of the branches of *Homo sapiens*, be they those carrying a bit of Neanderthal DNA or those carrying a bag of Denisovan DNA, can mix and mingle their DNA, bringing all kinds of advantages and challenges yet to be worked out. Here's to a future of coffee-coloured coffee drinkers by the million.

Whatever way you look at it, *Homo sapiens* is one big clever family sharing this planet, so stop all the fighting and try and get along with your brothers and sisters. After all, it took an awful lot of evolution, travel and sex to get to you.

CHAPTER 3

I WANT YOU, I WANT YOU SO BAD: THE SCIENCE OF FINDING LOVE

N THE LAST CHAPTER we saw that our ancestors who arrived in Europe around 40,000 years ago met Neanderthals. This turned out badly for the Neanderthals, as we killed them all off. But before we did, like the black widow spider, we had sex with them. Surprisingly, we are all descended from these couplings. Our DNA contains a small portion – around 1.8 per cent – of Neanderthal DNA. This idea that we would mate with hairy, brutish cavemen was derided by many scientists, as it was compared to us having sex with a chimpanzee. However, the evidence that we did is now compelling. What did we find attractive about them? Was it only women who were ovulating who found the cavemen attractive? How do we choose a prospective mate?

If you're a man, should you spray yourself with Old Spice, put a Mont Blanc pen in your breast pocket with the snowflake logo clearly showing, make sure your waist/hip ratio is 9:10, drink neat whiskey and strut your stuff on the dance floor? The science behind attraction has been a hot topic of late, with some surprising and enlightening findings that get to the very essence of who we are as a species. And when you do choose a mate, what are the odds that you'll stay faithful and have a happy relationship? Science might even have an answer to that.

The science of attraction is big business. Dating agencies have been around for a long time. In times past, the job of the matchmaker, who helped

couples get together, was an important one. In the late 20th century someone invented speed-dating as a way to make the whole process more efficient. In ancient Rome, the god Cupid was thought to

THE GOD OF LOVE SHOOTS AN ARROW AT THE LOVER, IN A 14TH-CENTURY DEPICTION OF THE LOVE POEM 'ROMAN DE LA ROSE'.

bring people together, as the process even then seemed mysterious. Why this person and not another? What dating agencies know is that interests, values and background are important. Although in a recent study, people filled in a detailed questionnaire about themselves and then, based on compatibility, predictions were made as to who might dig whom[1]. They were then put through a speed-dating process, and guess what? The predictions got it wrong. The authors of the study concluded that 'compatibility elements of human mating are challenging to predict before two people meet'.

We are, however, inclined to choose people like ourselves. In fact it has been shown that you are attracted to people who look like your own relatives[2]. First response: ew! Why this is the case isn't clear, but it could be down to a lower risk of being rejected. If you choose someone very different from you, they might see you as being from another tribe and might worry that you are going to harm them. Or perhaps someone who looks like a relative is more likely to stick around and help you raise the baby. In one study, it was shown that we are attracted to people who look like our parents. People born to older parents are attracted to older people. Maybe they make us feel safe. When it comes to instant physical attraction we are often unable to explain why it happened. One problem is studying it in a scientific way. It's almost impossible to replicate attraction in a laboratory context. Those bright lights and people in white coats are clearly off-putting. So what do we know about that moment when you see someone across a crowded room and think, hmmm, I like the look of that person?

First, there is our sense of smell. We find how other people smell either attractive or repellent. Welcome to the world of pheromones, the volatile chemicals that we exude mainly in our sweat. A lot of money has been spent on research into pheromones, as they could be the key to making perfumes more effective for attracting a mate. They are well known to play a role in the animal kingdom, so why not in humans? Female dogs in heat will release pheromones and male dogs many miles away can detect them and start howling. Insects mainly attract a mate by releasing pheromones. This type of communication is subconscious – we don't even know that it's happening.

One reasonably reputable study (and we must take these studies with a pinch of salt – or sweat) got men to sniff T-shirts from women at different times in their menstrual cycle. There was a statistically significant association with T-shirts being rated as smelling pleasant if the woman was ovulating (meaning that if sex should happen there's a good chance that she will conceive)[3]. This makes sense (or scents?). The woman will want to attract a mate when one of her eggs can be fertilised, so her body makes a pheromone which draws the man in (so to speak). The same thing happened when men were asked to evaluate a picture of a woman at two different times: when she was ovulating and when she wasn't[4]. Again ovulation drew the men in;

they rated the woman as more attractive when she was ovulating. No sense of smell was involved.

One possible difference was pupil dilation. An ovulating woman's pupils are likelier to be more dilated, and this is rated as more attractive. Pupil dilation is also a sign of sexual arousal. Tiny pinprick (so to speak) pupils are unattractive. Another feature of the ovulating woman is that she tends to expose more skin. The researchers got the women to take pictures of themselves over a number of days and then calculated how much skin was exposed. There was a clear correlation with more skin being exposed during ovulation. This was probably triggered by a slight increase in body temperature, but it could also be due to the woman's hormonal state, giving her more sexual confidence[5].

Again, men found women with more skin exposed more attractive. Men also rate women dressed in red as more attractive than those dressed in other colours[6]. For the same reason, bright red lipstick or rouge makes a woman's face more attractive. This is thought to be because a woman's body tends to become red/pink during sexual arousal and so the red clothing is interpreted by the man as the woman being turned on. It has also been shown that women are more likely to wear red when they are ovulating. Finally, a woman's voice is rated as more seductive when she is ovulating. Men are therefore pawns in a biological game whose mission it is to get a particular sperm to fertilise an egg, bringing the DNA of both people together to create new life.

What about the other way around? What attracts a woman to a man? Again, smell seems to play a crucial role. In one study, women were asked to smell men's sweaty vests, and there was a correlation with the smell being rated as pleasant and how symmetrical the man was[7]. Appropriately, the lead scientist on that particular study was called Randy Thornhill. Attempts have been made to identify the chemicals involved, and products of testosterone called androstenone, androstadioenone and androstenol are good candidates, although the evidence that if a man sprays this stuff on himself it makes him attractive is patchy at best. The mix of chemicals involved is important, as is

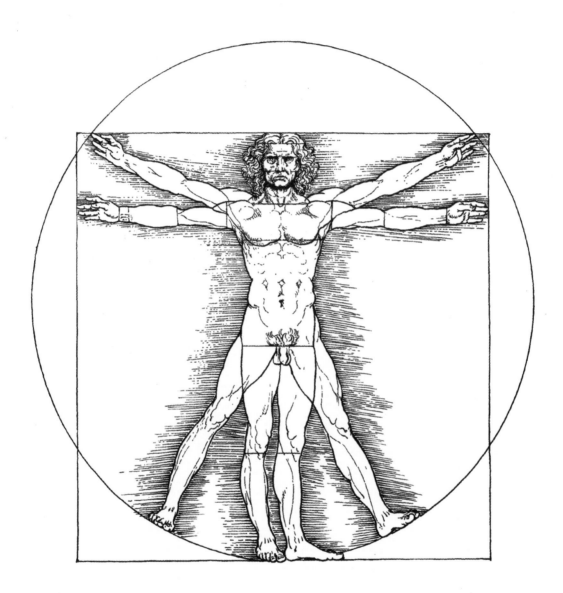

VITRUVIAN MAN, A DRAWING FROM C.
1490 BY LEONARDO DA VINCI, BASED
ON THE IDEAL HUMAN PROPORTIONS
AS DESCRIBED BY THE ANCIENT ROMAN
ARCHITECT VITRUVIUS.

the context in which they are being smelled by the woman. Perhaps they work best in a candlelit restaurant with Barry White playing in the background.

Several studies have shown that we find symmetry attractive. A beautiful face is one that is symmetrical. This sends a signal that the person has good genes – they didn't develop in an asymmetrical fashion, and therefore have robust bodies. This is good for attracting a mate who will have the best genes to pass on to your offspring. A lot of work has been done on symmetry. Women partnered to men with symmetrical bodies tend to have more orgasms[8], and women with symmetrical breasts are more fertile[9]. This may reflect normal and balanced oestrogen levels, which also promotes ovary function.

Apart from symmetry, another physical trait that was found to be linked to attractiveness in men was the length of the ring finger[10]. Women notice its length, probably subconsciously. Men, pay attention. A woman may not be looking at your ring finger to see if you're married. The length of the ring finger gives a strong indication of how much testosterone the man was exposed to in the womb. The longer it is relative to the index finger, the more testosterone was present. High levels of testosterone are linked to sperm count and increased fertility. However, women be warned. Men with long ring fingers are inclined to be more unfaithful, again most likely because of testosterone promoting an increase in libido.

The level of testosterone turns out to be a key difference between men and women, obvious as it may seem. It might give rise to slightly different brain structures, although that is controversial[11]. Whether a man's brain is hard-wired to be physically different from a woman's is a matter for debate. A large brain-imaging study recently carried out on this question found some differences, although there were more similarities than differences. There were 2,750 women and 2,466 men studied, and 68 regions within the brain were examined. A part of the brain called the cortex was thicker in women. A thicker cortex has been linked to higher scores in general intelligence tests. Men, however, on average had a larger hippocampus (the part of the brain involved in memory and spatial awareness), striatum (learning and reward processing) and thalamus (relaying sensory information to other parts of the brain). Men had a greater range of cortex sizes, which is consistent with men showing more variation in IQ tests than women. The study, although intriguing, doesn't resolve the controversy as to whether these differences mean anything in terms of the behaviour or intelligence of men compared to women.

We do know that men and women behave differently; throughout the animal kingdom males are more aggressive and men are inclined on average to have better spatial reasoning. Women tend on average to be more empathic and caring. This could be due to testosterone levels. The environmental influence on the development of men and women, however, can't be underestimated. One fascinating study showed that male babies elicit richer milk from a mother than female babies[12]. This could have all kinds of consequences for development, leading to male and female differences because of differences in nutrition.

Testosterone levels can vary widely in women, however, and this has become a bone of contention in sport. Some sportswomen have very high levels of testosterone naturally, and have better muscle mass and endurance as a result. The International Association of Athletics Federations is considering banning such women, but this is controversial. A well-known example is Caster Semenya, who won gold in the 800 metres in the 2012 and 2016 Olympics. She was subjected to gender tests that showed she had testosterone levels three times higher than average, and was ordered to take hormone-lowering drugs. But did we ban Usain Bolt because of his unnaturally springy legs? The problem is that there will always be athletes who have physiologies that place them in the top range, be it oxygen uptake or ability to tolerate high levels of lactic acid in their muscles.

Many studies have shown that women are attracted to more testosterone-driven, masculine-looking men, with above-average height, broad shoulders and a strong jaw all being rated highly. Women aren't necessarily choosing virile men, however. Not all women prefer masculine men, and it again seems to depend on where she is in her cycle[13]. One study found that when a woman is ovulating, she is more drawn to masculine men, but interestingly only if her partner is not masculine-looking. One interpretation of this study is that she will want her egg fertilised by a masculine man, but then wants a less masculine man (who will possibly be more caring) the rest of the time, as he might be a better father to the child and less inclined to stray. This, however, is pure speculation.

One fascinating aspect is that a man's smell tells a woman something about his major histocompatibility (MHC) genes[14]. His what? Well, these genes play a key role in your immune system. Women prefer a man whose MHC genes are different from hers because the children will have a more varied MHC, which means they will be better able to fight infection. It's like the MHC is a set of weapons. Variety is the spice of life. The more you have the more likely it is that you will kill an invader. However, it has also been shown that when a woman is using the contraceptive pill things change radically[15]. She prefers a less masculine man, and also a man whose MHC is more similar to her own.

TESTOSTERONE, THE PRIMARY MALE SEX HORMONE. IT PLAYS A KEY ROLE IN THE DEVELOPMENT OF MALE REPRODUCTIVE TISSUES AND PROMOTES SECONDARY SEXUAL CHARACTERISTICS SUCH AS INCREASED MUSCLE MASS AND BODY HAIR.

This is because the contraceptive pill makes her body think that she's pregnant, and so she is more drawn to a caring partner, which in the case of the MHC means a relative who is more likely to look after her offspring, as they will be related by blood. Another interesting finding with regard to the pill concerned sexual satisfaction. If a woman chose her mate while on the pill, she reports greater satisfaction with her partner as long as she stays on the pill. It's as if the pill has changed her perception of her partner in some way, perhaps by enhancing her sense of smell for the pheromones he exudes. If she comes off the pill, perhaps that smell is no longer attractive.

One other trait that comes up as attractive, at least for some women, and perhaps only when she is ovulating, is risk-taking behaviour[16]. Activities such as smoking were seen as sexually attractive, as they signalled strength. If my body can stand this, I must have good genes. Death-defying activities like skydiving or Formula One racing are attractive because they appear to advertise strength and bravery. So does confidence in either sex – but not overconfidence. Musicians are deemed attractive because they show bravery and confidence in standing up to play music. So are sportsmen and women. Part of this involves being admired by others, which indicates alpha status and possibly good genes. To be overconfident, however, suggests perhaps that you're hiding something, or that you're a narcissist.

The good news is we are not just crude machines programmed to scan someone's body, smell them and then go for it. Personality (as every Rose of Tralee knows) counts too. Certain personality traits play a role. Kindness has been shown to make someone more attractive[17]. People were asked to rate the attractiveness of photographs of faces. Two weeks later they were asked to evaluate them again, but this time some were labelled as 'kind' or 'honest'. And guess what? Those so labelled were more likely to be rated as attractive than they were the first time around.

What makes all these studies so difficult is that each of us seems to have individual preferences. Some prefer small feet, some prefer a business suit, some prefer bald men. There are some universal qualities that the majority of us rate highly, though: a clear complexion, shiny hair, cleanliness, as well as a female waist/hip ratio of 7:10 and a male waist/hip ratio of 9:10[18]. These seem to be universal across all cultures, and are seen as signs of health, youth and good genes. But again, personality traits can dominate. There really does seem to be someone for everyone.

So once you've chosen your partner, what happens next? Again, multiple studies have shown clear chemical involvement, in this case hormones[19]. The early phase is characterised by testosterone and oestrogen. These trigger sexual desire. Testosterone is also made in women, and, as in men, will stimulate sexual

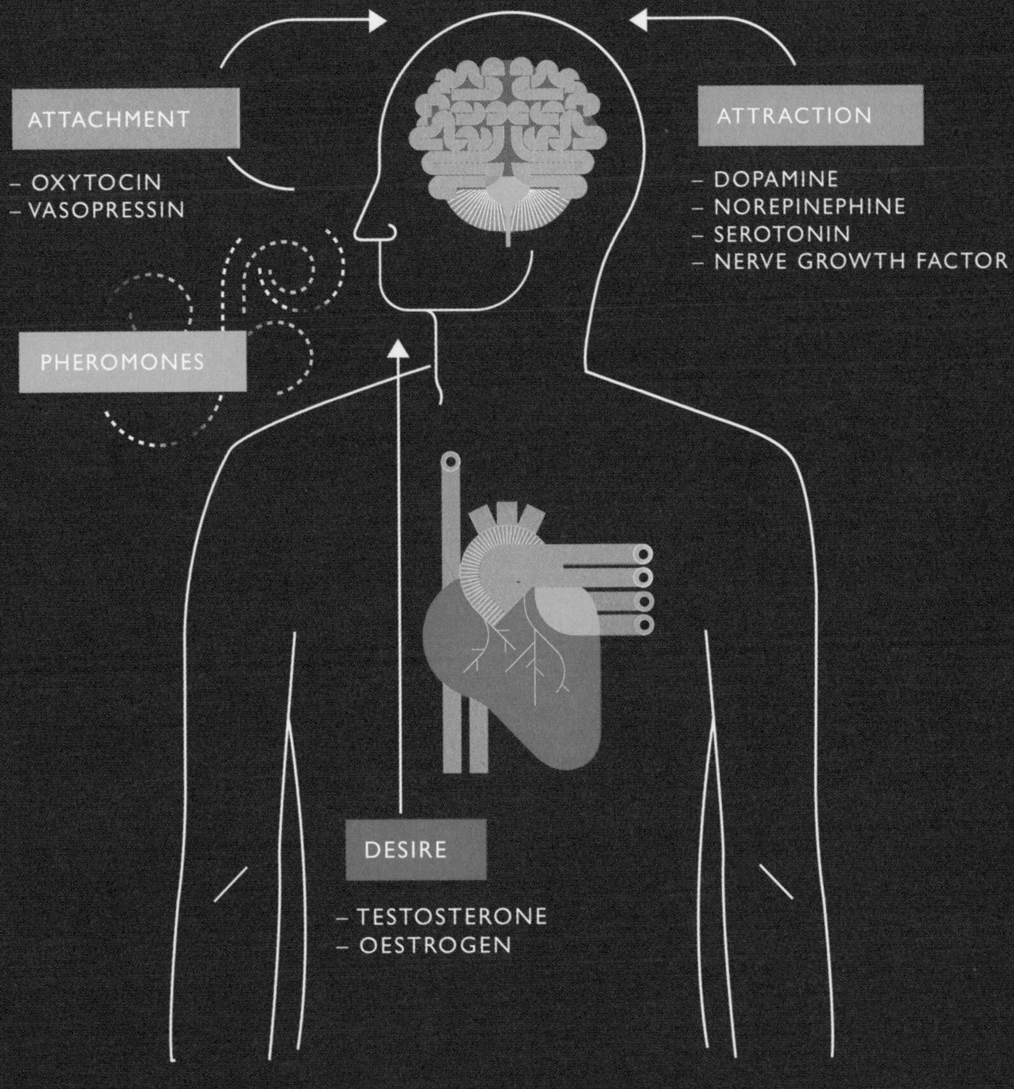

ATTACHMENT

– OXYTOCIN
– VASOPRESSIN

PHEROMONES

ATTRACTION

– DOPAMINE
– NOREPINEPHINE
– SEROTONIN
– NERVE GROWTH FACTOR

DESIRE

– TESTOSTERONE
– OESTROGEN

THE CHEMISTRY OF LOVE. IT STARTS
WITH PHEROMONES WHICH DRIVE
ATTRACTION. IN YOUR BRAIN, DIFFERENT
NEUROTRANSMITTERS THEN KICK IN,
CAUSING DESIRE, MAKING US FALL IN LOVE
AND KEEPING US TOGETHER.

desire. Oestrogen can have a similar effect, although it's weaker. Women report increased desire when they are ovulating, which is likely to be due to oestrogen.

Once attraction kicks in, neurotransmitters in the brain play a role, with dopamine, noradrenalin and serotonin all getting involved. They provoke reward sensations. They also make us lose our appetite and cause insomnia. A famous song from the 1980s – 'Addicted to Love' – had it right: 'You can't eat. You can't sleep. There's no doubt, you're in deep ... Might as well face it, you're addicted to love.' We effectively become addicted to the person. This is why we spend hours looking at their Facebook page or hang around in the rain to see them, or wait desperately for a text message, or are compelled to go home via their street. They are like heroin, and in fact addictive drugs like heroin mimic the effect of falling in love. They share that same intensity and behavioural change, where all we want is that other person, just as all a heroin addict wants is more heroin. Imaging studies of the brain of people in love have shown that the reward centre in the brain (the caudate nucleus) lights up like a beacon in people who are shown a photo of the one they are in love with. The exact same region lights up when a heroin addict is shown heroin[20]. Lou Reed got it right when he sang 'It's such a perfect day, I'm glad I spent it with you', which was actually about heroin *and* being in love with someone.

The involvement of serotonin is also no surprise. This is the neurotransmitter that causes obsessive-compulsive disorder, so again we see the link to total infatuation. All of these responses eventually wax and wane, the infatuation phase usually lasting from one to six months. They have to. Otherwise we would go nuts, and not do anything else all day other than gaze into the other person's eyes, or make decisions that will prove to be harmful in the long run. Evolution had to make sure this would stop, as otherwise we would be eaten by a sabre-toothed tiger.

The last phase is attachment, and that is driven by two more hormones: oxytocin and vasopressin. Oxytocin is especially important[21]. It is sometimes called the 'cuddle' or love hormone. Our bodies make it when we're forming attachments, meaning we bond to the person who is triggering it. We also

produce it after orgasm, and nursing mothers make it in abundance to bond them to their babies. When a baby sucks on its mother's breast, the stimulation triggers oxytocin's production, in a marvellous example of a feed-forward loop.

VOLES HAVE BEEN STUDIED TO HELP US UNDERSTAND THE BASIS OF MONOGAMY AND POLYGAMY IN MAMMALS. HUMANS ARE CLASSIFIED AS MILDLY POLYGAMOUS.

The suckling infant gets the mother's body to make a hormone that bonds the mother to the baby, so that the baby can get more milk. You can buy oxytocin spray which the manufacturers claim will make the person you are beside bond with you. Or develop a sudden thirst for milk.

Oxytocin also brings us to the topic of fidelity. What makes us stay with the person we've chosen? Psychologists classify humans as being 'mildly polygamous'. Most stay faithful but some stray, and there can be many reasons for this. The best scientific study carried out on polygamy and monogamy in animals involves the vole. These small furry creatures have been studied for decades for their behaviour, after it was noticed that two very closely related species (so related in fact that you can't tell them apart by sight) had wildly different behaviours.

The prairie vole, which, as the name suggests, lives on the open prairie, is monogamous, choosing a life partner and apparently never straying. The meadow vole, on the other hand, which lives in more lush grasslands, is a love rat. Meadow voles are polygamous. Scientists examined their DNA and found a striking difference. The genes that make the proteins that sense oxytocin and vasopressin (which is similar to oxytocin) are slightly different. In the monogamous prairie vole the genes become modified after sex, such that the level of the protein they make rises. The monogamous vole is therefore more strongly activated by vasopressin and oxytocin, because there are more of the sensor proteins in their brains.

So the theory goes that the prairie vole will keep seeking out the mate that triggered this pathway for the first time, as they will want the same 'bang for their buck', so to speak. It's like they have heard one particular song during sex and then want to hear it again and again to produce the same feeling. Strikingly, the researchers were able to boost the levels of these sensors promoting monogamy[22]. This would suggest that you can dial monogamy up and down by regulating the levels of proteins in your brain. The higher their levels, the more likely you will stay true.

Some scientists are of the view that alcohol suppresses this pathway. This may in part explain why people who are drunk might cheat – it's their vasopressin/oxytocin receptor protein being modified by alcohol that made them do it. Try telling your boyfriend that if he finds out. It also turns out that 'beer goggles' are real, especially for women drinkers[23]. We find people more attractive when we are drunk. We also find ourselves more attractive, which is the ultimate vanity. This can of course backfire badly, as we tell a prospective partner how great we are and think we are doing a great job of chatting them up.

Perhaps one way to test whether your relationship might survive is to test for the type of vasopressin or oxytocin receptor in your prospective partner. Another gene to test for is the serotonin transporter gene. Remember, serotonin is the happy neurotransmitter. It also makes us obsessively in love. It's made in the brain where it regulates mood, anxiety and happiness. Illicit mood-altering drugs such as ecstasy cause a significant rise in serotonin in the brain. Serotonin is multifunctional, though, as it is also made in the gastrointestinal tract, where it regulates bowel movements; it also promotes such things as blood clotting and bone density. The serotonin transporter (which removes serotonin from fluids in your body) comes in two flavours: a long and a short form. If you have the short form, you are more likely to report marital dissatisfaction over time than if you have the long form[24]. The researchers had more than 150 adults in the study and assessed them over a 13-year period. In the lab they watched how they spoke to each other, examined facial expressions, topics of discussion and tone of voice. From these assessments they could tell if the marriage was a satisfying one or not. The things scientists get up to …

What might the future hold? Well perhaps one day lots of traits and genetic markers will be put into an algorithm and the program will find your perfect partner. There will be a more elaborate form of online matchmaking. And you will be helped in your goal if you spray yourself with Love Potion No. 9. Surely it's more fun to find a mate in the wild, though? Do you believe in love at first sight? Yes, I'm certain it depends on testosterone, the serotonin transporter gene, ovulation and a 7:10 waist/hip ratio.

CHAPTER 4

SPERM MEETS EGG: THE SCIENCE OF FERTILITY

A S WE SAW IN THE LAST CHAPTER, the science of attraction is about all those signs and signals being transmitted and sensed in an attempt to draw us together. The purpose of this is simple: to get us to have sex and then look after the baby once it's born. And from all the ins and outs (as it were) and what have yous, it's clearly a highly complex process, without which our species would die out. All those trials and tribulations and worries and ruses to achieve one thing: to get the DNA from one tiny microscopic sperm to fuse with the DNA inside a tiny microscopic egg. And yet we're here to tell the tale that this process has worked for us as a species for at least 200,000 years. That's an awful lot of sperm and a lot of eggs stretching back over the millennia.

Some animals don't have it so easy. Take the panda bear. As adults these lovable black-and-white creatures live on their own and rarely meet another panda. Even then, studies have shown they mightn't even bother to have sex. And females are only in heat once a year in the spring for 12–25 days. But she's only actually fertile for up to 24 hours in that period – 24 hours in a whole year. Who invented that? How have they survived as a species? So even if a lumbering, cute male panda meets a female, he might miss that 24-hour period[1].

This is one reason why only around 1,600 pandas are left in the wild. It also presents a problem in trying to breed them in captivity. Even if the zookeeper creates the perfect ambience – they do their best to recreate the natural habitat for pandas, the equivalent of a romantic dinner for two with the Walrus of Love playing in the background – they still may not, in the immortal words of Marvin Gaye, get it on. Zookeepers have noticed they don't seem to have a clue how to do it. They've even tried Viagra to get them going, but to no avail. Two pandas were given to the National Zoo in Washington DC to mark Nixon's visit to China in 1972, but didn't have sex for 10 years.

LING-LING AND HSING-HSING AT THE NATIONAL ZOO. FEMALE PANDAS ARE ONLY IN HEAT ONCE A YEAR AND EVEN THEN RARELY MEET A MALE, MAKING PROCREATION DIFFICULT.

Pandas' main method for procreation now is artificial insemination. This is one reason why they aren't a dominant species in the world today. A panda may well eat, shoot and leave, but it's a perilously rare event, and might not result in a pregnancy. But if they do shoot, how likely is it that the sperm will make it to the egg and fertilise it? Again, this has a low probability, and likely much lower than us humans, who in our prime can expect a fertilisation to occur one in every four times[2].

This is the moment, the purpose of all the choosing what clothes to wear, staying late at a party where the music is too loud, the endless text-messaging, second-guessing, hassle and joy of the mating game – the moment when a sperm finally gets to the egg. Once there it dies as it squirts its DNA into the egg, joining the DNA from the mother. The now fertilised egg, at first a single cell, divides, and then the two cells that result divide, and so on and so on, until they get to a fully developed foetus. What's interesting about this is the fact that the cells begin to specialise. Some become cells in your brain, some become cells in your skin. Some become cells in your liver, some become cells in your blood. Finally all the cell types that make you are in place. Remember, every cell will have the entire DNA, since it gets copied in full every time a cell divides, starting with the fertilised egg.

What makes a specialised cell is that there is specific gene expression: a neuron turns on the genes that say 'I'm a neuron' but keep the genes that say 'I'm a liver cell' switched off. And vice versa. Trying to understand how this works is a very active area of research. It's still not fully understood. But because every cell in your body has all of the DNA, each can in principle be coaxed into becoming another cell type. This is the basis for stem cells: trying to take, say, a skin cell and reprogram it back into a cell like the fertilised egg, and then getting that cell to divide into a neuron or whatever specialised cell you want. This hasn't been fully achieved yet but is likely to be in the future when we might be able to grow a new liver to replace an old one, or grow neurons to repair a damaged spinal cord.

How the egg becomes fertilised has been a crucial area of research, mainly to help couples who have trouble conceiving. However, there is disturbing evidence that sperm numbers are dwindling in men in many countries, such

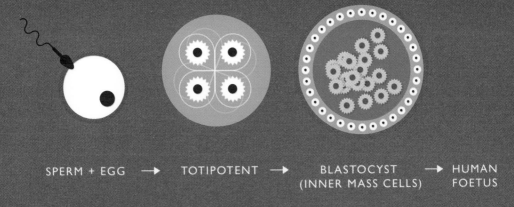

SPERM + EGG → TOTIPOTENT → BLASTOCYST (INNER MASS CELLS) → HUMAN FOETUS

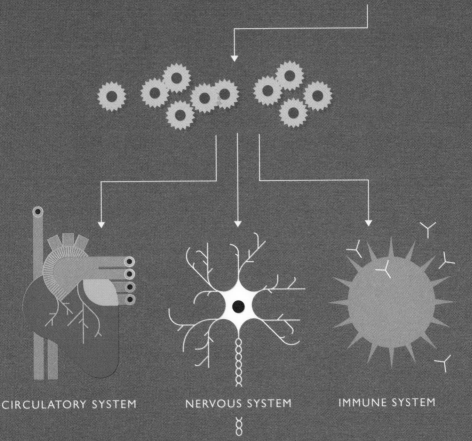

CIRCULATORY SYSTEM   NERVOUS SYSTEM   IMMUNE SYSTEM

CELLS DIVIDING AND SPECIALISING. THE FERTILISED EGG IS A SINGLE CELL THAT DIVIDES AND HAS ALL THE INFORMATION NEEDED TO MAKE THE CELL TYPES THAT GO ON TO FORM THE ORGAN SYSTEMS.

as the USA. How does the sperm fertilise the egg, and what might happen to us if sperm numbers become too low to do the job?

Not many movies feature sperm, much less a man dressed as a sperm, but Woody Allen made a movie called *Everything You Always Wanted to Know About Sex*, and played a sperm about to be ejaculated. He's waiting with all his fellow sperm, and in his usual neurotic way begins to worry. He's heard stories of how sometimes guys (meaning sperm) get their heads slammed up against a wall of hard rubber. And then he gets even more worried: 'What if he's masturbating? I'll end up on the ceiling.' These are the kind of thoughts Woody thinks a sperm might have. Of course sperm don't look like Woody Allen and can't think, but if they did maybe Woody is right.

Each ejaculate in humans contains up to 300 million sperm in an average volume of 10 ml – 300 million of them, each around 50 millionths of a metre long, swimming away in that milky ejaculate, and all looking for an egg. This may be where the rock band 10cc got their name (cc being an old way to represent ml). The primary mission of sex is for one of those sperm to make it to the egg and fertilise it, thus injecting its DNA into the egg. Every sperm may well be sacred but only one counts.

The odds are heavily stacked against a sperm meeting and fusing with an egg. It has a one in 300 million chance of making it, having to outswim all the others[3]. The distance the sperm has to swim is remarkable. To relate this to a human (say Woody Allen), by some estimates it would be the equivalent of swimming from Los Angeles to Hawaii. There are a whole host of obstacles. First the fluid in the vagina is somewhat acidic, so it's akin to swimming in vinegar. When a sperm reaches the cervix (the entrance to the womb), if it's lucky it will find sticky secretions there to help it. This is called cervical mucus, and the sperm can get added purchase by slipping along it. The sperm then reaches the Fallopian tube. Many sperm will not have made it, either running out of energy or stupidly swimming off in the wrong direction. Like the man who has produced them, sperm do not ask for directions. Only one in five sperm swim in the right direction, sensing a chemical come-hither

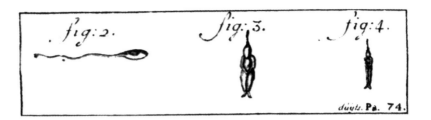

signal sent by the egg. Sperm actually burn fructose as a source of energy instead of glucose. This is a better fuel for them – a kind of energy drink. The seminal fluid is rich in it, giving it a somewhat bitter taste (apparently).

THERE WAS A TIME WHEN IT WAS THOUGHT THERE WAS A LITTLE MAN (HOMUNCULUS) INSIDE EVERY SPERM.

Some sperm also face being rejected. The woman sometimes has antibodies (immune molecules whose usual job is to latch onto microbes and help the immune system clear them) which bind to and neutralise the sperm. This type of rejection is happening without the man knowing. Having got to fourth base and not been rejected before having sex, a different type of rejection can happen when the sperm are finally released into the vagina. The man is oblivious to this (which equally applies to many aspects of male/female relations).

Having got within shooting distance, the sperm at the head of the pack now tries to find the egg. One piece of good news for that sperm is that there are unlikely to be sperm from another male coming up behind (so to speak). Many species have as part of their ejaculate a substance that plugs the vagina and prevents other males from injecting their sperm. Human sperm doesn't have this, and as a species we have what's termed low-to-intermediate levels of sperm competition. Primates with what are called multi-male breeding systems are more likely to have plugs or other chemicals in their sperm to kill off a subsequent ejaculate. This gives us evidence that humans are largely monogamous.

If the sperm that makes it is lucky, the woman will have ovulated. If not, the sperm can hang around, as sperm are hardy enough. The ambience in the cervical fluid is good for sperm and they can live for a few days. They take a brief vacation, probably view some of the sights, and wait for the egg to be delivered. When exposed to air outside the body they last only a few hours.

So now we get to the magic moment, when the sperm fuses with the egg. Even then there is a major obstacle called the zona pellucida, a tough skin around the egg. If the sperm manages to penetrate it, though, delivering its precious cargo of DNA, something interesting happens: the egg becomes impenetrable to other sperm. This means another sperm can't get in and the zygote (as it's called) will have the correct number of chromosomes. Despite the fact that sperm–egg fusion is critical for the whole process (and indeed for the survival of our species), the precise basis for this has only recently been worked out.

In 2005, a Japanese scientist called Okabe was studying the proteins that stud the surface of sperm[4]. These were likely to be the key to the process, as some proteins are very good at recognising other proteins – a bit like a key going inside a lock. This is because proteins have very complex and highly variable 3D shapes which allow them to do all kinds of interesting things. A bit like play dough, proteins can form into a huge number of shapes. A different shape might mean a different job, for example. Okabe discovered a protein that was critical for the fusion of the sperm with the egg. He had found the key on the surface of the sperm that seeks the lock on the surface of the egg. Sperm lacking this protein could not fuse, so this seemed to be the answer.

Proving that romance is alive and well in Japan, Okabe named the protein Izumo, after a Japanese shrine of marriage. Interestingly, Izumo only pops up on the surface of the sperm once it is in the acidic environment of the cervix. The sperm can sense the acid and then relay a signal to the gene for Izumo, which leads to its being made and going to the cell surface. This is an example of what is called in biochemistry 'signal transduction'. The acid leads to a signal being transduced inside the sperm that then turns on the production of Izumo. This is obviously a very efficient way to do things – no need to express Izumo if it's not needed.

When Okabe deleted the gene for Izumo in mice (it has become relatively straightforward to delete genes and see what happens), the males were infertile but the females weren't, confirming his overall discovery. The sperm that didn't have Izumo still made it to the egg, but they couldn't penetrate. They couldn't insert the Izumo key into the lock of the egg to open the door and let the sperm DNA in. At last the specific protein needed for penetration had been found.

SOME PRIMATES HAVE A MULTI-MALE BREEDING SYSTEM. ONCE THEY EJACULATE, A PLUG CAN FORM TO PREVENT THE ENTRY OF SPERM FROM A COMPETING MALE, ENSURING THAT ONE OF THEIR SPERM FERTILISES THE EGG.

But what was it recognising and inserting into on the egg? What was the lock to the Izumo key? A team in the UK led by Gavin Wright had been looking for just that[5]. Unlike sperm (which are very easy to come by: most adolescent males have a lot going spare), human eggs are more difficult to isolate and more precious, making the job of finding the lock difficult. The interaction between Izumo and an egg protein would also be fleeting, and

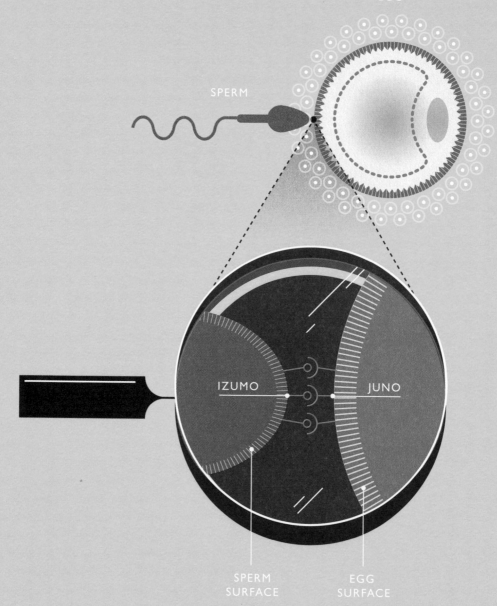

EGG

SPERM

IZUMO

JUNO

SPERM
SURFACE

EGG
SURFACE

A SPERM FERTILISING AN EGG. FOR THE SPERM TO PENETRATE THE
EGG IT HAS A 'KEY' CALLED IZUMO (NAMED AFTER A JAPANESE
SHRINE OF MARRIAGE), WHICH INSERTS INTO JUNO (NAMED
AFTER THE ROMAN GODDESS OF FERTILITY AND MARRIAGE). IT
CAN THEN GAIN ACCESS AND RELEASE ITS DNA TO MERGE WITH
THE DNA IN THE EGG: THE MAGICAL MOMENT OF FERTILISATION.

difficult to capture, as once the sperm hits the egg it gets inside very quickly. But with great perseverance and diligence they found it.

They used Izumo itself as a kind of bait to fish a possible lock out of a set of proteins. It was a protein that had been already reported 14 years earlier but in a totally different context, and with no known function. Once Wright realised its job was to interact with Izumo he gave it the name Juno, the Roman goddess of fertility and marriage. Scientists like to show off their knowledge. The name Juno may give a whole new meaning to that great Sean O'Casey play *Juno and the Paycock*.

Juno is only found on the surface of unfertilised eggs. Once a sperm inserts the Izumo key into the Juno lock it opens the door and goes inside, and all the other Juno locks rapidly disappear from the surface of the egg. This explains why other sperm can't get in. Juno is the lock to open the door to allow the sperm in, and once a sperm is in, as if by magic, all the other locks disappear. The discovery of Izumo and Juno, perhaps the molecular Adam and Eve, is an important one. First, a defect in either may be one explanation for why some couples can't conceive. And second, scientists are interested in developing ways to interfere with them as a new form of contraceptive which wouldn't be hormonal. Such a contraceptive might be preferable to some women, and if the Izumo key is covered over or blocked in some way, this might provide a viable male contraceptive.

So now the sperm is inside the egg and the DNA of the sperm can fuse with the DNA of the egg. What is interesting here is that sperm and eggs are unique among all the cells in our body. Every other cell has the DNA arranged in 23 pairs of chromosomes. For sperm and egg, only a single set of 23 chromosomes occurs. When the 23 chromosomes from the egg fuse with the 23 chromosomes of the sperm, we're back to 23 pairs. These are then copied, with one set of pairs going into one of the daughter cells, and another set of pairs going into the other daughter cell. When the developmental stage is reached to form sperm and egg, in those particular cells only one set of chromosomes occur. This is unique to sperm and egg, which have the attractive name of 'germ' cells, the word germ actually meaning 'seed'.

The fertilised egg will be either male or female, depending on the sperm. Male means it has a special chromosome called the Y chromosome. This means that the egg has been fertilised by a male sperm – a sperm carrying the Y chromosome. If the fertilised egg is female, it has been fertilised by a sperm that is female (i.e. has an X chromosome) – bet you didn't know there were female sperm. This means that in the male, there is an X (from the female egg) and a Y (from the male sperm) chromosome, whereas in the female, there are two X chromosomes, one from the female egg and one from the female sperm. That completely determines whether the baby will be male or female. This is laid down in the microscopically small fertilised egg, bursting with potential to develop into a fully fledged human being.

For largely unknown reasons, there are always slightly more boys than girls born, of the order of 51 per cent to 49 per cent. This may be because boys are slightly more expendable, whereas the mother is all important, as it is she who has to carry the foetus. There is however a disturbing recent trend. This ratio is changing. A study in Canada has revealed that, in communities which were exposed to pollution from oil refineries, metal smelters and pulp mills, the ratio shifts towards more females than males, a reversal of the normal sex ratio[6]. This is likely to be due to high levels of pollutants, possibly chemicals called dioxins, which have been shown to have such an effect on sex ratios. Studies in Russia and Italy have supported these findings. Whether the effect is due to a difference in ratio of male and female sperm or a lower ability of male sperm to fertilise the egg is not known. It could also be that miscarriages of male foetuses are slightly higher.

Another study, this one from Japan, has found that male foetuses are especially sensitive to the effects of climate change[7]. The researchers looked at monthly temperatures in Japan from 1968 to 2012, and in particular two extreme weather events: a very hot summer in 2010, and a very cold winter in 2011. Nine months after the hot summer there were clearly more females born than males. Similarly, nine months after the cold winter, there were more females born than males. Male foetuses appear to be more sensitive

MORE
MALES

MORE
FEMALES

EQUAL
NUMBERS

to extreme temperatures for as yet unknown reasons. This means that one unimagined consequence of global warming may be that more females than males will be born. Men may in fact become something of an endangered species – by not being born.

A MAP INDICATING MALE TO FEMALE SEX RATIOS IN DIFFERENT COUNTRIES.

A final threat is the current decrease in sperm count[8]. Researchers assessing 185 studies of sperm counts from men in North America, Europe, Australia and New Zealand between 1973 and 2011 have found a striking result – the number of sperm in an ejaculate seems to have halved in less than 40 years. And as the downward trend continues, this will be an increasing problem. In direct contrast, no decline was seen in South America, Asia or Africa. This allows for what is called an excellent control group.

Why are the numbers dropping in Western industrialised nations but not in poorer countries or countries in Asia? The decrease has been linked to exposure to chemicals used in pesticides, plastics, obesity and smoking. Some of these occur in countries not experiencing the decline, which suggests that it may be a combination of factors, or possibly certain genetic backgrounds are needed for the decrease to occur. One study suggested that it might be down to watching too much TV. Men who watched 20 hours or more of TV per week had lower sperm counts than men who did 15 hours or more of exercise. There is a consensus that this is a worrying trend, with a fear being expressed that we might become extinct.

Certain activities can transiently decrease sperm count, and couples trying to conceive are given guidelines on what the man should and shouldn't do in order to improve the sperm[9]. Temperature plays a big part. Sperm prefer cool conditions, so it's possible that sitting on the sofa doesn't allow enough air to circulate to keep the testicles cool. Another offender is wearing tight underwear. Mind you, if this were true in every case the world should be full of kilt-wearing Scotsmen. Too much time riding a bike is also a no-no, although it's not clear why. It appears that overall moderation in all things is your friend here. That might give you tiptop sperm in the right kind of quantities to go forth and multiply.

One projection from the falling sperm count is that Europeans and North Americans might be facing extinction. Or we will invite in Asian men to be the fathers of our children. One final possibility is to make sperm in a test tube. Crazy as it may sound, scientists have managed to do just that[10]. As above, this was all about stem cells, which, remember, have the capacity to become any cell in the body, provided we can programme them. Embryonic stem cells were the source of the sperm. The stem cells have the capacity to be turned into any cell type, provided they are coaxed in the right direction.

A team from Nanjing, China took embryonic stem cells and created what are called spermatids. These are immature sperm that, despite having no tail, are able to use their DNA to fertilise an egg. Researchers hadn't previously been able to push cells through a complicated dividing process in order to get rid of one set of chromosomes. That has now been achieved, with a spermatid made in this way being used to fertilise an egg. Mouse eggs were used in the study and, importantly, healthy baby mice were born. Work on this approach will continue, as will the effort to turn adult stem cells back to humans. It may one day be possible to take a skin cell, reprogramme it all the way back to a sperm cell, and then use that to fertilise an egg.

But will the world really turn into a place where there is no need for sex with your partner? Just scrape some skin off his foot when he's asleep, extract the cells, get them to revert to being a sperm cell, add it to one of your eggs in the dish, let Izumo insert into Juno, implant it into yourself and hey presto, nine months later a lovely baby? This may not be as much fun as the traditional method of getting sperm from him but hey, it might be an alternative.

However, if climate change and pollution aren't curbed, sperm counts will continue to fall, and the ratio of female to male will increase further. We might live in a strange world where there are no males left and sex (most likely with a robot) is no longer used to make babies. A Cyber-Jiggy world. Even if men still exist in this future, the need for men to provide sperm may not – and perhaps the world would be a happier place. Let's hope this doesn't come to pass, though, as most women agree that having men around can be diverting and maybe even at times useful. Men and their sperm aren't dead yet.

CHAPTER 5

IRISH MAMMIES GOT IT RIGHT

EVER SINCE *HOMO SAPIENS* evolved parents have worried about it. From the moment she knows that one of her eggs is fertilised, a mother worries about it. Teachers worry about it. Politicians worry about it. What is the best way to ensure our children have the best possible future? As a parent, what can I do to make sure I am sending the right signals and doing the right thing to turn my child into a successful adult? The shelves of bookshops are full of books to give you advice, preying on the vulnerable parents among us. Pet theories abound as to what should be done. Play Mozart. Play chess. Floss. But, as ever, what does science say? What do we know about the best way to make sure we are promoting well-being in our children such that they will grow up to live lives to the full?

Is it all about nature? Is the likelihood of success in life written in your genes? No matter what we do, can we overcome our preordained nature? Or does nurture play a more important role? Can we help any child to blossom? Can anyone succeed given a chance? These questions have been hotly debated by educationalists and pedagogists for decades, giving rise to all kinds of arguments and, often, bad science, with studies full of bias or not properly controlled. (For some reason I like the word 'pedagogy', which the Webster dictionary defines as 'the art, science or practice of teaching'. I love teaching pedagogists.)

If, for example, we think that it is mainly genetic, why bother educating children who have the wrong genes? Providing equality in an education system might seem like a good idea, but if success is predicated on genetics, it is doomed to failure, as different children will have different needs, and so an education system should be tailored to the individual. This of course is very difficult to achieve, expensive and time-consuming. And yet increasing evidence suggests that this should be the goal of an education system. To allow each individual child to engage with education in their own way, based on their abilities. Why try drumming drumming into a child who has no sense of rhythm?

The likely truth is that it's a combination of both nature and nurture – or, to be more precise, nature *via* nurture. You will reveal a person's genetic make-up by nurturing that person in a particular environment. If you nurture drumming in the child who has the precise genetics (meaning nature) to be a drummer, you will succeed as a teacher and the child will be happy, fulfilled in their drumming, with resulting happy parents (provided you supply soundproofing for the child's bedroom). The inherent skill that the child has for drumming only gets revealed by the teacher – hence nature *via* nurture. I would point out, however, that the precise genetic basis for being a good drummer (as with all complex traits) has yet to be uncovered. We should take DNA samples from Ringo Starr, Keith Moon (who could be exhumed for this purpose) and Larry Mullen to find out.

Another good analogy is cars. Let's say we are all cars with different engines – some more efficient than others. All cars need petrol. Some cars will run better than others (the nature of the engine dictates this), on the same petrol (the nurture to make them run). Hence again, nature via nurture – the nature of the engine will reveal itself based on how you nurture it with petrol. The 'environment' is therefore critical for different cars. This might mean petrol, or the state of the roads. If the roads are bad, the car won't go anywhere, no matter how souped-up the engine. The genes people have are therefore important. They are the things that make the brain (or in

ALFRED BINET (1857–1911), THE PSYCHOLOGIST WHO INVENTED THE FIRST PRACTICAL IQ TEST, DESIGNED TO REVEAL STUDENTS WHO NEEDED REMEDIAL HELP.

our analogy, the genes are the parts list for the engine). But the environment is also needed to get the car to perform. This means that we need to always think about the environment a child is brought up in, both at home and educationally, since there will be plenty of things that can be done to try to ensure that people have a chance.

What, however, might the relative importance of nature versus nurture be? The debate about success has been fuelled (enough already with the petrol analogy) by a study on twins led by Robert Plomin of King's College London[1]. Strikingly, this study found that differences in a child's academic performance in UK schools are more down to heritable traits than the teaching environment. The study showed that genes account for 58 per cent of how intelligent we are, with schooling having a 42 per cent contribution. This is an important study, as it suggests that no matter how great a school is, the genetics of the child will have a more important role in that child's academic performance.

Plomin is a world expert on the role of genetics in the variability in IQ, the measure of intelligence first devised by French psychologist Alfred Binet. Several studies have shown that if you're adopted, your IQ will correlate with that of your biological parents rather than your adopted parents[2]. 'Tiger mothering' (or indeed 'Irish Mammy-ing') might not make a huge amount of difference for an adopted child, at least when it comes to IQ. There is a slight effect when the child is young, but as they get older, their IQ tracks more and more to those of the blood relatives. Genes therefore appear to have an even greater effect as you get older – as much as 80 per cent. This may be because your real intelligence emerges as you age, and you choose to hang out with like-minded people, say. So the parental influence wanes and your true ability based on your genes emerges.

How did Plomin do his study? This is an important question, as study design is everything in psychology. There are plenty of studies which turned out not to be correct, because of some anomaly in the study or the studies being too small, poorly controlled or biased in some way. Plomin went big, examining GCSE results in over 10,000 sets of twins. This was a sufficiently large number to allow an average response to be reported, which would reflect the true situation. Large numbers such as these iron out what are called confounding variables – things that certain people do that you might not know about. He was able to show that 58 per cent of success in GSCEs, was heritable. Schools were different, but whatever the school might be, twins performed remarkably similarly.

This study was very much at odds with opinion on education in the UK. Most educators are of the view that teaching the same curriculum to all children will iron out any heritable advantages. In fact, it only makes them more significant. Think about the car engine again; give all the cars the same petrol (like the same education) and you will reveal differences between the engines. Using success at GCSEs, however, mainly measures performance as opposed to IQ, and so doesn't really capture the genetic basis of intelligence. This is important, because in truth the difference between us in intelligence is actually quite small. We know this by observing someone with genetically based mental retardation, who will show major differences in intelligence when compared to the general population. This makes the study of the heritability of intelligence difficult.

But this difficulty doesn't stop scientists from trying to find the genes that predict intelligence or exam performance[3], even though the difficulty is further compounded by the fact that intelligence is not easy to define. IQ tests can be performed, but they represent only one variety of test. For example, having a good memory is important for exam performance or appearing to be intelligent. Musical ability or the ability to read another person's emotions are also seen by some as important indicators of intelligence. And then there are problem-solving skills, which appear to be largely genetic, as identical twins (which occur when one egg is fertilised but splits to form two babies

The Pupil Becomes an Individual

A CARTOON FROM THE AMERICAN
SCHOOL BOARD IN 1922, ILLUSTRATING
THE PROBLEMS WITH CLASSIFYING PUPILS
BASED ON INTELLIGENCE TESTS.

which are genetically identical) tend to receive much more similar results to one another on problem-solving tests than do fraternal twins (which occur when two eggs are fertilised and therefore are like regular siblings). But these are difficult things to define and measure, and some psychologists have doubts about the tests used, which can be influenced by culture, education and experience. Most intelligence tests measure maths and verbal skills, as these are easy to measure.

If we ever find a clear genetic basis for variation in intelligence, this will create anxiety, as we then enter Aldous Huxley's Brave New World of alphas at the top, and epsilon-minus semi-morons at the bottom. Who wants to have a child that's an epsilon-minus semi-moron? It would allow us to tailor the teaching to help each child, however. This would mean that the true purpose of education – to allow a child to grow up and lead as full a life as possible – would be achievable for all. Scientists who favour this remind us of the awful harm done in the past when we didn't know about the genetic basis for something. There was a time when bad parenting was blamed for autism, which is estimated at 90 per cent genetic[4]. Those parents not only had to deal with their child, but also with others blaming them. It was the same with attention deficit hyperactivity disorder (ADHD), which was blamed on bad parenting or letting children have too many sugary drinks. We now know that ADHD is highly heritable[5].

The Plomin study however still shows an important environmental component – as much as 42 per cent. This means that the more equal the educational environment is, the more genes (as opposed to, say, how much money your parents have) matter. This presents a danger, since the same education given to everyone will result in the alphas, betas, gammas, deltas and epsilons of Huxley's Brave New World emerging unscathed from the education system. An equal education system for all will actually promote differences based on genetics. Money still counts for education in Ireland, the UK and many countries. Parents want the best for their children, so if they can they will spend their money on education, and they shouldn't be blamed for that. But in an ideal world, education should be free. It was Lenin who invented the phrase 'Education, Education, Education'. The Soviets provided mass free education and valued teachers and professors greatly.

So can we predict how well a child will do when they grow up? Recent studies have shown that a high IQ doesn't necessarily mean that a child will be a high achiever later in life. In a famous study, Lewis Terman, a psychologist at Stanford, recruited 1,528 children in California who had very high IQ scores[6]. He followed them, and found that many of them had indeed succeeded. They became known as 'Termites'. Between them they had written 2,000 research papers, lodged 230 patents, written 33 novels and had a median income three times the average in the US. But it wasn't all rosy. A quarter of them had less prestigious jobs that were often poorly paid, and none had matched the academic output of the intellectual elite in the US at that time. Also, no Termites went on to be entrepreneurs or 'wealth creators'. This meant that high IQ wasn't as good an indicator as people thought, and certainly wasn't a good predictor for who would drive innovation and economic growth. To paraphrase the Irish economist David McWilliams, it's the messers down the back of the class who are likely to be the entrepreneurs and businessmen.

The importance of environment can be seen in the overwhelming evidence that socio-economic status plays a key role in the future success of the child, however. In fact, the Terman study has been reanalysed, and the outcomes correlated with socio-economic status rather than IQ. Children with limited access to computers or books do worse in school[7]. Those who grow up in stimulating homes are much more likely to become entrepreneurs, leaders and artistic high achievers. It could be, though, that the parents of these high achievers have a genetic make-up which means the environment they establish is stimulating, and these genes pass on to their children. So ultimately, genetics remain a key aspect. But children under five who don't receive regular affection and responsive communication from parents or caregivers have impaired social and emotional development.

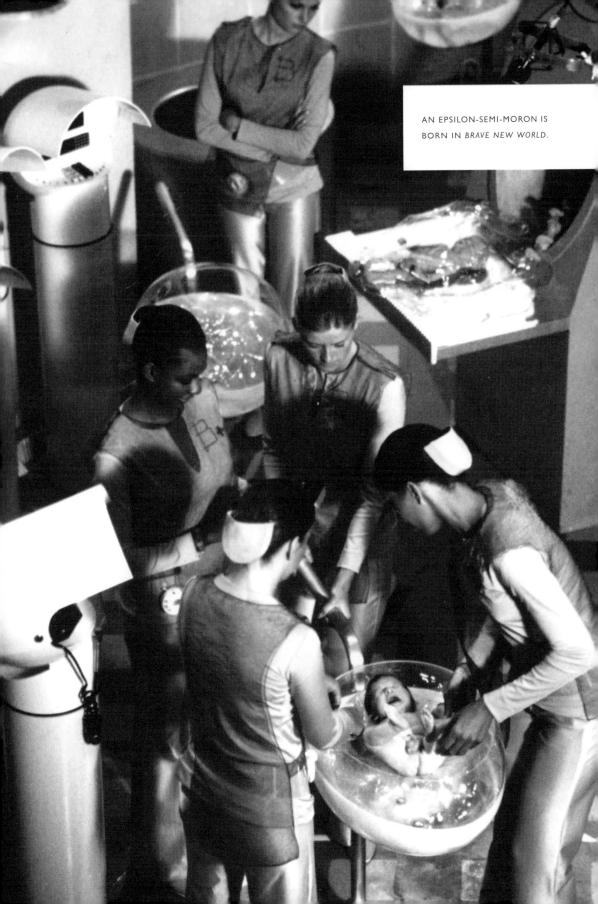

AN EPSILON-SEMI-MORON IS BORN IN *BRAVE NEW WORLD*.

The acquisition of language skills is especially important, and if it is delayed it can have disastrous knock-on effects. Language development helps boost cognitive development, literacy and educational attainment. It helps other parts of the brain too, not just those involved in language. The importance of early educational intervention is therefore critical. We have to be careful though, as, returning to our car analogy, all cars need fuel and maintenance, whatever their age; this also applies to children. The good will get very good, and the very good will get excellent, given a supportive environment. All boats will rise together (oops, I've moved off the car analogy into boats … how stupid of me).

And there is more to all this, as you might expect. A child may well have innate potential and the best parents ever, but they also need what's called 'focused practice'. The elite in every walk of life practised constantly, and continue to do so. This brings us to the idea of 10,000 hours as proposed by Malcolm Gladwell – that successful people spend at least 10,000 hours practising before achieving success. The Beatles did it in Hamburg. Björn Borg did it in Sweden. Of course, if any of us played tennis for hours and hours each day we might become champion tennis players too (or at a minimum go crazy).

So the question then becomes, Why do some people practise more than others? Pushy parents play a part in this, but a key trait is grit. And what makes people gritty? Part of the answer is motivation. If people are offered a financial reward for performing an IQ test, they score higher. IQ tests therefore not only measure intelligence, but also motivation. Grit means having the willpower to see something through to the bitter end. It involves hard work and the ability to resist distraction.

This means self-control, which turns out to be a key trait for future success. A study in New Zealand of 1,000 people from birth to 32 years old revealed that those who had better self-control in childhood were emotionally more stable as adults and were better off financially[8]. I remember as a teenager going into my house to study on a warm June evening, leaving my friends outside playing football. I really wanted to play football but I had the willpower not to. I still don't know why I had the willpower and blame my mother as a default. My friends all ended up in jail. I think.

The importance of self-control was superbly illustrated in a famous observation made by psychologist Walter Mischel. In the late 1960s, he offered young children a choice between eating a marshmallow immediately or holding off for 15 minutes and getting two marshmallows[9]. Years later, he found that those who had managed to wait did better in school, were more popular with their peers, were less likely to be overweight and earned higher salaries. This ability to resist temptation, to exhibit self-control, was a major predictor of future success. In the study around 30 per cent of the children resisted temptation. They did all kinds of things to distract themselves, from walking around the room to singing the theme tune to *Sesame Street* to putting their hands over their ears to hiding under the table.

There were 653 children who took part – again, a reasonable number for this kind of study. Fourteen years after the test, Mischel tracked down as many of those who took part as he could. He asked them about many traits, gauging their ability to cope with problems and their exam performance, using scores from the SATs (a standardised college admission test in the US). Those who went for the marshmallow early had more behavioural problems, lower SAT scores and trouble maintaining friendships. Those who could wait the 15 minutes had a SAT score on average 210 points higher (which is substantial) than those who couldn't wait.

These results were striking, as all of these things were measured 14 years after the marshmallow test (which only took 15 minutes). So a 15-minute session with a child could predict all kinds of complex things later in life. Mischel correctly interpreted this as all coming down to delayed gratification. He concluded that intelligence is important, but is also at the mercy of self-control. In this case, the self-control wasn't so much about not taking the marshmallow early as realising what was on offer (two marshmallows after 15 minutes) and coming up with strategies to make the situation work.

All children want the second marshmallow, but some figure out a way to get it. (And, one might add, the test wouldn't have worked on me – I hate marshmallows, so I would have waited and then annoyingly for the testers not eaten either marshmallow. If it had been a Twirl I would have eaten it immediately.)

The results also confirmed what psychologists have known for years – we can't control the world, but we can try and control how we think about it. Mischel concluded that the key skill was 'strategic allocation of attention'. They didn't kill their desire for the marshmallow. Instead they defeated it. They were able to avoid thinking about the marshmallow. Psychologists call this metacognition: thinking about thinking. As Mischel famously said, this wasn't about the marshmallows. It was about all kinds of skills – studying instead of playing football or saving money for your retirement. Smart moves.

What is also striking, and very important, is that a child can be taught self-control. There are T-shirts in the US stating 'Don't Eat the Marshmallow'. It's not enough, though, to teach a child mental tricks. They also have to form the *habit* of metacognition. This requires practice and constant reminding. This is where parenting comes in. It turns out that the most tedious things we have to put up with as children – not having dessert until after you've eaten your greens, saving your pocket money to buy something later, waiting for your birthday for the thing you want – are all training us in this important skill.

A great example can be found at Christmas. Your dad will tell you that if you behave well, on Christmas morning you will get gifts. A great scam if ever there was one, and yet it teaches a life lesson. You need to be patient, to wait, to distract yourself, and good things will happen. Tolerating waiting is in fact a very human trait. People are waiting for the Messiah and perhaps this is another trick to develop metacognition. Christmas is a sly exercise in metacognitive training. As Dan Bern sings in the song 'Jerusalem': 'Everybody is waiting for the Messiah. Christians are waiting. The Jews are waiting. Also the Muslims. It's like everybody's waiting. They've been waiting a long time … So I can just imagine, how darned impatient everybody must be getting.'

THE 'MARSHMALLOW TEST' DEVISED
FOR CHILDREN BY PSYCHOLOGIST
WALTER MISCHEL IS PREDICTIVE OF
LATER EVENTS IN LIFE.

And of course we have Samuel Beckett's *Waiting for Godot*, about two tramps who spend a whole play waiting for someone who never comes. This is a fitting depiction of the human condition. Meanwhile, Mischel wants marshmallows to be given out in every kindergarten with the instruction: 'You see this marshmallow. You don't have to eat it. You can wait. Here's how.' The smart kid listens, learns and gets two marshmallows (or the good, well-paying job).

Self-control, then, can be learnt. As ever, though, some people are better than others; but that may not have a genetic basis at all. Quick learners (which twin studies tell us is genetic) will out-compete slow ones. Self-control is also the key trait for focused practice. The child who will succeed most of all practises something they don't enjoy. They don't just go through the motions and drop out. They somehow know this will benefit them, and they learn the skill of metacognition, which they can apply to other aspects of their lives.

This all seems a bit too systematic, a bit too organised. To give us hope in our own humanity, we can turn to the last, perhaps surprising, trait that might predict future success: dreaming[10]. Another psychologist, Ellis Paul Torrance, studied several hundred creative high achievers, from secondary school to middle age. These people went on to be academics, writers, teachers, inventors and business executives, and one became a songwriter. And he noticed they all had one thing in common. It wasn't exam results or technical skills. Instead they all had a strong purpose. They fell in love with a dream and then pursued it with intensity. How can a parent encourage that kind of thing? This is difficult, as it won't be obvious where a child's talents lie. The best approach is encouragement for whatever inclinations they might have. Praise effort and progress, not intelligence and talent. Their lives aren't only set by their biology, but also by dreaming, dedication and practice.

A child might not be able to escape their genetics, but with support they might be able to learn impulse control, to practise and to be dedicated to something. They can dare to dream. Climb every mountain, wait 15 minutes for two marshmallows and dream the impossible dream. Sure, isn't that what Irish mammies have been teaching their children for generations?

CHAPTER 6

I AM WHAT I AM: THE SCIENCE OF GENDER AND SEXUAL ORIENTATION

T MIGHT COME AS A SURPRISE to people when they learn that sperm, the ultimate manly cell, can be male or female. The male sperm carry the Y chromosome, and the female sperm carry the X chromosome. No disputing that. As we read in Chapter 4, when the male sperm wins the swimming race to get to the egg, the resulting baby will be male. If the female sperm gets there first, the baby will be female. What this means ultimately is that information present on the Y chromosome will govern the development of male characteristics that we are well familiar with. The lack of this information will mean that female characteristics will emerge.

An unresolved question in science is whether there are major differences between males and females outside the obvious anatomical ones. A related question is the scientific basis for whether humans are heterosexual or homosexual or somewhere along the spectrum of these orientations. It can be a fraught topic, with scientists sometimes being accused of bias in their studies or their interpretation of data. All scientists carry baggage – they are human after all. And yet the scientific question as to what makes you a male or a female, or makes you straight or gay, is as valid as any other, and is one many people are interested in. And we still have no clear-cut answer, unusual as that may seem. I would plead with you to leave your own baggage in the closet, and go back and collect it after you've read this chapter. By the end of

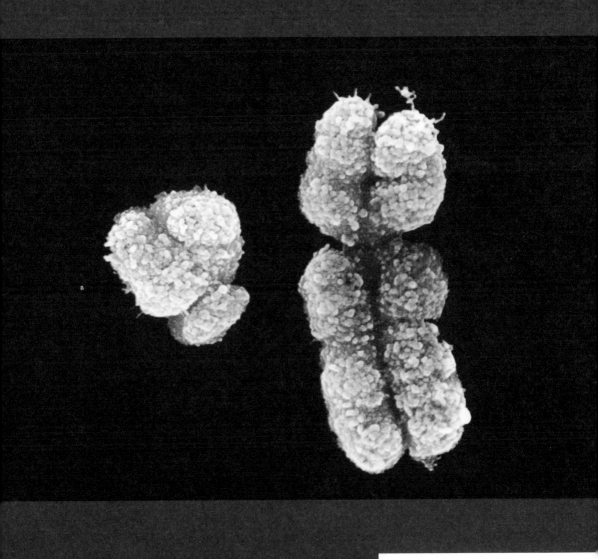

THE Y CHROMOSOME (LEFT) AND
THE X CHROMOSOME (RIGHT).
CARRYING THE Y CHROMOSOME
MAKES A MALE, ALTHOUGH THINGS
MAY NOT BE THAT SIMPLE.

MISS TIFFANY UNIVERSE, A BEAUTY CONTEST IN THAILAND WHERE ALL THE COMPETITORS WERE ONCE MEN.

it, you may wish to leave your baggage where it is, or add some rocks to it if I really annoy you.

First, let's look at gender. Once upon a time it seemed simple. In our species, as in nearly all species (barring creatures that, for example, don't have any gender and procreate by simply dividing, or where a single creature has both male and female parts and can have sex with itself), there were males and there were females. The males had more hair, deeper voices, more muscle mass, could produce sperm from testes and ejaculate them via a penis. Some of these features have obvious functions such as producing sperm and some have a secondary feature of helping to attract a mate. These include, for example, a deep voice and a six-pack (not of beer), and are called secondary sexual characteristics. But of course some males might have less muscle or body hair (as is the case with most Asian men), so the idea of a spectrum is therefore important here. But all men have testicles. Females tend on average to be smaller in stature, with less muscle mass, higher-pitched voices, mammary glands to produce milk for their young and help attract a mate, and the ability to produce eggs and become pregnant.

So far so good. But then it gets more complicated. It turns out there is huge diversity among humans when it comes to defining gender. Tolerating that diversity is what makes us truly human. At one point, Facebook users could choose from one of 71 gender options, including asexual, cisgender, transgender and polygender[1]. 'Man' and 'Woman' were only two options out of the 71. What Facebook recognised was that gender identities are complex, and that for many people, describing themselves as a man or a woman may be inadequate. It's certainly a mixed-up, muddled-up, shook-up world.

Our grandmothers would be very confused by this. But some people feel so fundamentally different they undergo gender reassignment, which is a combination of hormone therapy and surgery. Thailand is a particularly interesting country in this regard. There is a beauty contest there called Miss Tiffany Universe[2]. The women in this annual contest compete, as in other beauty contests, in swimsuits and ballgowns, but with one difference: they were all once men. The contest began 18 years ago in the hope that it would help break down the stigma that many in the Thai transgender community face. There are currently as many as 100,000 transgender women in South East Asia.

Gender identity is a person's private sense and subjective experience of their own gender rather than being purely based on their anatomy[3]. Psychologists tell us that gender identity is usually formed by the age of three and is extremely difficult to change after that. What governs it is complex. It can be driven by cues from the environment, such as a child observing and imitating gender-linked behaviours. For males, these behaviours include assertiveness, ambitiousness and competitiveness, while for females, more modest behaviour and a focus on relationships feature. The environment might also involve gender-specific toys and clothes. But there are also hormonal and genetic influences at play. Some people have a mix of sexual characteristics. For example, a person with female genitalia as well as a deep voice and facial hair may have difficulty in identifying with one particular gender. A survey of the literature covering the years 1955–2000 suggests that as many as one in every 100 have intersex characteristics.

So what does science tell us about gender? Whatever about private sense and subjective experience, we know that it is the Y chromosome that governs the appearance of the male physical characteristics. What is it on that chromosome that is responsible? There is in fact a single gene, called *SRY*, that acts as a signal to set the developmental pathway towards maleness[4]. The presence of this gene starts off the process of what is delightfully called virilisation. In females, the lack of the Y chromosome means this process can't begin.

Furthermore, females also undergo what is called X-inactivation: one of the two X chromosomes is actually shut off, as a double dose of the genes on the two X chromosomes might be dangerous. But humans can have a chromosomal arrangement that is inconsistent with their gender. For example there are XY females. They have a condition termed 'androgen insensitivity'. Androgens (a class of hormones that includes testosterone) drive the development of maleness, following the SRY cue from the Y chromosome. People with androgen insensitivity are not able to respond to androgens, and so the characteristics don't develop; instead the X chromosome in those people dominates and they become female.

Then there is the case of females (as defined by XX) whose bodies produce a lot of testosterone naturally. This could be because there are genetic changes in the genes for the proteins that make testosterone, and these changes step up production. Or perhaps the cells in the woman's body are much more sensitive to testosterone. She will then develop male secondary characteristics.

As we saw in Chapter 3, this has recently become an issue in athletics. A study of elite athletes in 2000 revealed that 4.7 per cent of females had a testosterone level in the male range[5]. Samples were taken from 2,127 elite male and female athletes from the 2011 and 2013 World Championships. High testosterone was shown to give a 'significant competitive advantages' to women running in the 400 m, 400 m hurdles and 800 m. Female hammer throwers and pole vaulters had a particularly high level. Exercise can actually influence the level of testosterone. Intense exercise boosts it, while endurance exercise lowers it. A question is whether women athletes with naturally high testosterone should be banned from competing because of what is called an 'androgen advantage'. Higher testosterone means more muscle mass and endurance, and perhaps a more aggressive competitive attitude to drive them, although this latter aspect hasn't been proven.

The International Olympic Committee is currently reviewing their opinion on this matter, with athletes such as Dutee Chand and Caster Semenya awaiting the verdict. Semenya was asked to take a gender test just before winning the 800 m in the 2009 World Championships. She went on to win gold in the 800 m in London in 2012 and Rio in 2016. One question is, If women who produce testosterone naturally are banned, where might that stop? Should an athlete be banned just because they have an optimal biology to allow them to win? (Take the case of swimmer Michael Phelps, who has a particular leg/upper body ratio.)

CASTER SEMENYA, A SOUTH AFRICAN MIDDLE-DISTANCE RUNNER AND 2016 OLYMPIC GOLD MEDALIST. FOLLOWING HER VICTORY AT THE 2009 WORLD CHAMPIONSHIPS, SHE WAS SUBJECTED TO GENDER TESTING. IN 2010 SHE WAS CLEARED TO RETURN TO COMPETITION.

One thing that is clear is that the issue of gender identity is now important for many people, and biochemistry alone will not be able to necessarily answer it. It has become so important that within international human rights law, the Yogyakarta Principles have been established. They came about following a 2006 international meeting of human rights groups in Yogyakarta in Indonesia, and were established due to a trend of people's human rights being violated because of their gender identity or sexual orientation. An Irish human rights expert, Michael O'Flaherty, led the drafting and development of the principles. They cover non-discrimination, personal security (including a specific statement on the death penalty, which is still applied in certain countries for sexual activity between persons of the same sex), economic, social and cultural rights, rights to expression and opinion, freedom of movement and rights of participation in family life. The Yogyakarta Principles are something of a milestone in the recognition of different gender identities and sexual orientation in humankind.

Sexual orientation and the issue of homosexuality has been a fraught topic for humans over the millennia. From antiquity, many cultures shunned homosexuality and punished those who were gay. Others, however, such as the ancient Greeks, were more tolerant. The first record of a homosexual couple was Khnumhotep and Niankhkhnum, ancient Egyptians who lived around 2400 BC. They are depicted in a nose-kissing position, which was the most intimate pose in Egyptian art. It was perfectly normal for Azande warriors in northern Congo to take young male lovers. Native Americans who were homosexual were revered as special shamans with particular magical powers. There are many accounts of same-sex relationships in ancient Chinese literature. But in some cultures and religions it remains a difficult topic, being labelled as deviant.

Homosexuality is a common trait that occurs throughout nature and may in fact have evolved to provide advantages to a social species such as ourselves. And there have been two main lines of investigation into the scientific basis for heterosexuality and homosexuality. As ever with something as complex as this, the issue of the environment is one aspect, while the biological basis (e.g. whether genetic variation explains its variation in human populations) forms the second, although the consensus once again is that it will be a combination of the two. The overall view is that there will be biological factors but that these will be modified based on environmental factors such as exposure to hormones in the uterus or social factors.

First, we should provide definitions. Heterosexuality is defined as romantic attraction, sexual attraction or sexual behaviour between persons of the opposite sex. It also refers to a sense of identity with others similarly inclined. Homosexuality is a preference in these things for one's own sex. What again has become clear is a continuum between the two, with bisexuality being defined as attraction to both sexes.

Factors that influence this trait concern exposure to testosterone in the womb. If there is androgen insensitivity then the brain might develop differently. Heterosexuality in females has been linked to a lower amount of masculinisation than that found in lesbians, for example. In one remarkable study, deletion of a single gene changed the orientation of female mice from straight to gay[6]. The gene in question has the highly appropriate name FucM, which was shown to be responsible for masculinising the mouse's brain. Females lacking this gene avoided the advances of male mice and tried to mate with females instead. Disappointingly, the gene for FucK does not appear to be involved.

A DEPICTION OF KHNUMHOTEP AND NIANKHKHNUM, A SAME-SEX COUPLE FROM ANCIENT EGYPT WHERE HOMOSEXUALITY WAS OPENLY PRACTISED.

A lot of effort has gone into finding 'the gay gene', but consensus has yet to be found. The idea that there would be a gene for such a complex trait is now seen as non sensical. There is however substantial evidence for there being a genetic basis, mainly based on identical and fraternal twin studies. These studies show that if one twin is gay, the partner twin is much more likely to also be gay if

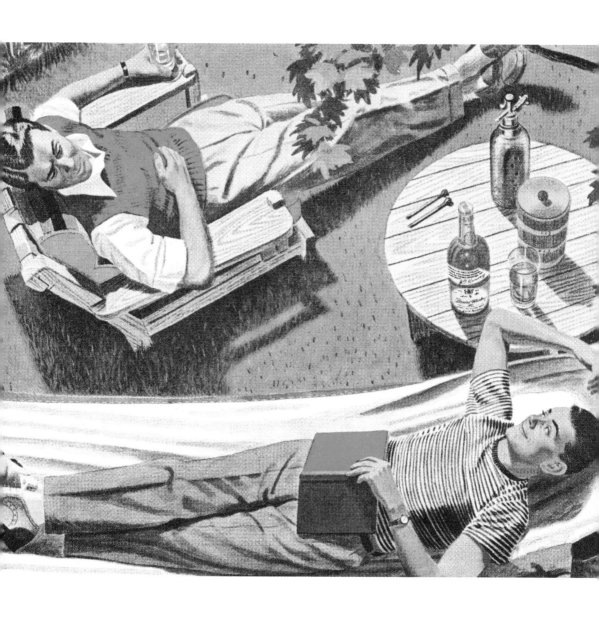

TWO BROTHERS SHARE A MANLY
DRINK. IS THE YOUNGER ONE
MORE LIKELY TO BE GAY?

they are identical rather than fraternal. The comparison between identical and fraternal twins is important, as identical twins share the exact same genes while fraternal twins don't. In both cases the reasonable assumption is that the twins will be raised in very similar environments, and so the fact that identical twins are more likely than fraternal twins to both be gay points to a genetic basis[7].

But what might that genetic basis be? As association has been found with regions on chromosome 8, and with the Xq28 gene in the X chromosome, and these are being explored further[8]. One interesting development is that there are marks on genes (chemical marks called methylations) which associate with sexual orientation, with five regions being marked in people who are gay, but not in straight people[9]. These markings are thought to act as volume controls on genes – how much a gene is active. This is the science of 'epigenetics', 'epi' meaning 'outside'. The gene is the same (in terms of DNA sequence), but it carries chemical markings. This pattern was able to predict sexual orientation in 67 per cent of cases, which is impressive, although the study needs to be replicated. The reason for such marks being there is not known, but it could be some environmental factor that attaches them. And they may well pass to the next generation, if the same markings are present in the sperm or egg, contributing to the heritability of homosexuality as a trait.

One interesting aspect of this concerns reproduction in the population as a whole. Why would genes persist in the population if their goal is to result in homosexuality, which could decrease the birth rate? Homosexuality seems to contradict the basic need for humans to reproduce. One reason is that the same gene variants that link to homosexuality may confer a reproductive advantage on heterosexual people. To support this, there is a study showing increased fertility in women related to gay people on their mother's side but, for some reason, not their father's[10]. The idea here is that the genes may confer being gay on the man, but if the woman has them she may not be gay but might be more fertile.

The second idea is that gay men make more diligent uncles, and so will help ensure the survival of their relatives, who are also carrying some of their DNA from their sister[11]. This would indeed make evolutionary sense, the mission here being to preserve the selfish genes of you and your family by being an attentive uncle – a 'guncle', as gay uncles are sometimes called. Your specific genes may not survive (you will have some genes that your siblings won't have), but some of your genes *will* survive, in your nieces and nephews. The selfish genes would like that.

Another interesting possibility concerns creativity. For this, we must remember that most genes have multiple effects. The same protein (remember, genes code for proteins) can do different things. If one gene increased the chance of creativity and also being gay, it might spread, as being creative might present an evolutionary advantage. There is evidence that gay people tend to be more creative, so this presents another possibility[12]. Some, however, view the increased creativity in gay people as a coping strategy rather than something directly linked to being gay. And the link is correlative rather than being cause and effect.

Finally, one of the strongest predictors of whether a man is likely to be gay or not is the order a man was born relative to his brothers[13]. This is called the 'fraternal birth order effect'. Several studies have shown that the more older brothers a man has, the more likely it is that he will be gay. It was noticed as far back as 1958 that gay men tend to have more older brothers. It didn't matter how many older sisters they had. It was also shown that each older brother increased the chances of a later-born brother of being gay by 33 per cent. Overall, one in seven gay men owe their sexual orientation to this birth order effect. There is no such effect on the orientation of women.

What might be going on here? Well, all the action is in the uterus. This was shown because it didn't matter if a gay brother was removed from his family at an early age. If a stepbrother came into a family with older brothers he didn't have an increased chance of being gay. It has also been shown to occur across different countries and cultures. All of this points to something happening during development. The best hypothesis is that the mother's immune system is somehow becoming sensitised to males as she has more pregnancies. Male foetuses produce what are called H-Y antigens, and these might be targeted by the female immune system as foreign. This somehow affects development in the foetus, and with each pregnancy this gets more pronounced, as the mother's immune system gets better able to recognised these H-Y antigens. It's almost as if the mother's immune system is getting vaccinated each time against male antigens, such that a point is reached where a later brother is now being fully targeted in some way. Exactly what is being targeted and how the fact that it's being targeted might alter sexual orientation is not known. But it remains a fascinating biological observation. And I wonder what it means for that most famous and magical of people in Irish folklore – the seventh son of a seventh son? He must always be fabulous ...

There is a school of thought that asks, Why do we need to know the precise basis of gender or why someone is straight or gay? This is a reasonable point, as there is no obvious benefit from the research being done in terms of, say, a new treatment for a disease. If a gene variant that predicts being straight or gay is found, why will that matter? Might people change that gene and alter their fate? This is unlikely, as being straight or gay is probably much more complex than being determined by one or even a few gene variants.

The main reason people research this area is not to be patronising, but out of pure curiosity – to discover why things are the way they are. Can we explain complex biological phenomena in molecular terms? The uncovering of the scientific basis for being straight or gay, or male or female or transgender, has to be seen as science providing ammunition against those who try to malign or suppress or discriminate against people who aren't like them.

One goal then is to promote a generally more tolerant society. All of these traits can be explained from our biology and our environments – part of what it is to be a member of the human race.. And most important, one thing that Mother Nature teaches us: without diversity, species die out. In spite of its best efforts, Facebook will most likely one day die, but we humans, in all our rich diversity, will hopefully prevail (see Chapter 19!).

CHAPTER 7

THE GOD
INVENTION

S THERE A SCIENTIFIC EXPLANATION for religious belief? Already I can hear hackles being raised (whatever a hackle is). I can hear accusations of a superior, conceited attitude from a scientist towards people of faith. The topic of science and religion has always been polarising, with – in my own experience – discussions rarely going anywhere and ending up entrenching people further in their views, especially when drink is taken. Richard Dawkins, writer of *The God Delusion*, has been attacked for daring to try to explain the basis for religious belief. Equally, in the US, religious battles are being fought over the teaching of evolution. Suffice to say, they don't get along. So I am already on dodgy ground here.

But for me, religion has always been a fascination. Why would people believe in reincarnation, life after death or that a man walked on water? One answer is that some or all of these are true. Another is that religious belief is just another trait, with similarities, say, to an avid Manchester United supporter (although that is much more hateful than believing in a god). And why is it that atheism is on the rise in Western societies? Is this a sign, as some believers say, of the end of days? Or is it just that religion no longer holds sway with some people in this age of cynicism, science and the electric light which banishes the darkness? As with all questions, scientists must approach this one with reasonableness. What have studies on religious belief told us? Might it be that faith in a higher power is a crucial part of being a human or is it, as Dawkins argues, just a delusion?

Let's start by saying that science never tries to answer the question of *why* we're here. It's mainly concerned with *how* we're here, that is to say, the process by which we evolved from the first lifeform that arose on Earth. And science has been spectacularly good at answering that question. Religion is mostly in the realm of *why* we come to be here (the answer being that a god or gods made us). The two areas are therefore separate from each other and when they try to mix, problems can arise.

Religious belief shouldn't need scientific evidence, and things can go badly wrong when it tries to find it. A good example is the attempt to date the Shroud of Turin. For the Catholic faith, this is one of the most important religious relics of

RICHARD DAWKINS, FORMER PROFESSOR FOR PUBLIC UNDERSTANDING OF SCIENCE AT OXFORD UNIVERSITY. IN HIS BOOK *THE GOD DELUSION* DAWKINS CONTENDS THAT RELIGIOUS FAITH IS A DELUSION.

all. The shroud was purported to have the imprint of the body of Christ after he was taken down off the cross. A pesky scientific invention called carbon dating (which can date organic material very precisely based on radioactive carbon isotopes which decay over time) dated the Shroud of Turin to between 1260 and 1390 AD, long after the time of Christ. Efforts like these give succour to the people who dismiss religion as a grand hoax, and holy relics as a scam that exploit the gullible and vulnerable. And why would a religion want to find scientific evidence of God? Would they say 'Ah-ha, there you have it — evidence!', which would only reveal the believer's own weakness of faith? No serious theologians are seeking scientific proof of God. This pursuit would risk falsifiability, and so theology has largely focused on questions of philosophy.

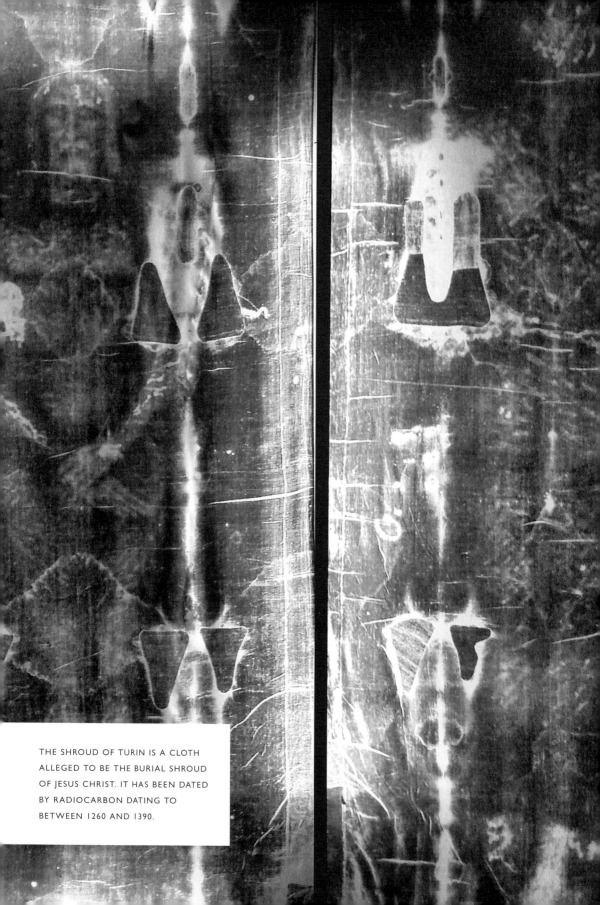

THE SHROUD OF TURIN IS A CLOTH
ALLEGED TO BE THE BURIAL SHROUD
OF JESUS CHRIST. IT HAS BEEN DATED
BY RADIOCARBON DATING TO
BETWEEN 1260 AND 1390.

The God question often concerns the emergence of life on Earth. Some believe that the laws of physics were set in motion by a higher power and left to simmer away. Others believe that we came from the splitting of a cosmic egg. But as we saw in Chapter 1, we now have a reasonable scientific explanation as to how life arose. It came down to a big bubbling cauldron full of rich organic chemicals that over the course of hundreds of millions of years eventually formed the first cell, which then divided and ultimately gave rise to us. That first cell was intensely complicated in terms of chemistry (or should I say biochemistry). It became a self-sustaining factory that could make copies of its own DNA. No mean feat, but there was no spark of life from the fingertip of a god. All that was needed were the laws of physics, chemistry and biology, and some random events.

That life can spring from the laws of science is perhaps best illustrated from attempts to make so-called synthetic life purely from chemical building blocks. A remarkable study has shown that DNA can be injected into a cell without DNA. The cell then 'boots up' and can make a copy of the new DNA and divide[2]. The contents of the cell still can't be assembled from scratch owing to their complexity, so this isn't quite synthesising life from first principles, but that prospect is getting closer. Perhaps scientists will be able to provide the 'spark' and create a living cell that will be able to reproduce and be subject to evolution.

In scientific terms, the main 'purpose' of life, if life can be said to have a purpose, is to survive so that DNA can be copied and passed on to the next generation. This can be achieved by reproducing at a high rate or by helping your relatives (who have copies of some of your genes too) to reproduce and survive. The mother who anxiously recommends possible suitors for her daughter (when did that ever work out?) is just playing out an instinct that evolved a long time ago. Copies of our genes in the bodies of our relatives are to be supported and encouraged and in that way some of our DNA carries on to the next generation.

This was quite simple when we lived in small tribes. We knew who our relatives were and it made sense to support them. Strangers were shunned and it is from this that our xenophobic instinct comes from. Anthropologists have evidence that we lived for a long time in small groups, with a maximum of probably 250 people[3]. One happy tribe, made up of you, your family and your in-laws. It's thought that it was in these kinds of groups that religion began[4], in the form of wisdom being passed down to the next generation. This advice is also thought to have taken the form of moral guidance – look after your neighbour, don't cause problems that might lead to trouble – in effect, love thy neighbour. This ensured that the copies of your DNA in your relatives would also get passed on.

Smart people in the tribe – the elders if you will – would have come up with ways to make members behave, since there is a natural tendency for people to stray from the path and become what in Ireland are called 'messers'. One way to convince them is to tell them the wisdom has come from some kind of super-being. We then get the concept of a supernatural being providing advice – a caring parent figure. This is a common concept in many religions. By obeying and serving this powerful figure, your own kin benefit and so the DNA passes on. There's always a risk of freeloaders not obeying these guidelines, but the risk is lessened because of the all-seeing father figure who can punish you. If the punishment doesn't materialise, it is up to the wise elders to provide it, under the guise of divine power, therefore creating the need for religious leaders and a hierarchy. Again, this is a common feature of many religions, although some (such as the Christian faith) have a father figure who is more of a provider who loves people who believe in him.

The survival of religion in our modern societies which aren't made up of tribes of 250 people is a puzzle. Again, a possible explanation is the survival of the fittest. Multiple studies have shown that religious people are on average healthier than non-believers. This could be because they receive more social support. If a *Homo sapiens* walked into Europe and met a Neanderthal, the spiritual ones with social awareness (which would allow them to form an army to fight) were more likely to survive the ensuing battle. These traits then passed on to the next generation, mostly via cultural transmission. Evidence for the effect religious faith has on people's health can be seen in the fact that Her Majesty Queen Elizabeth II is still alive. Is this because thousands of people every day pray 'God Save our Queen'? Maybe not. Maybe it's the social support she gets, including superb medical care.

Another suggestion for spirituality suggests that it might in part be genetic: you could carry a variant of a gene (or most likely several) which might predispose you to being spiritual in the right set of circumstances. Some of the evidence is based on twin studies, which show a 40 per cent genetic component to belief in a god[5]. This means the environment plays as much if not a bigger part in making someone spiritual. This set of genetic variants is likely to survive in a population because they will bring benefits, but only in a given cultural context, for example, the pre-agreed-upon rules of a religion. If you are a person who is genetically disposed to hate cheese, you are more likely to survive and thrive in an environment where it is agreed that cheese is bad. Hence the importance religions place on spreading the Good News and reminding the congregation of the rules and mission statement. This will mean that the tribe will look out for each other and promote social activities (such as religious ceremonies). We know social activity helps us a lot, decreasing the risk of heart disease, for example[6]. The loving feelings engendered by spirituality are related to the hormone oxytocin, which is the bonding hormone in humans. Oxytocin drives a feeling of warmth, and this in turn facilitates a large co-operative group functioning together. This kind of bonding is so much deeper than, say, the links between supporters of a football team, because it helps us deal with questions that are intrinsically human. Where did we come from? What happens after we die? These questions are in us because of intelligence and capacity to ponder on what might happen next to us – a defining trait of *Homo sapiens*.

Another piece in the puzzle is to do with the minds of children. A very telling phrase from Jesuit priests who ran certain schools in Ireland was 'Give me the boy of seven and I will give you the man'. What they were referring

THE CHI-RHO PAGE FROM THE BOOK
OF KELLS, ONE OF THE WORLD'S
GREATEST WORKS OF ART. IT
DEPICTS THE FIRST TWO LETTERS
OF CHRIST'S NAME IN GREEK. WHAT
INSPIRED ITS PSYCHEDELIC IMAGERY?

to was the remarkable plasticity and hunger for information of the mind of the developing child. This plasticity makes evolutionary sense. It arose to ensure that children, who were starting to explore the world and venture forth, would obey their elders. When the anxious father says to the seven-year-old,

THE PEYOTE CACTUS, NATIVE TO MEXICO AND SOUTHERN TEXAS. IT IS KNOWN FOR ITS PSYCHOACTIVE PROPERTIES AND WAS USED IN RITUALS BY INDIGENOUS NORTH AMERICANS.

'Don't go into that forest, there's a bogeyman in there,' the child will believe him. She won't seek evidence for the bogeyman, because her brain is set up to receive and believe the information. She will find it very hard to escape this belief in the bogeyman and might even carry it with her for the rest of her life, the imprinting on her mind being so powerful. What if the child is told that if he is naughty he will go to hell, in the Christian tradition, or Gehinnom in Judaism? He will believe those things too. If those things get reinforced (say every Sunday in church or by the chanting of mantras) as he moves through adolescence and on into adulthood, they might stick even more, especially as life's trials and tribulations take hold, and he will take comfort in the idea of a joyful afterlife.

Overall, we have a reasonable explanation for the origin of the tendency toward religious faith. We invented God subconsciously to promote our survival and the transmission of our DNA. God didn't invent us. But are we hardwired to believe in a higher power? Is there a neural map we can follow to explain what is going on when a person has a religious experience?

An interesting aspect of the mystical is the use of natural hallucinogens by many cultures during religious ceremonies. The peyote cactus was used by Native Americans and was considered to be a way for people to transcend reality and commune with God. It is interesting to speculate whether hallucinogenic mushrooms were used by the monks in Ireland, and whether they were the inspiration for the psychedelic imagery in the Book of Kells, most notably on the Chi-Rho page, which appears particularly trippy, full of kaleidoscope eyes. (Alternatively, this great work of art was inspired directly by faith in God, as was the case with the Renaissance.) The Salem witch trials that occurred in 1640 in the town of Salem, Massachusetts, may have been triggered by the consumption of bread that had become mouldy with ergot, a hallucinogenic fungus. These naturally occurring chemicals probably evolved as insect repellents, since they also cause behavioural changes in insects which protect the plant. The strategy here seems to be 'get the insect to have a trip, and it will wander off and not eat me'.

The synthetic hallucinogen LSD (or to give it its chemical name, lysergic acid diethylamide) was made accidentally by the chemist Albert Hoffman while working for the Swiss pharmaceutical company Sandoz, using chemicals derived from ergot. He took some by mistake and had the first recorded 'acid trip'. The key thing he reported was a spiritual awakening. He took a subsequent trip and took too high a dose (ten times the dose needed to cause changes) and thought that his neighbour was a 'malevolent witch'. It turns out that a religious experience is very common in people who have

ALBERT HOFFMANN (1906–2008) WAS THE FIRST PERSON TO SYNTHESISE AND INGEST LYSERGIC ACID DIETHYLAMIDE (LSD) AND EXPERIENCE THE FIRST ACID TRIP. HE CALLED LSD 'MEDICINE FOR THE SOUL'.

taken LSD – a sense of something greater, outside our own consciousness. The same effect can be triggered to some extent by starvation, which might explain why both Christianity and Islam involve their founders spending time isolated (40 days in the desert, for example) and starving. It might therefore be possible that there are certain neuronal pathways in our brains that when activated promote a religious sensibility. This might make us want to survive in times of stress and deprivation, and so yet again might be evidence of religious faith being a trait that promotes survival and gene transmission.

Religion has always thrived in places where there is great suffering. Poor people, or people in times of great trauma, are more inclined to believe in a god, possibly to give them hope and comfort. The problem has been, however, that such people are sometimes exploited by religious leaders who hold the money and the power. In the past, some supernatural religious experiences were possibly the manifestations of what we would now consider mental illness – a person heard voices or saw things that others didn't and ascribed these to a god. Many saints became famous for such things. One aspect of this that gives rise to suspicion is claims that the Virgin Mary appeared to girls who are entering puberty, as happened in Lourdes and Fatima. One explanation is that these girls are highly susceptible to such things and are making the stories up, or truly believe something has happened but are hallucinating. Teenage girls are known to be highly suggestive and there are many accounts of mass hysteria among them, most likely caused by social and cultural factors[7]. Another explanation is that the Virgin Mary chooses to appear to such girls on purpose. You can't win either way in that particular debate, but suffice to say which of these options science supports. Perhaps one reason for the decline in religion in Western societies is the increase in quality of life, with people facing less privation, and possibly less or better managed mental illness. Or perhaps it's all down to smartphones, which, let's face it, are pure magic.

This decline can be seen in recent surveys, which paint a disturbing picture for the religions involved. In the UK, a recent national census showed that 8.5 million people identify as Anglican, which is a significant drop from 13 million ten years ago[8]. The demographics of those of the Anglican faith present an even more worrying vista. About 40% of them are now over 70. Based on demographics alone, the number of Anglicans will decline to under 1 million people by 2050. And the Anglican faith is one of the most benign, demanding very little of its congregation. Its churches are now used mainly for weddings of people who don't believe in God, or for funerals for the bereaved who can think of no other option. It has, however, assets of more than £12 billion or has claimed that its investments outperform some hedge funds (could this be from divine intervention?), so its financial future seems secure. It has a great track record in helping the vulnerable, be it through poverty relief, education or health, and its main message (other than faith in scripture) is for compassion, tolerance and kindness. However, enthusiasts who are trying to maintain and revive it say that 'people are happy to listen when you talk about the good works done by the Church, but their eyes glaze over when you mention God.'

Where religion is dying out, it is being replaced by other things. Humans still have a need to be social, and to believe in something outside themselves to give their lives meaning. Some modern alternatives include Scientology, which has the singular feature of being neither scientific nor a religion. Kopimism is a congregation of file sharers who believe that copying information is a sacred virtue, and a high percentage of Australians say they are Jedis. This need for social grouping can also appear as support for a football team or a country (which has its own dangers) or for the welfare of fellow human beings. Humanism has all the characteristics of Christianity without the mystical parts and is sometimes derided by people of faith as being a sandwich with the meat taken out. It takes a lot of bravery (or, depending on how you see it, indoctrination) to declare faith in a man who came back from the dead and tried to convince humanity to be nice to each other, even though that is what every mother has been telling her children for a long time.

The development of science is another reason for religious faith declining. It provides people with answers as to how we came to be the way we are. It doesn't answer the big question of how all this got started (who invented those laws of chemistry and physics that gave rise to the first cell?) or why we're here, but those questions simply reveal how we are built: we are driven to ask questions and be curious, which is the reason why science got going in the first place. That very drive leaves us wanting when it comes to the big question of creation. Science and religion are, of course, not always mutually exclusive, and many scientists are devout believers. A good example is Francis Collins, who led the human genome project, and who is a devout Christian. Like him, some see what science reveals as actually being evidence for a god. Surveys have shown, however, that in general scientists are less likely to believe in god than the general public[9]. This is most likely because they are unable to hold two opposing views in their heads at the same time. Scientists need supporting data, which is lacking when it comes to religion.

One interesting development in the science/religion debate is the view of some that science is actually another religion anyway. Scientists shudder at this thought, since science is all about logic and reason and evidence, and couldn't possibly have any relation to what atheists believe to be mythical stories. Scratch a little deeper, however, and similarities emerge. First, scientists are often anthropocentric. Religion is similar. One of my favourite people to follow on Twitter is God. Yep, God tweets. Maybe that's where Trump got the idea. God currently has over 5 million followers (but only follows one person: Justin Bieber) and recently tweeted: 'You humans. You're so vain, I bet you think this universe is about you.' We thought the sun went around the Earth. Copernicus told us that was wrong, even though he couldn't get into a rocket and prove it. Some didn't believe it (and there are probably some people who still don't) but once we could go into space and actually observe the heliocentric nature of our solar system there was no disputing it – at least not when using our capacity for reason. So we learned that we are on a rock going around the sun, like the other rocks in our solar system. We then learned that our sun is just one of billions and billions of stars in billions and billions of galaxies. We are, as my wife Margaret

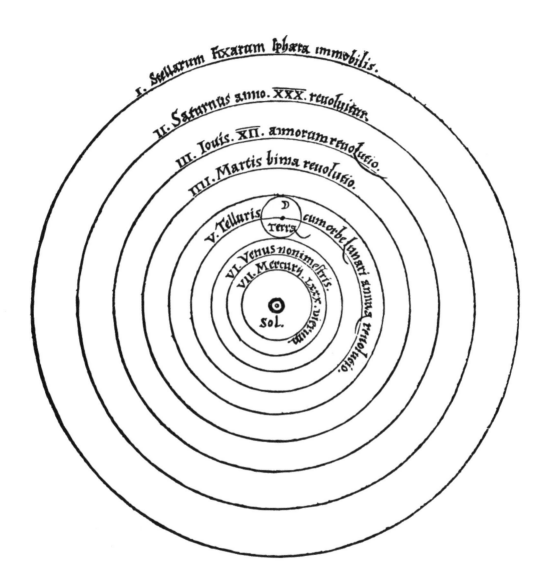

WHEN COPERNICUS (1473–1543) DESCRIBED HOW THE EARTH GOES AROUND THE SUN AND NOT THE OTHER WAY AROUND, THE PRIMACY OF HUMANS IN THE UNIVERSE WAS CHALLENGED.

THINGS WERE MUCH SIMPLER WHEN GOD HAD A LONG WHITE BEARD AND KEPT THE EARTH TURNING WITH HIS FEET.

has often said, 'a speck on a speck on a speck on a speck in the Universe'. The next kickback will be life on other planets. This will most likely be found, further decreasing our specialness. Having a God that created us and looks after us makes us feel important.

Other similarities between science and religion are the casting out of heretics (which usually happens when a radical new idea comes along), revering saints (Darwin, Newton and Einstein are the scientists who feature most on T-shirts) and a code of ethics (don't cheat in your research). Science also has its own priesthood who learn secrets (at university), wear special garments (white coats) and perform arcane ceremonies (experiments) in special rooms (laboratories). The scientific priesthood has, however, one big thing going for it: it is much more gender-inclusive. Much of science is also a complete mystery, with things like dark matter, dark energy and quantum strings (all top-line challenges in physics) going unexplained.

Finally, science requires a faith of sorts. When a scientist is asked to explain the existence of the universe, they'll invoke things like the Big Bang, superstrings and all sorts of concepts. When asked to explain any of them, they won't be able to, unless of course they are specialists. So they take it on faith, invoking other scientists. The big difference in this regard is that science has evidence to back up these explanations. As the astrophysicist Neil de Grasse Tyson has said: 'The good thing about science is that it's true whether or not you believe in it.' If science is to be viewed as a religion, however, it is one that looks outwards instead of inwards.

The men who went to the moon were interesting in this regard. Once they saw the enormity of the cosmos and the tiny blue dot of the Earth, some were said to marvel at it and praise God. Neil Armstrong said two particularly striking things after the Apollo mission: 'It suddenly struck me that that tiny pea, pretty and blue, was the Earth. I put up my thumb and shut one eye, and my thumb blotted out the planet Earth. I didn't feel like a giant. I felt very, very small.' He also said: 'Mystery creates wonder and wonder is the basis for man's desire to understand.' There may well be wonder in religion, but ultimately it is science that has the best chance of helping us understand more about where we came from, who we are and maybe even where we're going.

CHAPTER 8

HERE'S A GOOD ONE: WHY DO WE LAUGH?

UMANS LAUGH. A lot. Compared to other species, even the chimp and the supposed champion in the laughter league, the hyena, we are tops when it comes to laughing. Everyone likes a good laugh. But why do we laugh? Why do we find some things funny? What is the funniest joke ever? Why is most laughter not actually about finding something funny but rather fulfils a social function? And what happens when we 'corpse', or get a completely inappropriate fit of the giggles? The danger here is, as someone once said, that 'Trying to explain why something is funny is somewhat akin to dissecting a frog. Nobody laughs and the frog dies.' Still, we must be brave. Science knows no boundaries, and as long as you get a laugh out of it we'll be fine.

A good place to start is to consider what happens to our bodies when we laugh. In what is known as mirthful laughter, the type where our bellies vibrate, the muscles in our rib cage start to produce large contractions, which leads to air being squeezed out of our bodies – creating the sound of the laugh. When the contractions run close together, we emit a high-pitched wheeze. In contrast, the more social laughter that arises when we talk to someone doesn't involve these bodily changes.

That distinction is important when studying the purpose of laughter. One of the most telling experiments done to examine the function of laughter involved 33 women[1]. These women watched a humorous movie (in this case, perhaps inevitably, it was *When Harry Met Sally*). To measure how much they laughed they each had monitors put on their abdomens to measure their bellies moving. Why was this important? The scientists were interested in measuring mirthful laughter. This can be defined as real laughter – a belly laugh. They also watched a movie that wasn't funny (or at least not intentionally): a tourist video (luckily they weren't shown a video from Fáilte Ireland, as they might have laughed all the way through).

Watching *When Harry Met Sally* resulted in an average of 30 belly laughs per woman. The tourist video gave one belly laugh per woman on average. The scientists also took blood samples and looked at the immune systems of the women. The measure here was of a cell type called natural killer (NK) cells. These cells are important for fighting viruses. And guess what? After watching *When Harry Met Sally* the NK cell activity was enhanced, indicating a boost in the immune system. One effect of laughter therefore could be to make our immune systems work better. Perhaps it's a good idea for your doctor to prescribe you two tickets to see Dara Ó Briain.

Many previous studies had shown that negative emotions and stress can have a negative impact on the immune system. This is down to a stress hormone called cortisol, which is elevated when we are anxious or worried. High levels of cortisol have the negative effect of depressing our immune systems. In another study the scientists examined a section of the brain just behind your forehead called the prefrontal cortex, a brain region whose activity correlates with depression. If you have more activity on the right-hand side of this region you are inclined to be a 'glass half empty' kind of person. If the left-hand side is active, then you are 'glass half full'.

This is useful, because scientists can then categorise people into optimists or pessimists without having to resort to questionnaires, which can be unreliable. And they got a very striking result. Those with a more positive disposition (the ones whose glass is always half full) had a four times stronger response to a flu vaccine than those who were glass half empty[2]. This study provided compelling evidence that those who are inclined to positivity are likely to suffer less from colds and flus. One problem with this study is cause and effect. Maybe the fact that they were sick less often resulted in them having a more positive outlook, as reflected in the left-hand side of their prefrontal cortex being more active.

Either way, all of this suggests that good humour and laughter may well be the best medicine. And there are other health benefits to having a good laugh. Laughter can lower your blood pressure and increase blood flow to your heart. It is therefore a powerful ally in the fight against heart disease. It also turns out that it's actually a form of exercise. When you go to the gym don't be afraid to laugh at that middle-aged man in Lycra and a sweatband. In one study, laughing 100 times was the equivalent of 10 minutes on a rowing machine or 15 minutes cycling[3]. And a lot more fun.

Laughing can also lower your blood sugar levels, which is a good thing, as this will impact on your risk of developing type 2 diabetes[4]. This type of diabetes makes you resistant to your own insulin – which means that your cells can't take up as much glucose, and so your blood glucose level is too high, causing all kinds of health problems. In one study, people with type 2 diabetes ate a meal and then attended a boring lecture. The next day they had the same meal but this time went to a comedy show. Scientists measured the participants' blood glucose in both situations, and found that having a good laugh at the comedy show meant that blood sugar levels didn't rise after the meal as much as they did after the boring lecture. One possible reason is that the participants, muscles burned the glucose through laughing, but whatever the interpretation, there was a clear benefit. And then there's the effect laughter has on pain sensation (which is lowered), the easing of fear and anxiety being clear evidence that it helps us deal with bad situations.

But perhaps the most convincing work that has been done on laughter looks at its role in social bonding[5]. We all know that laughter is contagious. Have you ever caught a laugh from someone else simply because they are laughing and not because of what they are laughing at? And one bout of laughter will set us up to laugh again – this is why comedy shows have a warm-up comedian: once we start to laugh we are inclined to keep laughing. In a study at a shopping mall, scientists examined people laughing, eavesdropping on conversations. They then figured out the cause of the laughter. Strikingly, 80 per cent of laughter wasn't because of jokes or humorous anecdotes. Laughter was happening because of social

THE WESTCAR PAPRYUS (18TH–16TH CENTURY BC) CONTAINS ONE OF THE WORLD'S OLDEST JOKES, WHICH JUST LIKE TODAY INVOLVES POKING FUN AT A FIGURE OF AUTHORITY, IN THIS CASE A PHAROAH CALLED SNEFRU.

interaction. Watch out for this next time you are with people: often your laughter is not at something funny, but rather is saying, I'm friendly, you don't need to fear me, please keep talking to me!

Scientists are of the opinion that laughter allows humans to connect, bond and communicate with one another. The more relaxed you feel with someone, the easier it is to laugh. People are 30 times more likely to laugh in a social setting than if they are alone. This will be obvious to us all. When we watch a comedian on TV on our own, we rarely laugh. But watch a comedian with other people and we can't stop laughing. Laughter in that situation is a form of social bonding. As the great comedian Victor Borges said, 'Laugher is the shortest distance between two people.'

Laughter also boosts your interpersonal skills. It's true what they say: when you laugh the world laughs with you, but when you weep, you weep alone.

People are less likely to hang out with others who have nothing positive to say, so finding humour will improve your social skills. Laughter can also be about who is the most powerful in a group. One study examined laughter in work meetings[6]. It was easy to figure out who the boss was, because that person was more likely to generate laughter in the group. The plebs were inclined to laugh, indicating 'I know you're the alpha person here, please don't kill me (or fire me).' So laughter can have a function indicating status.

This leads us to one of the great unsolved mysteries in human psychology – why are some things funny? What makes a good joke? Again, we're reminded of the dissected frog, so we must proceed with caution. The earliest recorded joke is from 1900 BC[7]. It is a saying of the Sumerians, who lived in what is now southern Iraq, and it goes: 'Something which has never occurred since time immemorial; a young woman did not fart in her husband's lap.' Toilet humour. Funny back then, and still funny now.

The second-oldest joke dates to 1600 BC, and is a riddle found in the tomb of Pharaoh Snefru, who lived over 4,000 years ago. Egyptologists reckon it was written by a disgruntled architect. The joke was 'How do you entertain a bored pharaoh? You sail a boat down the Nile full of young women dressed only in fishing nets, and invite him to go and catch a fish.' This is a rather complex joke, it has to be said (as in, Do you get it? Because I don't). But one thing it has in common with our times is it is poking fun at authority, which is always fun. Along with toilet humour, this is a second category of joke. Ah, scientists, for ever trying to classify things. The other main category pertains to unexpected happenings in a story. Your mind is heading in one direction, but then the punchline takes you somewhere else, and for some reason the mind slip leads to a response that we call humour.

A few years ago there was a scientific attempt to find the world's funniest joke, and it had that characteristic[8]. Thousands of jokes were sent in and these were rated by 1.5 million people, with one joke emerging as the winner. You want to hear the joke, don't you? Well here it is. Two guys go on a hunting trip. One of them collapses, not breathing, skin turning blue.

GOOFY TEETH

JUMBO LIPS

LOTS OF FUN!

REAL LOOKING BUGS

SCARE MOM

CUT FINGER

FAKE $20.00 GOLD PIECE

SQUIRT FUN

FIRST PRIZE

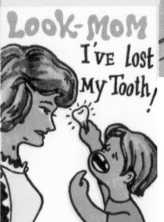

Look-MOM I'VE LOST MY TOOTH!

MAGNETIC RING

The CAT and The RAT

SQUIRT RING !!??

LOOK AT MY NEW RING

JOKE SHOPS – BETTER
THAN PHARMACIES FOR
MAKING PEOPLE FEEL GOOD?

VAMPIRE NAILS

OUCH!

NAIL TRICK

A Howling Trick!

The other guy calls emergency services and says 'You've got to help me! My friend has collapsed and appears to be dead.' The emergency services say, 'Calm down. We can help. First, let's make sure he's dead.' There's silence, followed by a gun shot. The guy gets back on the line and says 'OK, What now?' The comedy writer Spike Milligan gets the credit for writing that joke in 1951, for a radio programme called *The Goon Show*.

What is it that makes that joke funny? Well, Sigmund Freud had something to say about that. In his book *Jokes and Their Relation to the Unconscious* he argued that humour can be a way to relieve tension[9]. Freud speculated that humour is a safety catch for the expression of repressed sexual feelings (inevitably), or feelings of fear, hostility or unease. The above joke sets up an uneasy situation, involving a man and his dying friend, and then relieves the tension by turning it into an absurd situation. This is now known as the 'tension-relief theory'. Humour provides emotional arousal (usually in a story) with signals of safety – the recognition that the threat isn't real, that it's all 'just for fun'.

Just like a bungee jump, tension is built up, and then released. With jokes, humour will increase tension and then defuse it by trivialisation, triumph or humanisation. The two parts may occur in rapid succession. Take for example this joke: Did you hear the one about the honeymoon couple who couldn't tell the difference between K-Y Jelly and putty? All their windows fell out. The first line raises in your mind the prospect of something unpleasant, and that is then suddenly dispelled by the punchline. The reason why timing is so important in comedy is that tension needs to be released quickly. Mind you, Freud might have got it wrong. To paraphrase the English comedian Ken Dodd, Freud never had to play the second show at the Glasgow Empire on a wet Tuesday in November …

Another common function of jokes is to make fun of people who threaten us in some way. Hence the poking of fun at authority figures. In the bad old days this also meant racist jokes – about black people or Irish people. We are also inclined to laugh at the misfortune of others (which the Germans have a word for: *Schadenfreude*), especially when we don't like them or they are of high status. (Why do lawyers never play hide and seek? Because no one will try to find them.)

A third function is intellectual stimulation. Nonsense verse, clever word play or incongruous situations all amuse us. There is often a puzzle-solving aspect; the hunter joke above is like that. We're trying to figure out what happened and what might happen next. This puzzle-solving is actually central to humour, because it comes from a key evolved trait in us humans: the ability to anticipate what might happen next and to make corrections when expectations are not met. Laughter can happen when we debunk a presumption and then restructure perception – it's a reward for using a skill we evolved that promotes our survival.

Scientists have also pondered on the physical nature of laughter – the sound we make and the way our mouths open. It may have come from a threat to bite, strange as that may seem. Although it's playful, the sound our mouths make sends out a signal of triumph and aggression. Smiling is also interesting in that regard. Babies will start to smile at around eight weeks of age, and this is a hard-wired response. We know it's not learnt, because blind babies also smile. Smiling signals happiness with the situation, and pleasure. It also suggests appeasement. The mouth is closed, your teeth aren't bared and so you aren't a threat. Women smile a lot more than men because they are sending out empathic signals, or so one theory goes[10].

Some things are funny because they reveal an unspoken truth. Many comedians make observations about the hassles of everyday life, and we find this funny because it reassures us that we're not alone in experiencing these embarrassing things. A feeling of 'we are all in the same boat'. A lot of comedy also focuses on social awkwardness. This is to do with a fear of social exclusion that we all have. This is one of our greatest phobias, and reveals itself in fear of public speaking and stage fright. The great exponents of embarrassment being funny (on TV, at least) are Basil Fawlty, David Brent and Larry David (in *Curb Your Enthusiasm*).

One of the more complex forms of humour is satire. This pokes fun at stupidity and hypocrisy, and has the goal of driving social change. There was a huge growth in satire in the 1960s, as part of the movement for societal reform. It's been going on, though, since we became modern humans. The court jester was popular because he represented our desire to be eccentric and rebellious and to knock down 'sacred cows'. This can become a problem if the authority figure being lampooned doesn't like it. The Monty Python film *Life of Brian* had a very tough time and was banned in many parts of the world, including Ireland. The irony there was that the target wasn't Jesus Christ, but blind faith and the need to follow gurus. ('He's not the Messiah. He's a very naughty boy.')

We can see the different types of humour in the development of children, who generate humour from a very early age. To begin with it's in things like peekaboo and funny body movements (falling and sticking legs in the air is hilarious to a one-year-old). By the age of three, children will use objects in unexpected ways – putting underpants on their heads, for example. Early jokes will be influenced by their parents but will become increasingly original. But they begin by displaying the social function of humour: smiling, laughing and looking to their parents for a reaction.

Once we reach adulthood, we realise that humour can be useful to attract a mate, and perhaps this is a key reason why it evolved[11]. For men in particular, it is a thought of as a way of showing off intelligence and good genes. If a man is humorous, he must have good genes that give him that intelligence and status. We also judge people we are attracted to as being funny, and funniness enhances attractiveness. A French study (inevitably this was done in France) found that a woman was three times more likely to give a man their phone number if the man had just told a joke to his friends. It's a mystery how that study was done, as there is no record of French men ever telling jokes (apparently).

A study in the US concluded that women want men to have a GSOH (great sense of humour, for those of us unused to dating acronyms), but also to be receptive to her jokes[12]. A man doesn't tend to care if the woman is funny as long as she finds him funny. There is therefore some evidence that the production of humour is more of a male trait (at least in live performance), whereas receptiveness to humour is common to both men and women. Studies show that men are inclined to enjoy toilet humour, slapstick and competitive themes, whereas women favour nonsense jokes and clever word play[13]. And one thing both genders like is gallows humour – making a joke in the wake of something bad, or in anticipation of it. This seems to serve a cathartic function, allowing people to distance themselves from a difficult and upsetting situation. It is also used for social cohesion, especially among soldiers, undertakers and surgeons.

And then, once you find a mate, guess what? Studies into couples and how good their relationships are have revealed that a major indicator is couples laughing with each other[14]. The couple that laughs together stays together. It's an indicator of emotional support, closeness and high regard. Of course

KOKO THE GORILLA
HAS BEEN TAUGHT SIGN
LANGUAGE AND WILL
LAUGH WHEN HER KEEPER
SLIPS ON A BANANA SKIN.

there is a chicken-and-egg problem with this. Do we laugh first, and does that make us closer? Or are we close to begin with, and then we laugh more? Either way it's a very good sign.

Then there is the peculiar phenomenon of 'corpsing'. This happens when an actor suddenly starts to laugh uncontrollably during a performance. The same thing sometimes happens to radio presenters. A great example occurred during a cricket commentary on the BBC in 1991, when two commentators began laughing after one of them said, of a cricketer who stumbled on a wicket, that 'he just didn't quite get his leg over'. This may have given rise to a titter, but instead it led to both commentators laughing for a good two minutes. They fed off each other to keep it going. They didn't want to laugh but they couldn't stop. This was an extreme form of tension relief — commentating on a sporting event is a bit stressful, and the stress relief came in a torrent after an unintentional joke. Psychologists called this 'an involuntary vocal emotional expression'. If this was said to the pair of commentators it would have been a great way to stop them laughing in their tracks.

And finally we might examine another question that has persisted in the study of laughter, Why can't we tickle ourselves? Tickling activates a part of our brains that anticipates pain. It might therefore be a defence mechanism or a display of submissiveness. When you tickle yourself there is no danger, so you don't laugh. One bizarre study was recently carried out in order to examine

RATS HAVE BEEN SHOWN TO MAKE HAPPY NOISES WHEN THEY ARE TICKLED.

whether we can tickle animals. As far as we know, only two other animals get the giggles from tickling: apes and rats. Koko, a western lowland gorilla kept in the California-based Gorilla Foundation until her death in 2018, was studied a lot. She could be tickled, and would laugh when her keeper slipped on a banana skin. She had a special 'ho ho' laugh for visitors she was fond of. And then there was the study on tickling rats[15]. Scientists have shown that rats make happy noises when we tickle them. They make the same chirping noises as when they are playing (we all know how playful a rat can be). This has a serious side: it might be possible to develop a new antidepressant that makes rats laugh, and which from that basis might have utility in humans.

The scientists involved are currently tickling other animals to see whether it is possible to make them laugh too. Perhaps their next grant application will try to identify which joke animals find most funny. I'll put my money on my current favourite doing the job: 'If you're being chased by a pack of taxidermists, do not play dead.'

CHAPTER 9

I GOT THE MUSIC IN ME: WHY DO WE LISTEN TO MUSIC?

W HAT IS IT that makes us uniquely human? What sets us apart from other species? There may be many answers to this question but a good possible answer is our love of music. Humans all over the world love it, across all communities and ethnic groups. And yet we're not really sure what it does for us as a species. When scientists consider music all kinds of questions come into their heads. You might wonder: why can't they just listen to the music and enjoy it? Well, they can't. At least not all the time. This is the curse and the joy of being a scientist. We're always overthinking. And remember, everyone is a scientist; everyone wants to know about things and is curious.

So let's get back to the topic in hand (or ear) – can listening to music bring benefits? Why do some sounds suggest happiness (for example, Handel's *Water Music*) while others invoke sadness (for example, Albinoni's *Adagio*)? Why is a major key happy and a minor key sad? And is Nigel Tufnel from *Spinal Tap* correct when he says that D minor is the saddest chord of all? Whatever the reason, the musician in me wants to blame it on the boogie ...

Given how ubiquitous music is in our daily lives you might be surprised to hear that science has yet to come up with a convincing explanation of what it's all about. Archaeologists tell us that our species has been enjoying it for a long time. The oldest agreed-upon musical instrument is a flute made from

a mammoth bone dating to somewhere between 30,000 and 37,000 years ago[1], so music is clearly deep-seated in our psyche. The particular mammoth who gave his bone is long extinct, as are all his family and friends. But it seems that our ancestors loved the sound made by that punctured bone when someone blew into it.

ONE OF THE WORLD'S OLDEST MUSICAL INSTRUMENTS – A 35,000-YEAR-OLD FLUTE MADE FROM A SWAN'S WING BONE.

We have clear explanations for other pastimes. We play sport because it involves skills (such as throwing, hitting and moving in coordination in a group) that were crucial for our ancestors when they went on hunting expeditions or defended their tribe against other humans. We enjoy novels and films because they allow us to learn about the interpersonal dynamics crucial to our survival as a social species. But the enjoyment of music? This doesn't seem to help us do anything – or does it?

And then it becomes even stranger. We respond to music at an emotional level, and in some ways music is all about emotion. We don't need to think through our response. But deep in our subconscious mind things are afoot. The notes of a chord sound good together only if their frequencies obey

IN THAILAND THERE IS AN ELEPHANT
ORCHESTRA WHO CAN PLAY SONGS.
THEY ENJOY IT MORE WHEN THE
INSTRUMENTS ARE IN TUNE.

a strict mathematical relationship to each other. And the unfolding of a melody must obey its own law, revealing to the listener a gradually emerging pattern, which is occasionally broken. It seems to be the break in the pattern – that change or surprise – that we find especially enjoyable.

Psychologists have come up with a few ideas as to why we enjoy music. One is that music survives as a relic of a time before spoken language. Perhaps our ancestors made noises to each other across the valley to express sadness or joy or anger or loneliness. Music might therefore survive as a souvenir of an intermediary stage between hoots and chirps of animals and the full complexity of modern human language. And this is consistent with animals enjoying music, as all pet owners know. This phenomenon seems to depend on the frequency of the sounds. Labradors have vocal ranges similar to a human's and can make all kinds of noises that sound like singing. They take pleasure in music and will relax in response to classical music but become agitated in response to heavy metal[2]. (Don't we all?) Cats, superior beings that they are, don't respond much to music[3]. That is unless you play it at a frequency in their vocal range. Then they love it. I wonder what preferences cats have in music? Pussy Riot?

In Thailand there is even an orchestra of trained elephants. They learn to play in different keys and appear to enjoy it more when the instruments are in tune. Unsurprisingly, the instruments are adapted for heavy use. Recently in New York, a human orchestra played music that the elephants had composed. The audience were asked to guess the composer. To the elephant keeper's delight, several said it was John Cage.

Clearly humans can survive without an appreciation of music. We know this from studying those who have no understanding of music at all. About one person in 25 suffers from a condition called amusia, which in spite of its name is not amusing at all[4]. The effects of this range from tone-deafness to a total inability to find any pleasure in music. Some people are born with amusia[5] and some acquire it from a head injury or listening to too much Garth Brooks. However, people with this condition do not seem to suffer unduly or be at a disadvantage: 4 per cent of people are tone deaf; some of these also have amusia.

Those with tone deafness are unable to perceive pitch, by which is meant the highness or lowness of a sound[6]. If a violinist plays a note on a violin most people are hard pressed to tell you what that note is. That is until another note is played, and you can then tell if the first note is higher or lower than the second note. This helps you identify the note. Tone-deaf people can't do this – they can't tell a high note from a low note. Tone deafness seems to be strongly hereditary (in that it is likely to be governed by specific gene variants inherited from parents), since both twins in a set of identical twins have been shown to have it.

MRI scanning can find out which part of the brain is active in a partic- ular scenario. When we listen to music, a part of the brain called the arcuate fasciculus lights up. This means that this part of the brain burns more glucose (for energy) when you're listening to music. It is a set of nerves that relays information from one part of the brain to another. In tone-deaf people these bundles of nerves are much smaller, with one particular branch of the arcuate fasciculus missing. It may be that this is the part of the brain that is needed to tell notes apart based on pitch.

Then there are the people who have perfect pitch. One in 10,000 people in the US have this: they can sing in the right key without hearing any reference note. The rest of us have relative pitch – we can sing a note relative to another note. The part of the brain required for perfect pitch is not known.

The overarching proposal as to what music is for is that it brings us together as a community. If you have amusia, you may therefore not be at a particular disadvantage, so long as as you keep socialising in other ways, say by attending a sporting event. But for the rest of us, music turns a crowd into a community. It's no accident that soldiers once marched off into battle behind drummers and pipers, or that an entire stadium's worth of fans will belt out 'The Fields of Athenry'. Nothing can match the power of music in spreading an emotion across a crowd of people and binding them together. This might be the real purpose of music. It's easy to understand how such a trait would be selected for and become widespread, as it is our capacity for social activity that makes us the successful species we are.

We all know that going to a concert or music festival is a much more intense emotional and physical experience than simply listening at home. The sensing of rhythm is a key part of music, and this occurs partly through our sense of touch, as we pick up the vibrations. This can be especially vivid at a loud gig. In the communal environment of the concert hall, we don't just enjoy the music. We are swept away by it into something greater than ourselves, something ineffable. We get carried along in a great ocean of collective feeling.

Another theory has it that music helps us handle cognitive dissonance[7]. This is a feeling of unease that occurs when we hear two pieces of contra-dictory information. An experiment was carried out to test whether music

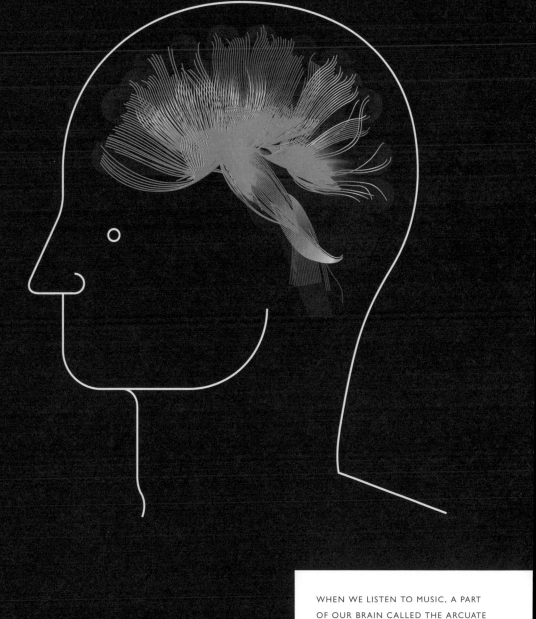

WHEN WE LISTEN TO MUSIC, A PART
OF OUR BRAIN CALLED THE ARCUATE
FASCICULUS BECOMES MORE ACTIVE. IN
TONE-DEAF PEOPLE, ONE BRANCH OF
THIS BRAIN REGION IS MISSING.

is able to soothe the feeling of cognitive dissonance. And guess what? It did. The experiment involved a group of four-year-olds (a heroic experiment if ever there was one) being asked to rate a group of toys from favourite to least favourite. Having chosen their favourite toy, they were then told to only play with their second-favourite toy. (Imagine the consternation, and the adult in charge saying 'Do what you're told. Why? Because I say so.')

Before the experiment the children didn't mind playing with their second-favourite toy, but then they were told that although the toy wasn't their favourite, they must keep playing with this second toy. This created the dissonance. Eventually though, the children lost interest in the second-favourite toy. They resolved the dissonance by agreeing with the adult telling them they didn't like that toy. However, things played out differently if there was music playing. The children learnt to handle the dissonance, and kept playing with the toy. Who thinks up these kinds of experiments? Psychologists, that's who.

In a somewhat similar study[8], the psychologists this time picked on 15-year-olds. They were asked to read through a multiple-choice test and to rate the questions based on difficulty, without actually doing the test. They then did the test, and the psychologists noticed that the students answered the difficult questions more quickly. This was because the students didn't want to spend too much time in a dissonant state – trying to choose the correct answer for a difficult question. However, when the students did the test with Mozart playing in the background, the students spent longer on the tricky questions, and were more likely to get them right. Perhaps music should be played in exam halls during the Leaving Cert to help the students.

One of the great puzzles of music is this: If you are sitting in a concert hall listening to music, and the orchestra plays a minor chord, why do you associate that with sadness? There is no obvious reason for this, and yet it's universal. Scientists have found that there is something similar about major and minor keys and the properties of happy and sad speech, respectively[9]. Sound spectra (the profile of different frequencies) were collected from Western classical music and Finnish folk songs, the thought being that their musical genres would be quite different. What was found was that the spectra in a major key resembled excited speech, while the spectra in a minor key resembled subdued speech. Perhaps excited speech and major chords mean 'Attack!', while subdued speech and minor chords mean it's time to go back to your cave to rest and recuperate.

WHY DO WE FIND SOME NOTE COMBINATIONS DISSONANT? RECENT STUDIES SUGGEST THAT THIS IS MAINLY CULTURAL.

This does seem to be a truly universal phenomenon. Westerners who listened to Kyrgyzstani, Hindustani and Navajo music were able to judge fairly accurately happy music and sad music, even though keys and rhythms and chord changes were different from Western music[10]. These relatively crude indicators of emotion therefore work across cultural boundaries. There are exceptions to the major/happy and minor/sad rule, however. Spanish music can be played in a minor key but appear happy. The same is true of Van Morrison's 'Moondance'.

Separately, dissonance is an unpleasant sound for most people. This is not to be confused with cognitive dissonance, as discussed above. Play two notes that are three steps away on a musical scale – say a C and an F-sharp – and it will sound dissonant. This was known as the 'devil's interval', and was used in medieval times to denote (so to speak) fear or evil. Good examples are the theme tune of *The Simpsons* or the intro to 'Purple Haze' by Jimi Hendrix.

Recent work has shown that we most likely learn to prefer harmonious music over dissonant music, rather than this preference being something we are born with. To Western ears, the difference between consonance and dissonance is clear – and we prefer consonance. This was previously thought to be innate. If you express the frequencies of two consonant notes played simultaneously, the result is a ratio. An octave interval has a ratio of 2:1, a fifth (say, a C and a G) has a ratio of 3:2. Dissonant notes can't be expressed in this way. And initially scientists were of the view that perhaps the brain prefers frequencies that can be expressed as those kinds of ratios.

But then they studied the Tsimané (pronounced 'chee-mah-nay'), who live in remote villages in the Amazon[11]. They have had little exposure to Western music and, to the scientists' surprise, aren't disturbed by dissonance. The Tsimané can tell the difference between consonance and dissonance, but they don't value one over the other. This study is seen as important because, up until that point, as is often the case in psychology, the main types of people who are studied are WEIRD (which stands for those from Western, Educated, Industrialised, Rich and Democratic nations), and therefore not necessarily representative of the human race.

The Tsimané live in villages with no electricity or tap water, and only meet Westerners when they make rare visits to nearby towns. Sixty-four villagers were studied and asked to rate the pleasantness of music. Unlike US citizens, or indeed Native Americans living in La Paz and rural Bolivia, the Tsimané didn't rate consonant sounds over dissonant ones. There is evidence for a similar phenomenon in other cultures. Balinese musicians will mistune their instruments and no one is concerned. Croatian singers will sing the same melody but one semitone apart, which to Western ears sounds dissonant.

So the preference of consonant over dissonant sounds would appear to be cultural. But why does consonant music have those perfect ratios? One theory is that the Greeks, who loved ratios and mathematical precision, began making music with those ratios and it caught on – although quite how they would have figured out the ratios is not known. Perhaps all Western music is descended from Ancient Greece, the original *Greece, The Musical*. They began making music that way (if the theory is correct) and we've been doing it that way ever since. We're unlikely to stop now.

When do we learn about this? When do we learn to prefer consonance over dissonance, or associate a major key with happiness? Well, the evidence is that this kicks in in the womb, when the foetus is five to six months old. So play that funky music to the foetus in the womb and the baby will come out all funked up.

Whatever the function of music might be, study after study has shown its health benefits. More than 400 studies have been done (perhaps scientists like listening to the music as part of each study), and the overwhelming conclusion is that listening to music is good for your immune system and lowers levels of the stress hormone cortisol to a greater extent than anti-anxiety drugs. It has been shown that music boosts the production of an antibody called IgA, which is present in the secretions of our inner tissues – in the gut and in the mouth for instance[12]. IgA maintains the health of these tissues. Music also increases the number of NK cells – a cell type very important for handling viruses and killing tumours[13] (among other things – see Chapter 8). Evidence suggests that combining music therapy with standard care also can be useful for addressing depression.

Perhaps unsurprisingly, music has also been shown to promote social cohesion. If you are in a group of people and you are all listening to background music, your heart rate will synchronise with those of others in the group. This is thought to promote feelings of affection through the bonding hormone oxytocin, which is elevated when you listen to music in a group. It further appears that singing in a choir is especially good for us. In the US alone, 28.5 million people are in a total of 250,000 choirs. That's an awful lot of Hallelujah choruses.

Several studies have shown that choral singing brings huge benefits, including physical and physiological benefits (specifically respiratory health), cognitive stimulation and improved mental health[14]. When nursing home residents take part in a singing session once a month they have less anxiety and depression. The act of singing has been shown to release the 'happy hormones': endorphins. Singing in front of a crowd has an even stronger effect. It builds confidence and has been shown to have long-lasting effects. Singing in public is likely to affect the brain differently from singing on your own in the shower. This has even been shown with birds. When male songbirds sing for females, their brains' pleasure centres register, but only in the presence of a female.

So singing is at its best when you don't do it on your own. Another reason for the beneficial effects singing in a choir brings is that if you are in a choir you have to concentrate on the music and technique. This means that you won't be worrying about the usual stressful things such as relationships, finances or work. As a result choral singers have what is called a 'stress-free zone'. They will also be learning new songs, harmonies and tempos, and all that learning has a wonderfully beneficial effect on the brain, and might fend off depression, especially in older people. Learning to play a musical instrument can have a similarly positive effect. Not only is it a distraction, but it also involves motor skills, coordination and timing skills. All of these are manna to the hungry brain.

Music can have more practical applications. Studies have shown that having music in the background actually improves learning. In one study people learning a foreign language with background music were able to learn 8.7 per cent more words in a set time, compared to those not listening to music[15]. This is similar to the so-called Mozart effect, where listening to Mozart has been shown to improve performance in spatial reasoning tests.

On the more negative side, music has been used as torture. A Canadian police force on Prince Edward Island is threatening drink-drivers with the music of Nickelback. Police in the town of Kensington have told these drink-drivers that, as well as a large fine, criminal charge and a year's driving suspension, they will also be subjected to the latest Nickelback album as punishment. In Rockdale near Sydney, the music of Barry Manilow has been used to stop teenagers loitering outside shops. A US judge recently sentenced antisocial young adults who were playing music too loud from their cars to music immersion, the music being the theme tune from *Barney & Friends* and, yet again, Barry Manilow. There is also a device called Teen Away, which generates high-frequency noises that people over about the age of 30 can't hear. Whether it actually works is another matter. However, teens are also known to use this different perception of frequencies to their advantage – they can use a ring tone that their parents can't hear.

Teen Away is somewhat similar to ultrasonic devices which send out powerful sounds beyond the human ear's range to repel insects. This works

Wolfgang Amade Mozart.
Geb. 27. Jan. 1756 in Salzburg, gest. 5. Dez. 1791 in Wien.

PLAYING MOZART IN THE
BACKGROUND HAS BEEN SHOWN
TO IMPROVE PERFORMANCE.

especially well with crickets. It also works with rats but only for a short time, as they soon get accustomed to the new frequency. And what about cows? Not so much to repel them (pesky cows hanging around shopping malls …) but to get them to produce more milk. A detailed study has shown that playing them soothing music increases milk yield by 3 per cent.

Music has actually also been used systematically as a weapon. Merchant ships will play Britney Spears music very loudly if under attack by Somali pirates. This method was proposed by Steven Jones, of the Security Association for the Maritime Industry. He is on record as saying 'I'd imagine using Justin Bieber would be against the Geneva Convention.' The former leader of Panama, Manuel Noriega, eventually surrendered from hiding in the house of the Papal Nuncio in Panama City when the opera-loving general was subjected to deafening heavy metal music. And during the war in Iraq, US troops fitted powerful speakers to their military vehicles and played loud heavy metal at the enemy. This might be somewhat akin to Scottish bagpipers in World War I, who were known by the Germans as 'The Screaming Ladies' given their kilts and loud bagpipes.

Studies have also shown that as we get older, we are more likely to be irritated by music, and less likely to become huge fans of certain types of music, as we did when we were teenagers. Part of the reason for this is that as we get older our hearing range becomes much shorter. We are less able to hear higher frequencies. Sadly, the decline begins at age eight. One study has examined people over 40 and people under 40[16]. Those over 40 were less able to detect subtle differences in tone and rhythm. Their perception of the difference between consonance and dissonance also lessens. The peak age of music perception is between 17 and 22, which is perhaps why the music we hear at that age stays with us for ever as our firm favourite. This is why Baby Boomers can't get over the music of the 1960s, while Generation Xers are trapped in punk and ska.

Finally, a bone of contention in surgical circles has arisen regarding surgeons playing music in the operating theatre. As long as a hundred years

A SCOTTISH BAGPIPER (OR 'LADY
FROM HELL') LEADS TROOPS
INTO BATTLE IN WORLD WAR I.

ago, the US surgeon Evan Kane, who was from Pennsylvania, wrote a letter to the esteemed *American Association for Medicine Journal*, describing the 'beneficial effects of the phonograph in the operating room'. We've come a long way from the phonograph, and surgeons are now more likely to play tracks off Spotify on their iPhones. Kane felt that the music was good for calming the patient. One wonders if it also calmed him when he became the first person to take his own appendix out, which he did in 1920. The question as to whether music in the theatre is a good or bad thing can divide teams. 'I will not operate with that Ed Sheeran playing in the background,' says the angry old surgeon.

One obvious benefit is to the patient. Music and healing have in fact been intertwined from antiquity. Six thousand years ago, booking a harp player to entertain everyone was seen as payment for medical services. The Greeks made Apollo their god of healing and music. Music has been shown to be better at calming the patient than a sedative. These benefits even extend to patients having ventilation in an intensive care unit[17].

And what about the effect of music on the surgeon and the nursing staff? As many as 72 per cent of operations are done with music playing, and 80 per cent of staff report beneficial effects, from team-building to reducing anxiety and, most compellingly, improving the performance of the surgeon[18]. Some studies have shown that music helps the surgeon focus on the task in hand, aiding task completion while lowering muscle fatigue. However, there are detractors who worry that the music is a distraction, and this does seem to be the case with trainees. It also increases what one study called 'general irritation', which can't be a good thing in the operating theatre.

The question then becomes what music to play in the operating room. How about 'Getting Better' by The Beatles? Perhaps 'Stayin' Alive' by the Bee Gees, or 'Comfortably Numb' by Pink Floyd. Songs to avoid would be 'Another One Bites the Dust' by Queen, or 'Let It Bleed' by the Rolling Stones.

MUSIC TO CUT BY: WHICH
SONGS WORK BEST IN THE
OPERATING THEATRE?

CHAPTER 10

SLEEP AND THE DAILY RHYTHMS OF LIFE

W HETHER YOU ARE A SEVERE INSOMNIAC, a teenager who never leaves their bedroom before 3 pm, or a siesta-loving Spaniard, sleep is a fascination. Why do we need it? What happens when we sleep? Why did this unusual and potentially dangerous behaviour evolve? It doesn't seem to make sense, as we are especially vulnerable when we sleep. Is it to do with allowing our brains to dream? Or maybe it's a time to clear out the garbage from our brains that has built up during the day? And what about the daily biological rhythms of our lives? What are they for? My goal in this chapter is to keep you awake long enough to ponder sleep and our circadian rhythm.

Everybody needs to sleep. When you go without it you become irritable, crave sweet or fatty foods, become a bit loopy and will eventually die. This is true – mice kept awake will die after a few days. It's not really clear what they die from (other than their brains and hearts ceasing to work), so we can't find out what sleep is actually for, other than keeping us from becoming very irritable and ultimately dying.

Scientists have known for some time that there are different phases to sleep[1]. A machine called an electroencephalograph (EEG) allowed people to see what was happening electrically inside brains. It measures electrical activity, which is read out as brainwave patterns. What is striking is that there are five distinct

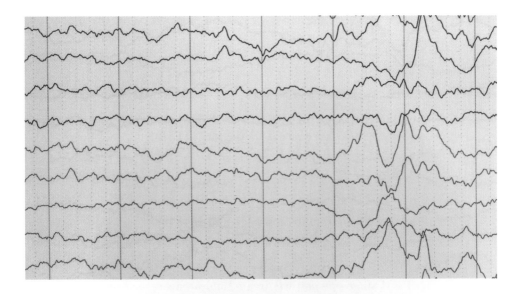

brainwave patterns during sleep. In the first phase, you are still relatively awake. The electrical wave patterns are small and fast, like rapid ripples on water. These NORMAL ADULT BRAIN WAVES WHEN AWAKE AND ASLEEP.

are known as beta waves. The brain begins to relax, and the waves get bigger and slower, as your brain heads to the deep blue depths of sleep. These are called alpha waves, and are observed in Stage 2 of sleep.

In this stage you aren't yet asleep, but you might experience vivid dreams, which are called hypnagogic hallucinations. It is this kind of state that hypnotists can induce. They somehow, usually with a calm voice getting you to focus on something like a swinging watch, provoke slow waves in your brain. You become prone to suggestion too, which is why a hypnotist can make you search for a leprechaun, or maybe get you to stop smoking. Sometimes you'll feel like you're falling, or your body will writhe suddenly. This is known as a myoclonic jerk, which is actually quite common and has no explanation.

Your brain then moves into the second phase of sleep, which usually lasts about 30 minutes: you are now entering Stage 3 and Stage 4 of sleep. Your body temperature starts to drop (and so you might feel cold and pull the duvet tight). Heart rate also begins to slow during this phase. Your brain is now entering into a deep sleep, a stage that lasts around 30 minutes. The brainwaves are now even slower and are called delta waves. Stage 4 gets you in even deeper. Bed-wetting and sleepwalking occur at the end of this phase, although why these occur then is not fully understood. Finally, your brain enters Stage 5, which is known as the 'active' phase of sleep, where something peculiar starts to happen – your eyes start to rapidly move back and forth. This is known as rapid eye movement, or REM for short. Your breathing rate can go up in this stage and your brain will show increased activity again. What's paradoxical here is in spite of your brain being very active, the opposite is true for your muscles, which are very relaxed.

The REM stage is when we dream, and on average we will enter it 90 minutes after falling asleep. We have no idea why we dream, but theories include that it might have something to do with ordering and storage of thoughts, or more simply a consequence of the slowing down of neurons, which somehow triggers memories to be vivid and jumbled. If undisturbed you will cycle four or five times through these stages in a night.

What is going on here? Why is this highly ordered and predictable course of different brain activities happening? A few theories have been proposed[2]. First is the evolutionary theory, which states that sleep evolved to get us out of harm's way. At night we might be especially vulnerable to predators, and so we evolved to sleep, where we might retire to a nice warm cave and stay very still. We were also less likely to injure ourselves in the dark. Darwinian natural selection led to this behaviour, which then dominated in the population. We may have survived because our early immediate ancestors evolved to sleep, perchance to dream.

The second idea is called the energy conservation theory[3]. We fall asleep to save us having to eat, at a time when trying to catch prey is difficult because of the dark. There is some evidence for this. Energy demand drops by 10 per cent when we are asleep. Evolution could work its magic again and

randomly select this trait, providing an advantage over those who don't sleep and therefore persist. The primary function of sleep might therefore be conservation of energy.

THE NIGHTMARE (1791), BY ANGLO-SWISS ARTIST HENRY FUSELI.

Idea number three (they come thick and fast – I hope you're still awake) is the restorative theory, in which the brain repairs and rejuvenates cells and tissues. This will clear out any debris that has built up during the day. Furthermore, muscle growth, repair of tissues and the making of new proteins all occur more prominently when we are asleep. A good example here is to do with a chemical called adenosine. This is made during the daytime as a by-product of the activity of cells. Its build-up is what makes us sleepy, and eventually fall asleep. There is a 'drive to sleep' in response to adenosine. When we sleep

WHY IS SLEEP IMPORTANT?
FUNCTIONS OF SLEEP

 CLEANING THE BRAIN OF TOXINS

 PHYSICAL RESTORATION

 INFORMATION PROCESSING
& MEMORISATION

 MOOD REGULARISATION

 STRENGTHENING IMMUNE SYSTEM

we then clear the adenosine. That life-saver of a substance caffeine works by counteracting the effect of adenosine, making us more alert.

When we are young, sleep appears to have an especially important role in brain development. Infants will sleep for up to 14 hours per day, and at least half that time is spent in REM sleep. Lots of electrical activity happens, perhaps akin to a building site where the electrics are being installed and tested.

In 2013 scientists provided evidence for the restorative function of sleep[+]. They have found that when we sleep, the refuse trucks come out in our brains to help clear the debris that build up during the day, adenosine being a prime example of refuse. Our brains work very hard. Neurons are constantly firing, being pared back and interacting with each other via what are called synapses. Chemicals called neurotransmitters leap across synapses in order for one neuron to communicate with another. Neurons also communicate with another important cell type in the brain called glial cells. All this frenzy of activity is happening right now, as you read this stimulating chapter, leading to a build-up of refuse − by-products from all the activity. This refuse is cleared by glial cells, the brain's garbage trucks.

It's been thought for a long time that when glial cells go rogue and stop doing their job, nasty proteins can build up. Most noticeably this occurs in Alzheimer's disease, where a protein called beta-amyloid builds up in a part of our brains called the hippocampus (named after the Latin word for seahorse, due to its shape). It's a bit like rubbish building up to block a road. In the case of the hippocampus, the build-up affects personality and memory through still-mysterious processes. And remember, scientists love mysterious processes.

At night, however, the sluice gates in the channels of the brain open, and cerebrospinal fluid rushes though, bringing the refuse-collecting cells, and acting to flush out the things that have built up during the day. The refuse is then flushed down to your liver to be digested. What the scientists found was that this process runs twice as fast when you sleep, because your neurons shrink, making the channels between them wider. Scientists have observed tiny fluid-filled channels in the brain. To see them, they had to train mice

MARGARET THATCHER (1925–2013),
FORMER BRITISH PRIME MINISTER,
IS OFTEN CITED AS NEEDING ONLY
FOUR HOURS OF SLEEP PER NIGHT.

to fall asleep on top of a two-photon microscope. They then injected a dye into their brains and watched it flowing in the channels.

Also it is thought that the barrier between the brain and the rest of the body, called the 'blood–brain barrier', opens a little more during sleep, allowing the refuse to be cleared out of the brain. This is when they saw the increased flow, when the mice were asleep. They also injected a labelled version of beta-amyloid, and could see it being cleared at twice the rate when the mice were asleep. Sleep thereby restores us because it clears out all this junk after a hard day's thinking. Sleep deprivation and insomnia are known risk factors for Alzheimer's disease, and we now perhaps know why: less refuse collection, because of lack of sleep, clogging up the hippocampus. So a major function of sleep has been found. Sleep is all about clean-up time, a bit like putting on your dishwasher or washing machine at night. This doesn't mean that the other functions don't also occur, as sleep is likely to have a number of functions, all equally important.

Another area of study is the power nap. During the day, we sometimes feel sleepy. This again may be due to a build-up in adenosine, which caffeine can counteract. A power nap can do the trick too, however, and has been shown to be tremendously beneficial[5]. Just 20 to 30 minutes of sleep can reset your system and give you a burst of alertness. Studies have shown an increase in so-called motor skills (for example typing or playing the piano) following a 20-minute power nap. Importantly, though, no more than 30 minutes. If you go beyond that into Stage 3 sleep and then are woken up, you will perform worse at motor skills, including driving. However, higher-order activity such as memory is boosted by a sleep of around 60 minutes, even though you may feel groggy.

Power napping becomes all the more important if you are sleep-deprived. The question that often arises is, how many hours sleep a night is best[6]? This has huge variability. Some need 10 hours and some get away with five hours or less. We are the only species on the planet that we know of that intentionally deprives itself of sleep. Margaret Thatcher, the former British prime minister, is often cited as someone who got only four hours sleep a night. This may in fact be one of the reasons she eventually developed Alzheimer's disease, although we can't be sure of that. In a study of 54,269 adults (which is a huge number, and so the averages that emerge are probably correct), 31 per cent slept for six hours or less, 64.8 per cent slept for seven to nine hours and 4.2 per cent slept for 10 hours[7]. Those at either end of this range were more likely to be obese and suffer from anxiety and diabetes.

At any event, many people report being sleep-deprived, especially middle-aged men. Studies have shown that one in five Irish people are sleep-deprived. Sleep deprivation is actually a serious health matter. It leads to a weakening of your bones through osteoporosis. It can be assessed by measuring a protein (P1NP) that is released by your bones when they are strong. Levels of this protein were 28 per cent lower in young men who were sleep-deprived[8].

Sleep deprivation also increases the craving for junk food, which in turn leads to obesity and all its consequences of increased risk of diabetes and cancer. It could also be a simple matter of time: the more hours we are awake the more time we have at our disposal to eat. Our bodies also make more of a chemical called endocannabinoids. These are your own form of the cannabinoids found in cannabis, and they cause a natural form of the 'munchies', which those who have had cannabis will recognise. If you are sleep-deprived you make more of this, and so eat more, again leading to obesity. Instead of smoking a joint, sleep for only four hours a night and you might make your own chemicals to give you a high.

An International Bedroom Poll has been done (now there's a great title for a survey) across several countries[9]. The US and Japan have it worst, sleeping on average 40 minutes less than people in other countries. The

Japanese average 6 hours and 22 minutes, while the Americans average 6 hours and 31 minutes. Germans, Mexicans and Canadians report the longest time asleep, with over seven hours in each country. Every country reports sleeping on at weekends, with an average of an extra 45 minutes on days they do not work.

Other intriguing findings to emerge from the survey were that more than half of Mexicans and Americans pray or meditate before sleep. Apparently 43 per cent of people in the UK have a soothing drink before bed, and one-third of them sleep naked. In most countries, however, at least two-thirds watch TV just before bed, and for many people the last thing they do before sleeping is to check their smartphone. The Japanese are more likely to sleep in the same bed as their children, and people in the US are most likely to sleep in the same bed as their pets. And which country is most likely to have people sleeping with their socks on? The US and Canada again. Perhaps it's the cold winters in parts of those countries.

Another recent study used an app on its subjects' smartphones to get an even better picture of sleep habits. This study broadly confirmed findings in the International Bedroom Poll. Other interesting findings were that women on average sleep 30 minutes longer than men[10]. Also, the study confirmed that as you get older you need less and less sleep. Sleep patterns varied widely among young people, but in older people the amount of time asleep narrowed to around six hours on average.

Why is there such variation in how much sleep different people need? Why do some people become sleepy at certain times during the day? And why do we feel sleepy at night anyway? Also, why are some people more alert at night (scientists call them 'night owls') while others are more alert in the morning (they are termed 'morning larks')? It all comes down to our in-built biological clock[11]. The scientific term for how our body changes over the course of the day is 'circadian rhythm' — 'circadian' meaning 'about a day'. Just like our ability to look at our wristwatch, our bodies have evolved this neat little system of internal clocks so that our bodies know what time of day it is. Since life began, the Earth has been spinning on its axis, bringing with it the daily changes that we are now so familiar with. Sunrise, sunset.

Our body clock allows us to schedule things at the right time of day. It's like your internal daily planner. Practically all animals on Earth have it. We are all familiar with this. We feel hungry at certain times, mostly when it's bright. We feel sleepy at other times, mostly when it's dark. When we are jet-lagged these rhythms go out of whack, making us sleepy at the wrong time, with disrupted appetite and mood changes. Shift workers also have disruptions in the normal rhythms of daily life, which can in fact damage their overall health. The study of circadian rhythm has relevance to our overall health and well-being, with fascinating aspects being discovered.

First, let's define the typical events that happen in our bodies over the course of a day. Between 6 am and 9 am, most people wake up. We are of course excluding that strange creature the teenager, who has very different patterns from others. My own mother realised I had entered adolescence when quite quickly I went from a lively young boy, up with the lark, running around and smiling, to a teenager who only emerged from his bedroom after 2 pm. She wondered what had happened to her lovely little boy. But for most other ages, we are all awake by around 9 am. Testosterone also peaks at this time, perhaps to get us ready for the day ahead. However it is also the time when we are at risk of a heart attack, as our blood is slightly thicker and our blood pressure slightly higher.

These changes seem to be to get us ready for the day ahead and prepare us for the activities that face us. Between 9 am and 12 noon, the stress hormone cortisol peaks, which gives our brains a boost of alertness. We tend to be most productive at work before lunch, when our short-term memory is at its best. Our body makes digestive enzymes in anticipation of eating and we feel hungry because of the release of hormones such as ghrelin, which stimulates the parts of our brain that then say 'you're hungry'. Between 12 noon and 3 pm, our bellies will be full of food.

And of course once we've eaten we experience that familiar early-after-noon slump, the post-lunch dip. Our alertness takes a nose-dive at this time,

7.30
MELATONIN
SECRETION
STOPS

8.30
BOWEL
MOVEMENT
LIKELY

9.00
HIGHEST
TESTOSTERONE
SECRETION

10.00
HIGH
ALERTNESS

15.30
FASTEST
REACTION TIME

14.30
BEST
COORDINATION

18.30
HIGHEST
BLOOD PRESSURE

17.00
GREATEST
CARDIOVASCULAR
EFFECIENCY
& MUSCLE
STRENGTH

NOON 12.00

06.00

18.00

MIDNIGHT 12.00

4.30
LOWEST
BODY
TEMPERATURE

6.45
SHARPEST
RISE IN BLOOD
PRESSURE

2.00
DEEPEST
SLEEP

21.00
MELATONIN
SECRETION STARTS

22.30
BOWEL
MOVEMENT
SUPRESSED

19.00
HIGHEST BODY
TEMPERATURE

THE RHYTHM OF LIFE. WE ARE EFFECTIVELY
MACHINES, WITH OUR BODIES AND BEHAVIOUR
CHANGING ACCORDING TO A CIRCADIAN CLOCK
THROUGHOUT THE DAY AND NIGHT.

and there are more accidents on the roads. It's also the worst time to drink alcohol, as it makes you even groggier. Between 3 pm and 6 pm our body temperature rises slightly, our hearts and lungs work better and our muscles are 6 per cent stronger, so now is a good time for physical work or a workout. Some athletes actually try to get a personal best in sport at this time because of this difference.

Between 6 pm and 9 pm you are ready for dinner. However, don't leave this too late, as the way the body handles food changes as we get closer to night-time. We are more likely to store food as fat, so it's a bad idea to eat at night[12]. A bag of chips eaten at night will pile on more fat than when eaten earlier. This is in part because we are more active during the day and burn it off, but it also appears to be due to storage of fat being more prominent at night. One useful thing, though, is that our liver can break down alcohol at this time, so now is the safest time to drink. From 9 pm to midnight, bedtime is looming.

This is perhaps the most dramatic thing to happen, as our bodies make our own sleeping tablet in the form of melatonin. When our eyes detect the dimming light, melatonin is secreted by the pineal gland in our brains and makes us fall asleep. When we travel across time zones this gets made at the wrong time compared to local time and so we fall asleep and lose vitality at the wrong time – this is what we call jet lag. Sunlight shining in through our eyes affects its production – it is made in low light, and so eventually our bodies acclimatise in the new time zone.

Blue light suppresses its production and is the wavelength of light emitted from computer screens or smartphones, so it is not a good idea to be looking at devices at night-time if you want to sleep. Shift workers working at night have to defy their own melatonin, and then have trouble sleeping at other times. They are also more likely to be obese, as they eat at night. One reason therefore for the current obesity epidemic is that people have disrupted sleep or are sleep-deprived and are eating at the wrong time.

Melatonin gets made earlier if you are a morning lark and later if you are a night owl, although what controls this isn't known. Genes that make proteins that control our circadian rhythm, and one called PER2 seems to play a prominent role. PER2 appears to be one of the key cogs in our body clock. If you have one type (called the long type), you will be more likely to be a morning lark, whereas if you've the short type you will be a night owl. There is also a condition called familial advanced sleep phase syndrome, where people fall asleep at 7.30 pm and wake at 4.30 am on average. This runs in families, so if you happen to have a family near you with this condition, don't call around at 7.30 pm, as they will all be snoring. It is caused by a particular mutation in PER2, further highlighting the importance of this protein for controlling our sleep/wake cycle[13]. PER2 and other components are responding to sunlight, which therefore sets our body clocks. It's almost as if sunlight is the key that winds up the daily spring in our body clock, with PER2 running as the spring unwinds.

The role of sunlight in maintaining our body clocks is likely to be important when we consider seasonal affective disorder (SAD). This is a mood disorder in which people who have good mental health for most of the year have depression in the winter. They sleep too much and have less energy. This is likely to be caused by less sunlight. In the US it affects 1.4 per cent in Florida but 9.9 per cent in Alaska. Similar rates have been reported in Nordic countries. This response may have evolved to make us less active in the winter, when food is scarcer. Light therapy can be a useful treatment for SAD, as can dawn simulation, which involves a device that gives gradually increased light in the morning when it would otherwise be dark. The long, dark winter may limit the production of melatonin, which light therapy appears to restore. Melatonin itself can be a useful therapy.

What is also interesting regarding circadian rhythm and mood is that if you are a night owl, you have a higher risk of depression and cancer[14]. Night owls are also inclined to be more outgoing, sociable, narcissistic and promiscuous. One interpretation of this is that it's to do with what zoologists call 'mate poaching' – if you are awake at night and your rival isn't you might poach his or her partner. Marital breakdown has also been shown to be higher if two night owls marry or if two larks marry. This could be because they get in each other's way (and on each other's nerves). The ideal marriage is an owl and a lark, as they will only meet up at certain times, and might have complementary personalities. Perhaps the ability to stagger responsibilities such as childcare and household chores over a longer day leads to harmonious relationships.

Owls and larks to one side, there are some creatures that don't rely on sunlight to set their clocks. Bristle worms, which live in the sea, use moonlight to set theirs, and sea lice use the tides to set theirs, so any regular environmental cue will do.

From midnight to 3 am you are asleep, and the sluice gates open to flush out the debris from your brain that has built up during the day. If you're still awake, however, you need to be careful. You may well have the long dark night of the soul, as the hormones in your body are making you feel tired and somewhat low in mood. Industrial accidents are much more common during these hours, for obvious reasons. From 3 am to 6 am you are still hopefully asleep, but melatonin levels start to fall to get you ready to wake up. Your core body temperature is also cooler, as energy is diverted away from maintaining a body temperature at 37°C, to other activities like skin repair.

Sleep may well promote beauty by making your skin look better. The energy might also be needed to keep the flush on in the brain. It has recently been shown that our immune systems are more active at night and less active during the day[15]. This seems odd, as we might need our immune systems to defend us when we are up and about, since we might be more likely to get infections. It may be that a slightly less active immune system might stop us from overreacting to mild infections, which can do more harm than good. It is also thought that during the night the immune system is creating memories of what it encountered during the day, so that if we see the same infection again we will respond to it appropriately.

This feature, however, also has consequences for diseases involving our immune system. Rheumatoid arthritis is a disease where our immune systems attack our own joints, causing destruction and pain. It's worse at night, and people wake up very stiff and sore. Asthma attacks are also more common at night, and again this could be due to an overactive allergic response in our lungs, at the same time when our lung function is at its lowest.

And so, having gone through a 24-hour cycle, we wake up again, to the beat of a drum, or in this case your body clock. This circadian rhythm reveals how we are actually machines, and how our moods, appetites and sleep patterns are governed not by choice but by the workings of clock proteins in our bodies.

There is of course variation in the human population, as the general distinction of the night owl and morning lark reveals. People who need very little sleep and yet appear to be healthy have been the subject of a recent study. A genetic basis for what are called 'short sleepers' has been found[16]. Many of these people who only need four to six hours a night share a mutation in a gene known as DEC2. Mice that were created with this mutation also needed very little sleep, and when their brains were examined, a very interesting finding was made: they had enhanced connections between the parts of the brain that connect sensation and memory. The mice were also less likely to be overweight, which is similar to humans who are short sleepers. How can they get away with half the amount of sleep as the rest of us? It appears they get more bang for their buck when it comes to sleep. The enhanced connections might enhance the sluicing of debris or allow for memory consolidation, which is thought to be another important function of sleep.

The discovery of this mutated gene promoting short sleep is an intriguing development, and scientists would love to know exactly what it does. It may well be the master regulator of the sluicing, which as we have seen is a key purpose behind why we sleep at all.

Would you like the short-sleep DEC2? What would you do with the extra time it would give you? Who knows, the future might have lots of genetically modified short sleepers, up all night to get lucky, enjoying themselves, and truly seizing the day.

AFTER SLEEPING BEAUTY HITS THE
SNOOZE BUTTON FOR THE FIFTH
TIME ON HER SMARTPHONE, PRINCE
CHARMING INTERVENES.

CHAPTER 11

OUR DESPERATE RELATIONSHIP WITH FOOD

A LL LIFE ON EARTH consumes nutrients. We eat to take in molecules that we use to build more of us, and also to provide us with the energy that our bodies need to work. Food provides the fuel in the tank but also the parts we need to make a new car. This all seems very simple. And yet the science of food and nutrition is often dogged with controversy. It is full of bad science, commercial interests and torment. Our relationship with food in the 21st century has become ever more complex, and the developed world is currently suffering from an obesity epidemic.

We now have a deeper understanding of what it is about food that makes us crave it, and efforts are under way to make synthetic food that is healthier and that will cut out the middle man (or in this case the middle cow). Who would have thought that something our ancestors thought of as a simple thing (I'm hungry, I must eat) would have become so complex and disturbing?

A lot of scientific progress has given insight into what controls our appetite, why we crave certain foods and why some people are prone to obesity. It's a very important medical question, as current analysis shows that 25 per cent of Irish people are overweight or obese, with that percentage set to rise[1]. Being overweight brings with it all kinds of health problems, from heart disease to diabetes to an increased risk of cancer. Governments are trying to do things

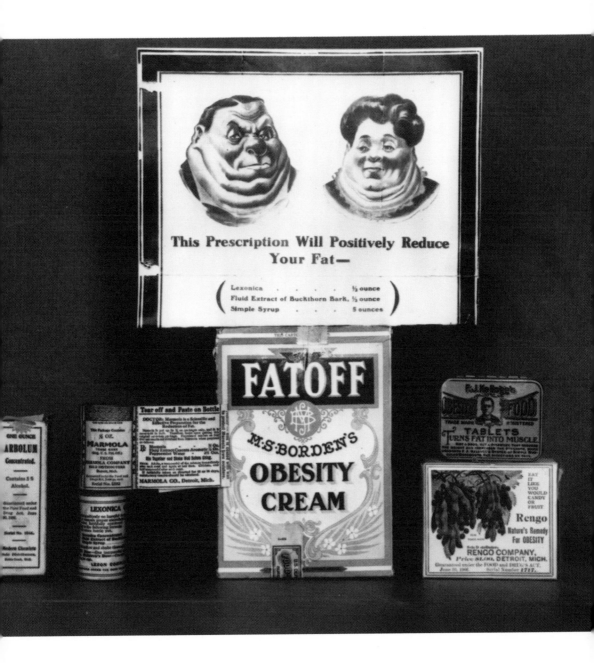

ON SALE IN THE US IN THE
1800S, FAT OFF CREAM CLAIMED
TO 'REDUCE SUPERFLUOUS FLESH
WHEREVER NEEDED'.

to stem this tide of obesity, whether it be a tax on sugar or a decrease in fat content in processed foods. There appears to be a constant battle between food producers and regulators. Food producers want to maintain their businesses, while regulators want to make sure the public don't get sick.

But there is no doubt that high sugar consumption promotes obesity. The reason is simple. We live in Stone Age bodies – that is to say, bodies that evolved for conditions that prevailed 200,000 years ago. Food was relatively scarce, so when we got some, we ate as much of it as we could. When we had our fill, any extra was stored as fat. Our bodies are especially good at changing sugar into fat, since fat is a great way to store food. The energy released when we burn fat is huge – at least ten times more than burning the same amount of sugar, and so we store fat from sugar for the rainy day when we're starving.

The modern situation, however, is that we are rarely starving and we're always gorging. Result? We become obese. Added to this is the fact that our primitive ancestors had a lifestyle where they hunted, caught the animal to eat, ate it and then ran on. Run, eat, run. As opposed to *Run, Fatboy, Run*. Life today therefore has a deadly combination: no running and a lot of eating. Our sedentary lifestyle is working against us. Eating is one of Maslow's primary needs, and so it's little wonder that in our current land of plenty (at least in most countries) we keep on eating.

But is it really as simple as that? Recent work has identified hormones that control our appetite, our desire for certain foods and also the off-switch – the response that says 'stop eating'. These can go out of kilter too, and lead to obesity. Some sound like the names of the seven dwarves – for example, leptin and ghrelin. Others have more complex names such as FGF21, a hormone that stops us having a sweet tooth. Work on them is giving us some fascinating insights into when we eat, why we eat, what we eat and when we decide to stop eating.

Scientists have been studying hunger and satiety (feeling full) for decades. These are sensations, with hunger being the physiological need to eat food,

and satiety the absence of hunger. Feeling hungry generally happens after only a few hours without eating, and is sufficiently unpleasant to motivate us to seek food. Satiety happens five to 20 minutes after eating. A breakthrough happened with the discovery of a hormone called leptin[2]. This hormone is mainly

THE OB/OB MOUSE (LEFT) IS GENETICALLY OBESE. IT CAN'T MAKE A HORMONE CALLED LEPTIN WHICH LIMITS HUNGER, CAUSING THE MOUSE TO OVEREAT.

made by fat cells and regulates energy balance in your body by stopping you from feeling hungry. The discovery of leptin gave rise to great excitement. Might it be possible to give it to people to stop them eating? Sadly things didn't turn out as simple as that.

Leptin was discovered from studies on obese mice. In 1949, scientists in the US found a laboratory strain of mice that ate voraciously and were massively obese; these mice were called ob/ob mice ('ob' being short for 'obese'). Then another strain of obese mice was found that developed diabetes; these were called db/db mice, 'db' standing for diabetes. And then in 1990, the defective gene in the ob/ob mouse was found, and was shown to be responsible for making leptin (the name is from the Greek meaning 'thin'). The ob/ob mice turned out to be missing leptin, and the db/db mouse was shown to be missing the leptin sensor (called a 'receptor') on cells, and so couldn't respond to their own leptin. Both mice were therefore obese because of a defect in leptin – ob/ob mice couldn't make any, and db/db mice couldn't respond to their own leptin.

An Irish scientist, Stephen O'Rahilly, then made an important discovery in humans, describing severely obese children who were obese because they couldn't make any leptin, a bit like the ob/ob mouse. These patients were treated with leptin, and lost weight dramatically. They remain of normal weight to this day, but require daily leptin injections. Leptin was then investigated as a treatment for more common forms of obesity. Surely if it was given to obese people they would then feel full and stop eating? But as ever with science and medicine, there is many a slip twixt cup and lip (a particularly apt analogy if the cup holds a sugary drink). It turns out that most obese people have high circulating levels of leptin anyway, because they have a higher percentage of body fat. Remember, it's your fat cells that make the leptin. They have actually become resistant to their own leptin. The elevated levels of leptin therefore fail to control hunger and regulate weight gain.

Although leptin may not quite be the hormone to allow you to have your cake and eat it, work on it has revealed the complexities of how hormones can regulate obesity. Leptin may in fact be a starvation signal sent when levels are low, provoking us to get some food. When it's made normally, it says 'Stop looking for food because you have plenty of fat in storage.' And obesity may be partly about our bodies not responding to our own leptin. Studies are trying to make obese people more responsive to their own leptin, as occurs in type 2 diabetes, where several of the existing drugs that are used work by making people more sensitive to their own insulin.

So if leptin isn't crucial to making you feel full, then what is? This involves a special region in your brain called the ventromedial nucleus, which is in a

GO ON ... IGNORE YOUR FGF21
AND HAVE SOME.

part of your brain called the hypothalamus. It turns out that this part of the brain can actually sense the levels of nutrients in your blood, including rising blood glucose, fats and the levels of amino acids (which come from protein). It is especially sensitive to the level of amino acids. All those amino acids in your bloodstream regulate your appetite and get you to eat less overall. This might explain why a high-protein diet helps us lose weight.

Psychology can also play a role, however. If you repeatedly see a picture of a foodstuff, you actually go off it, at least for a short time. This is probably to stop you eating too much of the same food, which might lead to a deficiency in nutrients. Work on leptin led to the discovery of another hormone that regulates appetite: ghrelin. Low levels of leptin (which occur when you have insufficient stores of fat) trigger the release of ghrelin, which is therefore described as a secondary hormone to leptin[3].

Ghrelin actually makes you feel hungry. Studies have shown that increased production of ghrelin will enhance appetite when we actually see food. When you see an advertisement for food and you feel hungry it is probably ghrelin that is making you want that food. Also of interest are studies showing that when you are stressed, ghrelin is made. This may explain why hunger can prevail during a stressful situation. To lose your appetite then might be negative, as you risk being malnourished in a stressful situation when you might need energy. There are currently studies exploring the use of ghrelin to stimulate appetite in the elderly, or in cancer patients who lose their appetite. GLP1 is another, possibly even more important, substance made that stimulates appetite, so this is a very active area of research.

One of the most interesting recent studies described another hormone called FGF21, which is made after we've eaten sugar. Its job is to regulate how much sugar we eat. For those of us who make plenty of it, it is easier not to be tempted by the vending machine in the corridor. For those with less of it, however, the temptation to eat all the biscuits in the packet is too strong. Studies have shown that no matter how careful you are with your diet, some of us just find it too hard to overcome the desire for more sweet things, and it could be down to FGF21 levels. This hormone had been found to reduce sugar ingestion in rats, but now the same has been shown to be the case in humans.

In a study in Denmark involving 6,500 Danes[4], scientists found that those with a particular type of FGF21 were 20 per cent more likely to be high consumers of sweets. These people were carrying a defective form of FGF21, hence the increased tendency to eat cakes and sweets. The liver can sense how much sugar there is in your blood and starts to make and send out FGF21, which goes to your brain and says 'Stop eating sugar.' Our craving for sugar decreases and we find it less appealing.

This kind of research might be useful in helping people to lose weight, as giving FGF21 will suppress the desire for sugar and so lower the production of fat. However, as ever with science, unexpected results crop up. It turns out that people with defective FGF21 were actually less obese. This was a surprise, as it was the opposite of what we might expect, since these people ate more sugar. Clearly obesity is not just down to sugar consumption; a sedentary lifestyle is a big factor. Perhaps FGF21 has other roles, such as promoting exercise – maybe the type of exercise that involves running to the shop to buy more sugary foods.

The work did highlight how a hormone can control how much sweet food we eat, though. That said, the likelihood of simply injecting yourself with a hormone to help you lose weight by affecting your appetite seems challenging, but this is an active area of research. Meanwhile several diets have been proven to help, including the low-carbohydrate diet (which might be due to all the amino acids in the proteins being eaten, making you feel full), the Mediterranean diet (which involves a lot of olive oil, vegetables, fish and berries) and the Paleo (or Stone Age) diet, which has no processed foods[5]. These have been shown to help people lose weight or put on less weight. However the simplest advice is to eat less and exercise more.

Although FGF21 makes sure you eat less sugar, what do we know about cravings? We all have these, and they can suddenly jump up on you. Seemingly out of nowhere you will have a craving for some salt and vinegar crisps or a bag of toffees. Some will crave a type of food which others won't like at all.

WE TASTE FOOD THROUGH
TASTE BUDS ON OUR TONGUES
BUT WE ALSO USE OUR SENSE OF
SMELL.

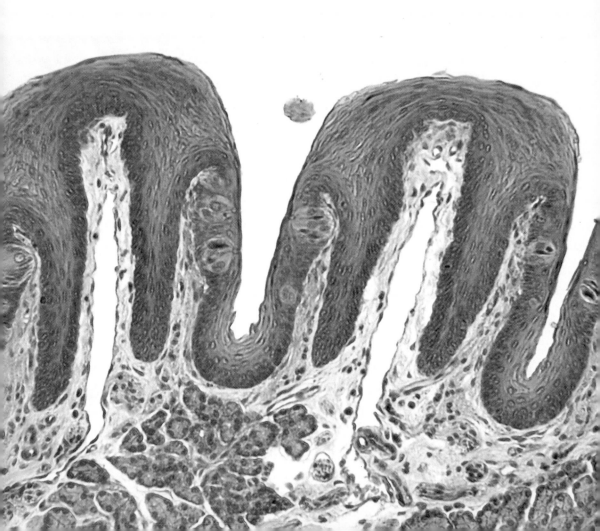

What is it that gives us these appetites? Preferences might be formed in part while we are still in our mother's womb. A fan of carrots, for example, will give birth to one (a fan that is, not a carrot). And all mammals have a craving for sweet things, perhaps because it is the main taste in their mother's milk.

Studies have also shown that babies born to mothers who have diets high in fat and sugar are inclined to become obese, but also they are at a higher risk of being addicted to other substances, including alcohol and drugs[6]. So if you want you can blame your mother for your Krispy Kreme Donuts, Jack Daniels or speed habit (although it must be said the science behind all this is not especially robust). One possible mechanism here is the dopamine rush that we get in our brains when we eat food, which we find pleasurable.

Dopamine is the reward neurotransmitter that is also triggered by alcohol and drugs, and so we may also crave those. This gives rise to the question – can we become addicted to food? In a way we can. Brain scans of teenagers who have eaten chocolate ice cream are revealing. Those who had it as an occasional treat had huge activity in their brains. But those who ate it all the time had a much lower signal, showing that they had become desensitised. This might mean that they will overindulge next time to get the same kick as they got before they developed tolerance.

Psychology again plays a role here. For some unknown reason, if you eat food off a round plate you will think it is sweeter than if you eat it off a square plate[7]. A copper spoon can make food taste bitter. Strawberry mousse tastes 10 per cent sweeter on a white plate, while coffee tastes less bitter if you serve it in a transparent blue glass. A red soft drink will be rated as being sweeter, while a yellow drink will be rated as more sour. A colourless cola sold under the name 'Tab Clear' bombed, even though it had the exact same flavour as the regular version. It's not known why this happens, as we taste food on the taste buds on our tongues.

And a lot of taste also involves smell. A good thing to try is to eat some mint leaves while pinching your nose. The mint will taste bland, until you unpinch your nose, after which the sensation of mint rushes to your brain.

You are tasting the mint via your taste buds but also through your sense of smell. We only have five types of receptors for taste on our taste buds: salt, sweet, bitter, sour and savoury (also called umami). But our noses have thousands of receptors for what we smell, so there is much more diversity there. We mainly 'taste' melons and pineapples from our sense of smell.

As we get older, our sense of smell starts to fail, which is one reason why older people will complain that food has no flavour. And one place where all our senses of taste and smell are compromised is in an aeroplane[8]. The senses of taste and smell are the first things to go at 30,000 feet. This is a recipe for disaster when combined with that wonderful airline food that we all love. Our perception of saltiness and sweetness fall by as much as 30 per cent when we are in a pressurised cabin. This is driven by a lack of humidity, lower air pressure and even the background noise. Airlines add more salt and spice to the food to make it more palatable. Fruity wines retain some of their flavour at altitude, but one drink that really suffers is champagne, which tastes much more acidic at altitude.

So what might the future look like for food? For the obesity epidemic dietary change and more exercise are key, but both are difficult to achieve because of our hard-wired desire for sugar, salt and fat, and how our hormones can get the better of us. Perhaps the future is in synthetic food[9]. This is a very active area of research. One reason for decreasing meat production is to save the planet. Meat production is a huge cause of greenhouse gases. In Ireland, one-third of our greenhouse gases come from farm animals belching methane, which as a greenhouse gas is eight times as damaging as carbon dioxide.

If we can make meat synthetically, we can alter its composition to make it healthier and more nutritious. In 2015, the first ever synthetic burger was reported. It took five years to make and involved taking cells from organic cows, culturing them in a nutrient solution to allow them to grow into a type of muscle tissue, and then teasing them into strands of meat. The burger needed tens of billions of cells, egg powder, beetroot juice, breadcrumbs, salt and

saffron to add flavour and texture. It also cost $330,000, and so won't be in a shop near you anytime soon.

Several companies have been set up to explore synthetic food, however. One of the more notable ones, 'Impossible Foods', is backed by Bill Gates and Larry Page of Google fame[10]. Like other Silicon Valley ventures, they sold themselves on the principal of 'disintermediation' – removing the middle man. Just as Amazon removed the bookstore, Impossible Foods will remove the middle cow. Gates's investment was inspired by the growing number of middle-class people in the developing world, as a feature of wealth is the desire for meat. This company has sold its burgers in several restaurants in the US, with what are claimed to be promising results. How did it crack the challenge at a price that people could afford?

Patrick Brown, the biochemist founder of Impossible Foods, knew that a key ingredient in meat is a substance called haem. Haem gives meat its red

IN 2015, THE FIRST COMPLETELY SYNTHETIC BURGER WAS MADE BY GROWING BILLIONS OF CELLS FROM COWS AND ADDING EGG POWDER, BEETROOT JUICE AND OTHER INGREDIENTS. COST: $330,000.

colour and some of its protein content. Brown realised that a similar protein could be found in clover, and so he collected clover from a hill near his house and extracted the haem. He then combined it with fibre from wheat and potatoes, coconut oil instead of animal fat and an Asian plant called konjac as a replacement for gelatin. These burgers will be considerably less fattening, with a lot less cholesterol than regular burgers, and could lead to less obesity. He is now producing synthetic burgers in a company employing 140 staff. In effect he has removed the cow from the chain of events that begins with them eating clover to help make meat. He now makes the 'meat' directly from the clover.

A key issue is of course flavour. The burger has to trigger the same pleasure sensations and dopamine rush as a regular burger. The company is working on the 'sizzle' – the way a burger reacts to cooking and mouth-coating, the aftertaste that makes a burger so appealing. To identify the chemicals that give rise to these flavours, extracts of regular barbecued meat were fed into a mass spectrometer (a machine that identifies chemicals at a very high sensitivity). Human noses also smelt the sizzling meat and listed flavours which included, alongside 'buttery' and 'burnt', more unusual descriptors such as 'skunk' and 'smelly diaper'. The company has managed to recreate some of these flavours in their burger. They are also working on pork and chicken, but beef burgers are the main focus. This is because burger meat is consumed in huge quantities. McDonald's sells 500,000 tonnes of beef per year. If some of these could be substituted with the synthetic burger, and if soft drinks with a lot less glucose syrup could be sold, there is likely to be a major effect on levels of obesity.

Synthetic food is of course nothing new. Processed cheese has been sold for years, containing fillers, oils and emulsifiers and often no cheese. Similarly, butter substitutes with no butter are common, as is orange juice that is not orange juice but rather extracts of various fruit concentrates with flavours added. These stimulate the same pathways in our brains as natural foods, but with fewer nutritional benefits. A synthetic juice drink will still stimulate the production of FGF21, which hopefully does its job and stops you drinking too much of it.

With the prospect of synthetic food and the advent of food as a major business proposition looking for innovation and new markets, food fraud has also emerged as a concern[11]. How do you know that what you're eating is what it says on the label? Food fraud is said to cost the global food industry $49 billion per year, with the top three foods that are adulterated being oil, milk and honey. Europe was beset in 2013 by the horse meat scandal, where foods advertised as beef were found to contain horse meat[12]. This revealed a major breakdown in the traceability of the food supply. In the UK, of 27 beef burgers tested, 37 per cent tested positive for horse DNA, and 85 per cent for pig DNA. An Irish company called Identigen has led the way with using DNA testing to prove the origin of beef, and through their work and that of companies like them, food fraud, at least in the meat industry, should be less common.

The horse meat scandal at least gave us one of the funnier jokes of 2013: What is HAMBURGERS an anagram of? SHERGAR BUM. And when it comes to food perhaps we should remember what Alex Levine, a well-known science writer, said: 'Only Irish coffee provides in a single glass all four essential food groups: alcohol, caffeine, sugar and fat.' Ireland can therefore rejoice as the provider of excellent food and drink. If only we could get rid of the obesity epidemic we might become the poster children of Europe when it comes to the food industry and nutrition.

CHAPTER 12

SUPERHUMANS REAL AND IMAGINED

COMIC BOOKS AND HOLLYWOOD have always had a great time with enhanced humans created by genetic engineering – stories featuring a dystopian future where modified humans go out of control. One example of how an attempt to predict the future got it terribly wrong was the 1982 movie *Blade Runner*. This movie depicts a dystopian Los Angeles in 2019 where 'replicants' – as genetically engineered humans are termed – are made to work in off-world colonies. Some escape and return to Earth and Harrison Ford plays a special policeman (a 'blade runner') whose job it is to hunt them down. The movie is therefore very high tech, with one exception. At one point, Ford has to make a phone call, and guess what? He uses a pay phone. All that tremendous science and yet no mobile phones. It illustrates how predicting the future can be dangerous.

However, recent advances in genetic engineering, notably a technique called CRISPR, have made the prospect of altering humans genetically a more feasible occurrence. Might it be possible to make humans disease-resistant by correcting faulty genes? And how about existing humans who are naturally superior in terms of resisting diseases? Can we use that information to make everyone disease-resistant? Would it be possible to make a human like Fionn MacCumhaill or Spiderman? Can we make humans with stronger muscles or vision or hearing?

You actually don't need technology that is too advanced to try to make a superhuman. Humans have been trying to do this since boy met girl all those years ago on the plains of Africa. As we saw in Chapter 3, the woman will select her mate based on her guessing of certain traits, such as intelligence or likelihood to stay around to help raise the offspring. The man on the other hand will select his mate based on her perceived fertility, such as shiny hair or a curvy body indicating fat stores. Both sexes like symmetry in the face, because this correlates with normal development and so good genes.

The future though might involve parents-to-be selecting traits that their babies will have, based on testing sperm and egg. The company 23andMe was recently given a patent called 'Family Traits Inheritance Calculator' (patent #8543339), which allows them to use genetic and computer technologies that would allow prospective parents to hand-pick a sperm or egg donor. The chosen donor would be likely to produce a child born with certain traits based on genetic features of the donor. Sperm banks already provide a wide range of information on the man who produced the sperm. Things like socio-economic status, pedigree (number of siblings, nieces and nephews and the like), level of intelligence and many other features can be listed.

There is a huge premium on sperm from very successful men, including Nobel laureates, who regularly get asked for sperm donations. One laureate supposedly responded by saying, 'It's not my sperm you want. It's my dad's, as he produced me. He's a cab driver in New York.' An IVF clinic in the US will charge $2,500 for you to select the gender of your child, based on whether you use a male (XY) or female (XX) sperm. However, 23andMe allows for genetic testing to select a 'preferred donor', which when combined with the genetics of the person who is selecting the sperm or egg is most likely to give rise to a child with selected traits where genetics plays a big role. Diseases with a strong genetic basis such as cystic fibrosis or Huntington's disease can also be predicted. And there is no need to worry about the morality of what's happening, because selection happens before fertilisation (unless, of course, you believe that every sperm is sacred).

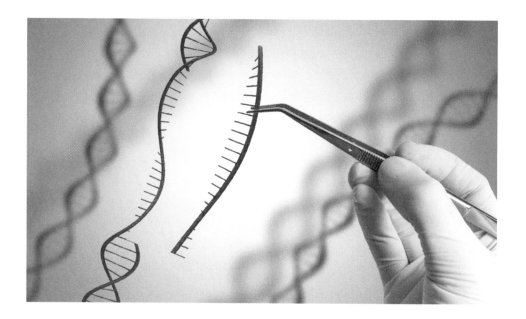

A TECHNOLOGY CALLED CRISPR HAS MADE GENETIC ENGINEERING MUCH EASIER.

But the 23andMe patent goes beyond issues of health and includes such traits as height, weight, eye colour, 'personality characteristics' like warmth and sense of humour, and the kind of muscle performance that would make the person better at endurance sports. These can't be fully guaranteed, however, as the precise genetic basis for these things is not fully known, and there are environmental influences that are probably as important, or at least work in tandem with, the genetic traits.

The science isn't there yet, though. At the moment, 23andMe aren't providing this service, but the fact that they have patented it indicates that they or someone else will. If there is a hefty profit to be made they may well pursue it. Market research reported on a parent who said, 'If I am going to spend $100K to send my kid to Princeton, I'll spend $20K to give my kid an increased chance of success in life at the genetic level.' This of course brings us closer to a *Brave New World* situation, where the rich can afford to make sure their kids have the best traits.

And 23andMe can at the moment provide you with a range of information on your own DNA, including predicting your risk of over 200 diseases. I had my DNA tested and learnt that I am hypersensitive to the blood-thinning drug warfarin. I am also sensitive to norovirus, the winter vomiting virus, and I have a higher risk of blindness in old age. I also found out that I am distantly related to the actress Susan Sarandon. Based on my genetics, the chances of me starring in a film with Susan as 'Blind Vomiting Clot-Man' seem remote.

If we know that certain genetic variants result in certain traits, how close are we to actually making designer babies, where we engineer traits into eggs, sperm or the fertilised egg? How close is 'Gucci Gucci Goo'? The discovery of a technique called CRISPR has brought us closer than ever. CRISPR has made genetic engineering relatively easy. You can almost do it in your kitchen. It's a bit like going from a hand-operated whisk to a food processor. It was first discovered in bacteria, in an enzyme called Cas9, which are able to chop out viral genes from their genomes as a means of self-defence. The same machinery can be used on any cell, though, and scientists can now remove genes, or replace broken ones with fixed ones. Human embryos were recently tested, and a gene linked to heart attacks was fixed[1]. The embryo wasn't implanted but could have been.

Dogs, goats and monkeys have all been modified, but pigs have been at the heart of some eye-catching work. So-called micro-pigs have been made that weigh six times less than normal pigs, and are sold as pets. Pigs with more muscle (and hence more pork) have also been made, as has a pig whose DNA has been modified in 62 places, the aim being to make organs that might be usable in humans[2]. This is a laudable goal, as many transplant patients are waiting for a donor, so if a pig kidney could be used that matches those in humans, a lot more transplants could be performed. Less importantly, goats have been made with longer hair to produce more cashmere. And in a particularly exciting development, mosquitoes are being engineered to be sterile. They will compete with other mosquitoes in the wild and may eventually dominate the population, potentially getting rid of malaria, which they transmit.

MOSQUITOES THAT ARE MODIFIED USING CRISPR SO THAT THEY CAN NO LONGER TRANSMIT DISEASES SUCH AS MALARIA ARE CURRENTLY BEING TESTED. THIS HAS THE POTENTIAL TO ERADICATE MALARIA WITHIN ONE YEAR OF THEIR RELEASE.

The ethics of using CRISPR on humans, however, has been hotly debated, and has been banned in many countries. International guidelines state that humans shouldn't be altered using CRISPR. The fear is that once it starts it won't stop, and the population of the Earth will be dramatically changed for various traits. For the first time ever, there is a species on Earth (i.e. us) who can tamper with genetics with relative ease, not through the usual way of natural selection allowing for survival of the fittest, but by directed intervention.

No one knows where that will lead. These kinds of things scare some people, as they raise the prospect of eugenics. Previously, discussions on genetic enhancement were largely viewed as theoretical, but CRISPR is seen as something of a game changer. It's more flexible, accurate, cheaper and easier to use than previous techniques. Scientists in China recently successfully applied CRISPR to human embryos, although the embryos were later destroyed, in compliance with Chinese ethical guidelines. Next came the UK, where human embryos were also modified, in a study of early development. So far only Denmark and German have banned using CRISPR on human embryos.

There is a strong lobby to allow CRISPR to correct genes that will cause birth defects. Every year an estimated 7.9 million children are born with such defects. Potentially CRISPR could stop all that suffering. Clearly the recent success of editing a gene in human embryos by CRISPR must mean that this will eventually come to pass, although it will have to be tightly regulated.

So what genes would we modify if we could? We might be able to make a superhuman that is resistant to diseases. This could involve correcting or deleting a broken gene. A good example is cystic fibrosis, where a gene making a protein called CFTR is defective. The job of this protein is to keep the salt balance in your lungs normal – it is a chloride ion channel. In people with cystic fibrosis, however, it behaves abnormally. There are drugs available that help it work better, by binding to CFTR and getting it to perform. The best known is Vertex's Ivacaftor, which has made a big difference to people with cystic fibrosis. But if you could fix the gene in the embryo using CRISPR, that would solve the problem at source and permanently. There are many diseases up for grabs that afflict humanity caused by a genetic defect.

One interesting study took a different approach. Usually doctors study someone who is sick, find out what is wrong with them and then treat them. Recently, however, doctors have been examining people who should be sick but who aren't. Some people never get AIDS in spite of being infected regularly. Why? And we all know the granny who smoked all her life but didn't die of lung cancer. This is an interesting group of people to examine. One study recently looked at 13 people who have genetic mutations that mean they should be dead[3]. These people have defied their own biology – but the big question is how?

The study involved almost 600,000 people. One of these people should have had cystic fibrosis but didn't. Another should have had Pfeiffer syndrome (a disease affecting skull growth) but didn't. These people must have had other genetic changes that protect them, and scientists are now trying to find out what those changes are. They are basically making their own medicine of sorts to stop themselves from getting sick. The gene variant responsible could potentially be engineered into people to prevent disease. A bigger study called 'Resilience' is under way to find more of these people, specifically those who should have more common diseases based on their genetics but don't. These resilient people could prove to be quite useful.

In the case of AIDS, people were found who had been heavily exposed to the virus but never succumbed[4]. Their genetics was studied, and some of them were found to have a mutation in the gene for a protein called CCR5.

This protein is on the surface of T lymphocytes – the cell type infected by the human immunodeficiency virus (HIV), which causes AIDS. The virus locks onto it and then gets inside the T lymphocyte. Those people who weren't infected had a version that the virus could not lock onto. It was a bit like changing the locks on the door – the old key no longer fits and the virus can't get in.

This led to the development of a drug called Maraviroc, which binds to CCR5 to prevent viral entry and has shown some success. That resistant CCR5 variant could be engineered into humans, making HIV infection a thing of the past. We are all inheritors of an immune system built up by our ancestors over many generations in order to survive in the face of infection.

Genes of the immune system are the fastest-evolving genes in humans because of this constant battle with infectious bacteria, viruses and fungi. So if AIDS had been allowed to continue to kill so many people, only those with the CCR5 mutation would have survived.

And what about smokers? People who live to a ripe old age despite being heavy smokers have been studied in detail, and a set of genes has been found that seems to protect them[5]. These genes are involved in repairing damage to DNA. Smoking will damage DNA, causing mutations that promote cancer. But in those who are resistant, that damage is corrected, providing some protection against cancer developing. It's as though these people have a spellchecker that corrects the mistakes in the DNA code caused by smoking. This souped-up spellchecker might prevent damage from all kinds of environmental toxins and pollutants, and could be engineered into humans to prevent them from getting a whole range of environmental cancers. Smoking kills half of the people who smoke, so understanding how to prevent the damage it causes could be most useful.

Britain's oldest smoker died at the age of 102, and doctors estimated that she smoked her way through 170,000 cigarettes[6]. Winnie Langley took up the habit days after World War I broke out. She was seven years old. Winnie outlived her husband Robert and her son Donald. She cut down from five cigarettes a day to one a year before she died because of what she said was 'the credit crunch'. This may have been the cause of her demise. Her genetics would certainly be interesting to probe.

Sporting prowess has also been studied extensively. Scientists are trying to help our muscles work better. This might involve strengthening muscles in the elderly or helping devise new treatments for muscle-wasting diseases such as Duchenne muscular dystrophy (DMD). Genetics again plays a part in some of these diseases, with DMD involving a mutation in a gene for a muscle protein called dystrophin. However, if we could intervene would we want to make a superhuman who had huge sprinting abilities or endurance?

MARAVIROC, A TREATMENT TO PREVENT AIDS, WAS DISCOVERED FROM WORK ON PATIENTS WHO ARE NATURALLY RESISTANT TO THE HUMAN IMMUNODEFICIENCY VIRUS.

Athletes from East Africa have long been known to be superb performers over long distances. Why is this? It is often assumed that it comes down to genetics, since a small community in areas with few resources has produced a disproportionate number of medallists at the Olympics. There is some evidence that the typical body type of East Africans – e.g. long slender legs – may be part of this success, but distinct genetic traits have yet to be found to explain the performance[7]. A possible reason is that they run a lot in childhood. One study has shown that the distance to school for these successful athletes varied from three to 12 miles each way, with the future athletes running both ways every day. This may have built up stamina and endurance. Training at altitude may also play a part, but a major motivation is the desire for economic success for them and their communities. This drives them on. There is also evidence of a gene encoding a protein (ACTN3) in muscle being involved in running skills. The non-mutant version is associated with sprinting, while a mutant form is linked to endurance. We may well find a large part of the genetic basis for sports performance.

One hormone that is used in doping is erythropoietin, or EPO. Its job is to stimulate your bone marrow to make erythrocytes, also known as red blood cells. These carry oxygen around our bodies. If you inject EPO you make a lot more red blood cells, and this brings more oxygen to muscles, making them burn more fuel and generating more power and stamina. The only problem is that EPO makes your blood very thick with red blood cells, and so increases pressure on your heart, leading to a much higher risk of heart disease.

There are, however, some people who naturally make more EPO than others, and have muscles that work better. Similarly, a protein called NCOR1 was found which can generate muscle mass. When this was engineered into a mouse, the mouse had muscles that were three times stronger than an ordinary mouse[8]. It had in effect become Supermouse. People have therefore speculated whether gene doping might come into sport, where athletes have the natural gene inserted into their tissues, causing them to make the natural proteins, and so there will be no evidence of doping. The risks of such approaches are wholly unknown.

Given that it's been possible to make Supermouse, scientists have had fun speculating on whether it might actually be possible to make superheroes[9]. There are many legends of heroes with huge strength. The Irish hero Fionn Mac Cumhaill could throw rocks the size of the Isle of Man. In the US, comic books and Hollywood have provided a way to give humans superpowers. We've all seen the movie where a scientist is working in the lab late one night (and no doubt about to do the Monster Mash). An unfortunate mishap happens, with some science attached to it – exposure to radiation, some toxic chemical, or some form of high energy with a fly in the chamber, and hey presto we get the Hulk or Spiderman.

Notably, superheroes often start off as scientists. Bruce Banner, who became the Incredible Hulk, is a good example. They are inclined to be handsome, rugged types, which immediately puts us on alert that this can't be true, given that, as we all know, scientist are awkward wimps with glasses and buck teeth, who spend all their time in the lab doing incredibly tedious

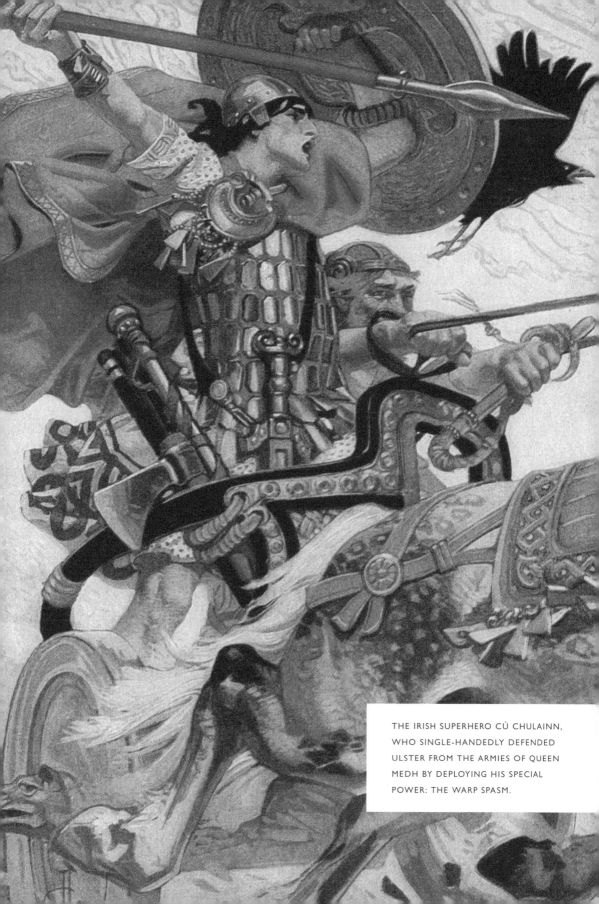

THE IRISH SUPERHERO CÚ CHULAINN,
WHO SINGLE-HANDEDLY DEFENDED
ULSTER FROM THE ARMIES OF QUEEN
MEDH BY DEPLOYING HIS SPECIAL
POWER: THE WARP SPASM.

things that require huge amounts of intelligence, and precious little in the way of social skills. Is there any likelihood that we could turn scientists into superheroes (which of course they are already)?

Creating someone with Superman's powers would be impossible to achieve. His ability to lift heavy objects is put down to gravity being much stronger on his home planet of Krypton. His ability to fly comes down to willpower alone, which sadly will never be achieved.

With Spiderman we are on slightly more solid ground. Peter Parker is the human who is transformed by the bite of a spider that has been exposed to radiation. This might have changed the DNA in the spider, with the venom that is injected into Peter then altering genes. Maybe the writer of Spiderman foresaw CRISPR! He has a super-grip, and is able to walk up walls and across ceilings. Insects can do this in part by having specialised hairs at the base of their feet that allow them to grip. The gecko, a type of lizard, is also able to walk across almost any surface. This comes down again to thousands and thousands of hair-like structures at the base of its toes, which actually penetrate the surface the gecko walks on, causing an attractive force that maintains adhesiveness.

And what about the web he weaves? A spider's web is made of silk which is rich in a protein called keratin. It has huge strength, so it might even be possible for Spiderman to catch criminals with the silk he fires out, and string them up. Scientists are currently examining the silk spiders make to see what they can learn from it in order to make stronger materials for bags and other applications.

And what about his special Spidey Sense? Spiders do have special hairs called setae, which are connected directly to the spider's nervous system and can detect changes in air pressure and temperature. Perhaps Spiderman has these too, and can therefore detect subtle compression changes in the air that are akin to acute hearing abilities. So who knows, if we wanted to we could perhaps make a Spiderman.

The Incredible Hulk also draws on some real science. In the recent version Bruce Banner's father, who is tampering with DNA, modifies his own, which is passed down. Again, did the writers see the advent of CRISPR? Bruce is then exposed to gamma rays – a very high-energy form of radiation. This leads to further changes. This could all build up muscle mass, especially if the gene for NCOR1 was modified. But the business of suddenly building such mass is too far-fetched, as it takes years for such transformations to occur.

So sadly it seems unlikely that we'll turn humans into superheroes any time soon, although exactly where CRISPR – or perhaps follow-on technologies that might be even better – might lead is intriguing to speculate on. The likelihood is that some parents will choose traits for their offspring based on DNA testing prior to IVF. Or it might be permissible to do this kind of testing in utero. What might happen then is that if potential defects are found, the wonder of CRISPR will be brought to bear in utero, and the embryo fixed. Whether such traits as intelligence, beauty, musical ability and empathy will ever be shown to have a genetic component which might be modifiable is not certain either, given the complexities of these traits, and the fact that we are all pretty close to each other in these traits anyway. One thing that is obvious is that people will still want to make babies in the old-fashioned way, as evolution made sure that we are all strongly motivated to do it.

CHAPTER 13

ARE THE ROBOTS COMING TO SAVE US OR ENSLAVE US?

ROBOTS ARE THE STUFF of many movies and many worrying predictions about the future. Robots will become more intelligent than us and kill us. There will be few jobs in the future as robots will take them. Driverless cars will revolutionise transport and lead to huge job losses. Well, guess what, at least some of this is coming true. Should we be afraid? Very afraid? Or should we embrace all of this and become freer and happier as a result?

The scaremongerers have been out in force when it comes to robots. The fear that robots will destroy jobs and leave masses of people idle (and as we well know, the devil finds work for idle hands to do) has been with us for decades and is as old as automation itself. And yet, from the Luddites on, the fears have eventually been proven to be wrong, with economies actually ending up stronger than before because of technology. But still, the Bank of England's chief economist recently predicted that robots threaten 15 million jobs in the UK.

But what jobs are most at risk? Obviously we see this already where any kind of repetitive job that can be automated has been replaced by machines, notable examples being in car manufacturing and retail. But more generally, job losses may be evident in places you hadn't thought of. Scientists themselves may be at risk. Recently, in a collaboration between Aberystwyth and Cambridge universities, a robot called Adam discovered new scientific knowledge[1]. The robot was able to design an experiment, carry it out and then interpret the results. Meanwhile, another robot called Eve working in Manchester University has been trying to identify anti-malarial drugs[2].

Often these robots perform repetitive analyses, say, on millions of different drugs, adding them to experimental systems that resemble disease (on cells taken from patients, for example) and trying to find ones that work. They still need to be given a question and programmed to solve it, though, so there will still be a function for at least a few humans.

The second area that is somewhat surprisingly at risk is entertainment. You would think that machines could never disrupt the worlds of art and music, where to be creative needs huge insight and that thing in music called 'soul'. The

EVEN THOUGH HE HAD BEEN DEAD FOR 16 YEARS, IN 2012 TUPAC COULD STILL PLAY 'LIVE' IN THE FORM OF A HOLOGRAM.

art of performing is a direct connection between the performer on the stage and the audience, where something magical happens that a robot couldn't replace. Right? Well yes, until you build a highly effective hologram. In 2012 a hologram of Tupac Shakur performed in Las Vegas, 16 years after his death.

Similarly, Abba have been approached on numerous occasions to reform, and almost did some years ago with the temptation of a pay cheque of $1 billion dollars, which they said they would use to fund a hospital. The deal fell apart, however. But now they are about to go on the road virtually, in the form of very effective holograms that really do look as if they are performing on stage. Mamma Mia! Will people go and watch them? The Abba tour, with all of its state-of-the-art technology, is a real testing ground for this technology, given the appetite the fans have to see Abba in one form or another. It's only a matter of time before we see holograms of U2 performing, and the first

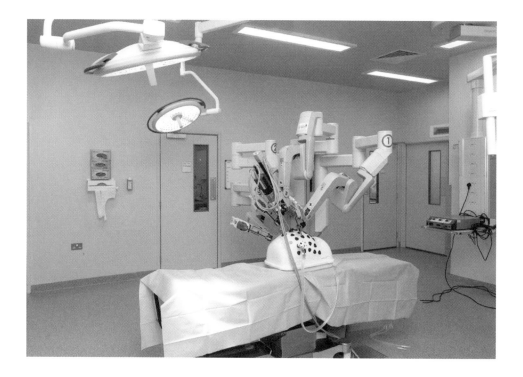

THE DA VINCI SURGICAL
SYSTEM IS MADE BY THE
AMERICAN COMPANY
INTUITIVE SURGICAL.

song they perform will no doubt be 'Even Better Than the Real Thing'.

Art is also being performed by machines with artificial intelligence. This is termed 'generative art', where robots endlessly create paintings or music, out-producing any human. Instead of humans 'mashing up' songs, as for example happened on the Beatles' *Love* album, maybe machines will do it and extract even more out of the Beatles back catalogue.

Another area where robots are increasingly being used is medicine. Right now, robots can diagnose a disease and then prescribe the correct medicine, and even perform surgery. It's just a matter of detecting the indicators of the disease and then, from a vast amount of data, issuing the most effective therapy. Medicine could become a long list of diseases on one side of the page, and the various treatments on the other, with robotic doctors figuring it all out.

But one profession where humans will most likely still be needed is nursing. A career like nursing is in fact the perfect mixture of almost everything a machine finds difficult: fine motor skills (e.g. putting a line into a vein), specialist knowledge, a wide variety of potential complications in the course of the job, and the need to have empathy and put on a friendly face. This means that the profession of nursing is likely to persist.

It will be the doctors who will become unwanted, while the nurses will thrive. Doctors are very expensive to train and hire, which means they are in the front line for replacement. They also make mistakes, being only human. An estimated 215,000 people died in 2013 in the US from medical errors[3]. One interesting statistical study has shown that when doctors go on strike the death rate goes down[4]. The so-called Da Vinci robot can perform surgeries no human can because of its high precision. It can be remotely operated, allowing a surgeon in one hospital to perform an operation in another. The future of surgery may therefore be one highly eminent surgeon overseeing multiple operations carried out by robotic surgeons at remote locations. Most impressively, there is Mabu, the personal healthcare companion. Mabu will engage the patient in conversation and pass the data on to doctors, affording the patient (and doctor) a situation where they don't have to engage with a human being if they don't want to, and still get treated.

Apart from doctors, there are many aspects of the healthcare industry where we will see more and more robots. The Japanese are especially interested in this, as they have an ageing population: a quarter of their 128 million people are over 65. Innovations there are making life easier for the elderly and their caregivers. A 'muscle suit' has been developed that gives the carer extra power when lifting a bed-bound patient. It looks like a backpack and takes off as much as 30 per cent of the strain of lifting someone.

The Japanese have also developed a walking-stick-like device called the 'LIGHTBOT' which will guide visually impaired people to their destination, watching out for trip hazards along the way. In a good example of necessity being the mother of invention, it was developed because of a shortage of guide dogs in Japan, and the difficulties of keeping dogs as pets in Tokyo. Another robot that is proving popular is the 'Robo Nailist'. This is an industrial robot which uses incredible precision to paint people's nails. Elderly women like it because their hands might shake slightly, making putting on nail varnish a challenge.

Journalism is also under threat. A Chicago-based firm called Narrative Science has a product called Quill. If you enter data structured in a certain way it will produce a convincing and original news story. It is currently in use by some news outlets, and is especially good at generating stories in sport and finance, where the information comes in in a predictable format (e.g. goals scored or stock market prices moving). How do you know that what you are reading right now wasn't written by a robot ... written by a robot ... written by a ...?

And what about lawyers? That much-maligned profession might also see itself defunct as robot technology advances. Will lawyers be missed? Law should be the ultimate human-only field. Much of the law is concerned with the precision of common language or the interplay between the theoretical world of textbooks and the real world. Or trying to present complex evidence to a jury to convince them of where the truth lies. Robots have trouble with all of these. But a lot of what happens in law is actually surprisingly rote. Conveyancing, drawing up employment contracts and preparing wills can now all be done online. What is clear is that as artificial intelligence progresses, the need for a human lawyer in many situations where they are currently needed will disappear.

But there is good news too. Robots can actually create employment. A recent study showed that the robotics industry currently employs over 200,000 people worldwide, and this is growing as work in artificial intelligence proceeds. The Chinese are yet again leading the way, with multibillion investments from the government to spur on results. And artificial intelligence is already widespread, be it in your smartphone, GPS or heating system. The Chinese want it to be as ubiquitous as electricity. They are planning for a true internet of things, where every device is connected to every other device, and is always learning. The great line is that Google knows more about you than you do, and also if you're a woman it can also know that you're pregnant before you do, based on what you are searching for or buying.

Robots have been shown to be responsible for an annual growth of labour productivity and GDP by 0.36 and 0.37 percentage points, respectively, between 1993 and 2007[5]. This translates into 10 per cent of total GDP growth in the countries studied, and 16 per cent of labour productivity growth over that time. And people are getting more comfortable at having robots around. An EU survey revealed that 35 per cent of people would be happy in a driverless car. Fifty-seven per cent believe that drones are a convenient way to transport goods. Bill Gates thinks we should tax them.

One emerging idea is that robots will spare us the need to talk to other people – something some of us would cherish. Silicon Valley Robotics (where else?) has a robot that will check you into your hotel room. Their analysis shows that people enjoy interacting with robots, but what they enjoy even more is not to have a social interaction with someone at a time when they are not feeling sociable. Some hardware stores in the US have OSHbot, a robot that will bring you to the right shelf and initiate a video call with human experts if there are specific issues that it can't address.

Given that over $3 billion is currently being spent in China on robotics and artificial intelligence, we are bound to see major advances in many areas. The Agricultural Bank of China is rolling out facial recognition at its ATM machines which are highly sophisticated and won't recognise masks. Fast food places, restaurants and hotels are introducing this technology, and you may soon pay by having your face scanned. In banks it's called 'Smile & Pay': you smile and the ATM pays. Universities are using facial scans to allow students access to their dorms or lecture theatres, with no need for a card swipe. Twenty automated bookstores staffed with robots are opening in Beijing. They are open 24 hours a day. The robot offers 'precise and humanised' book suggestions

I, Robot

STORIES OF SCIENCE FICTION

ISAAC ASIMOV'S *I, ROBOT* TELLS THE FICTIONAL STORY OF DR SUSAN CALVIN IN THE 21ST CENTURY AND HER INTERACTION WITH ROBOTS.

ISAAC ASIMOV

to customers. Staffless convenience stores and supermarkets are also opening around the city. And there's even a robotic Buddhist monk in a monastery in Beijing called Xian'er who people can consult. He is dressed in a saffron-yellow robe and has a shaved head. His role is to help people who are more connected to their smartphones than they are to their inner selves. He can answer 20 questions displayed on his chest on a touchscreen. Perhaps this will solve the vocational crisis gripping churches around the world. I wonder what the Vatican will make of a robotic priest? Bless me robot, for I have sinned.

We already see robots doing household chores. The vacuuming Roomba or window-washing Windoro are more and more common. There are also stain-removing robots. But caution is needed. Revenge of the robots may have begun. In Australia, a woman put a cleaning robot on the counter in her kitchen to clear up a cereal spill. She switched it off after the job was done. The robot, however, was clearly in despair with its life of drudgery and had an existential crisis. It switched itself back on, went over to the hotplate, pushed over a coffee pot and then sat there until it burst into flames, destroying most of the apartment, in what is recorded as the first robot suicide.

Is there any prospect of robots making us their slaves? This seems unlikely, and safeguards can be built in. Drones going crazy and attacking innocent targets were a concern, but we're assured there are too many checks and balances to allow that to happen. The term 'AI takeover' is used to describe a scenario where computers and robots take control of the planet away from us humans. A typical Hollywood version of this storyline goes something like this: superintelligent robots decide that humans are a risk or a waste of Earth's resources and so should be killed off. One example of this that is used involves a thought experiment called the 'paperclip maximiser', whereby robots that are programmed to make paperclips use all the Earth's resources to achieve this goal, which might involve eliminating humans, who are a drain on the system and might shut the robots down.

How likely is this? The late Stephen Hawking, Bill Gates and SpaceX founder Elon Musk have all expressed concerns that AI might develop beyond our control, so perhaps we should be worried. There is evidence of robots cooperating with one another. Robots that act together without humans is a scary prospect, especially if they learn and develop. In one study in the US a thousand robots, each the size of a quarter dollar, came together and formed squares and letters[6]. Ten robotic helicopters (called quadcopters) communicated with each other constantly and avoided collisions. A group of boat robots cooperated in manoeuvres that were highly elaborate. These are self-organising machines, programmed to behave in these ways, and may well become more and more sophisticated.

One thing everyone agrees on is that the future includes driverless cars. This began with companies putting computers in cars to improve engine efficiency. Things got more and more elaborate, and as the airline industry invented the autopilot carmakers began to follow suit. Huge amounts of money are now being spent on research, with Google leading the way with a current spend of $1.1 billion[7]. Most futurologists are predicting a time when all cars on our roads will be driverless. Experts are saying this will be the last generation to own a car. Driverless cars will revamp our lives, destroy millions of jobs and suddenly be as ubiquitous and transformative as the smartphone[8].

It will begin on bus routes in the centre of cities. Lyon already has driverless buses. Driverless cars are predicted to be on our roads in the coming decade. Paris is planning on making the inner part of the city driverless by 2024, when it hosts the Olympics. Initially they will coexist with human-driven cars. Trucks delivering goods will be next. Driverless cars and trucks will mainly run on electricity provided by batteries. The batteries will be solar-powered and will recharge as the vehicles run, by running over charging strips on the roads. There will be a boom in racetracks as a leisure pursuit, where petrol heads will go to burn rubber, since some people will still want to drive. The incentives to have driverless cars will be many, including hefty charges if you should want to drive your car in a city. Thirty per cent of people surveyed have said they would prefer it if the world had driverless cars. Eighty-six per cent said yes to this if insurance was cheaper.

Google are ahead of the competition. Their self-driving cars have now been involved in 12 accidents while covering more than 1.7 million miles during the past six years, according to the company[9]. The cars have eight cameras on board and 12 ultrasonic sensors. They also carry a 'prior'. This is a Google map of the area, which the car constantly compares to the current situation. Any changes mean it can react instantly. It's likely therefore that all driverless cars will have a prior map loaded into the system. I saw Google's driverless car in action when I was on the Google campus. A blind man (or at least a man with a stick and dark glasses) got into the passenger seat and the car drove off. It drove around the block and into the car park. The blind man got out to rapturous applause.

THE FUTURE WILL BELONG TO DRIVERLESS CARS.

The predictions when they are fully adopted are startling. First the total number of vehicles on our roads will drop by 90 per cent. This is because they are so efficient and will act like a constant taxi service, dropping off and picking up. It's only a small step to turn Uber into a fully automated taxi service. As they will be taxis, car ownership will plummet. Why own a car when you can summon one to take you anywhere you want to go at an affordable price? The predicted saving for the average person who gets rid of their own car and uses driverless cars is €6,000 per annum.

Accidents will also plummet. These are usually caused by slow reaction times, tailgating and rubbernecking, all human flaws. One estimate puts the drop at 90 per cent – this represents 1.2 million lives. Imagine, 1.2 million people won't die from traffic accidents once driverless cars are widespread. This will also mean a saving of $190 billion. There will be some accidents, but the technology is developing at such a rate that these will be few and far between, and most likely won't be caused directly by the driverless car malfunctioning. Since the cars will all be electric, pollution levels will plummet. Traffic jams will be a thing of the past, as the position and speed of each and every car in a network will be known, and speeds adjusted to ensure a smooth flow of traffic. Congestion will effectively be abolished, as much of that is caused by people trying to find parking or getting lost.

The cars will be optimally spaced and run at a density that will make them seem like trains with carriages. The need for parking will also be a thing of the past, as the cars will rarely stop, or at least will only stop to let you out. There are currently 150,000 cars parked in Paris city centre. Imagine what the freeing up of that space would do – new parks, playgrounds, walks. Instead of a car taking up space, leaking oil and sitting there, there will now be a lovely park. Travelling to work in a driverless car will be a pleasure. You will be able to have your coffee, do your make-up, check out the news, or just sleep. Driverless cars will be a particular boon to older people. They will become much more mobile, travelling to see their friends and family in comfort. Disabled people will also have an opening up of possibilities. Driverless cars will also help teenagers. Imagine, the taxi service that many parents turn into during the teen years will no longer be needed.

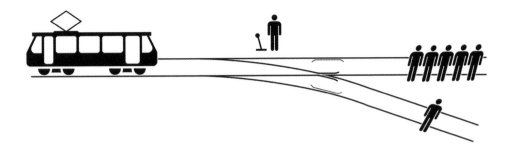

So where are the downsides? Well, there are some. There is a fear that a driverless car might make an 'ethical' decision in certain circumstances. Let us say for example that the car might swerve to miss a child but in doing so will kill the occupants who comprise, say, four adults. What decision will the car make? Kill

A THOUGHT EXPERIMENT CALLED THE TROLLEY PROBLEM. IS IT MORE ETHICAL TO INTERVENE TO PULL THE LEVER OR TAKE NO ACTION?

the child and spare the adults or let the adults die and save the child? Some predict it will be possible to deal with these kinds of dilemmas. For example, MIT are using a website called Moral Machine which allows you to input different scenarios for driverless cars. You make a moral decision based on a given scenario, and then the programme compares your decision to other people, possibly correcting a bad decision. This might run automatically in the driverless car, leading to a decision on a given situation based on a consensus of how a human would react[10]. A second fear is that people won't take them up, as they prefer the power of a petrol engine and actually enjoy driving. Price may sort out the former and racetracks the latter.

But the big downside is likely to be job losses. The existing automotive industry is huge in all developed countries. For Germany it makes up fully one-third of the German economy. Truck and taxi drivers will see their jobs disappear. Carmakers will be taken over by technology giants such as Google, who have the money and the information to make it work. Governments will lose out on parking fines, speeding fines and petrol tax, so an important stream of income will go. One industry that is also predicted to suffer a lot is the insurance industry. For some of them, over 50 per cent of their income comes from car insurance, the people in the cars and the people who might get hurt. That will no longer be needed to the same extent. This means insurance companies will have less money to invest in other businesses, slowing economic growth.

All of these concerns are felt to be overstated, and certainly not insurmountable. Insurance companies will surely find something else to insure. We have some records of what happened when the horseless carriages first appeared, to the horror of people working in the horse trade. A man with a red flag had to walk in front of a car back then. Lots of jobs were lost, but look what happened. A massive new industry was spawned, enriching the lives of millions and millions. This is happening again, but now without the risk of destroying lives and the planet.

We can look forward to a world full of robots helping us in so many ways, checking our health, painting our nails and driving us in a most leisurely way to anywhere we want to go. We will sit there in comfort watching reruns of great Grand Prix races, reminding us of a bygone age when the mass of people worked in jobs of quiet desperation, often stuck for hours in traffic jams while polluting the Earth with fumes. Roll on robots, we humans have nothing to lose but our chains.

PARENTS OF EARTH, ARE YOUR CHILDREN FULLY IMMUNIZED?

TWO OF THE WORLD'S FAVORITE ROBOTS, C-3PO AND R2D2, HELPING HUMANS OUT.

MAKE SURE— CALL YOUR DOCTOR OR HEALTH DEPARTMENT TODAY. AND MAY THE FORCE BE WITH YOU.

U.S. Department of Health, Education, and Welfare / Public Health Service / Center for Disease Control

CHAPTER 14

THE BIGGEST AND MOST EXPENSIVE MACHINES EVER BUILT

.

N THE YEAR 1712 a strange noise, never before heard on Earth, started coming from a mine near Dudley in the West Midlands of England[1]. The noise was a repetitive chugging sound, and it set off the greatest change the world has ever seen: the Industrial Revolution. This machine had been made by Thomas Newcomen to pump water from the mine. It was fuelled by coal and worked by steam. It was the first steam engine.

The energy needed to do work of the kind being done by what was called the 'atmospheric engine' had up to that point mainly come from muscle power, either human or animal. Flowing water or wind power had been used to turn wheels to grind wheat into flour, but here was something very different. This machine didn't rely on gravity or flowing water or wind. It relied on energy coming from coal. It made an infernal noise and spewed out noxious fumes. It set in train a cacophony of noise that has never abated. Many more machines have since been built that make modern life possible: trains, planes, automobiles, electricity generators, iPhones. Even noise-cancelling headphones to stop all the noise. They are a testament to the ingenuity of humans.

But two machines leave us gaping in awe at what we humans have been able to achieve: the International Space Station (ISS) and the Large Hadron Collider (LHC)[2]. The ISS is the most expensive single item ever made. The current estimated cost is $150 billion. The LHC is the most expensive single

machine ever built, coming in at €7.5 billion. What are they and why did we make them?

THE INTERNATIONAL SPACE
STATION: AN AMAZING
FEAT OF ENGINEERING AND
INTERNATIONAL COOPERATION.

The ISS is a habitable space station in low Earth orbit. This means it is between 330 km and 435 km above the Earth, though sometimes it has to come in a little closer, usually during space shuttle visits[3]. It goes all the way around the Earth 15.54 times a day. The first component of the ISS was launched in 1998. It is so big that it can be seen with the naked eye scooting across the sky. There are human beings in it right now, and their job is to do experiments in biology, physics, astronomy and meteorology. It is visited regularly by Russian, American, European and Japanese vehicles. It is a marvellous example of countries on Earth working together instead of fighting or bickering. Astronauts or cosmonauts (as they are called in Russia) from 17 different countries have stayed on it and hopefully stayed friends.

The construction of the ISS was an amazing feat of international cooperation and engineering. Science and technology brought humans together as never before. It began in 1998 with the launch of the Russian modules, which were docked robotically. Yet again the Russians beat the Americans at something in space. All other modules, though, were delivered by an American-built space shuttle. There were 159 components laboriously added, involving more than 1,000 hours of space walks. In 2000, the Russian spacecraft *Zvezda* (meaning 'Star') was launched and robotically added sleeping quarters, a toilet, a kitchen, carbon dioxide scrubbers to clean the air, oxygen generators, exercise equipment and communications equipment. The first resident crew were Russian, and the American Bill Shepherd was then brought to the ISS on the Russian spacecraft Soyuz TM-31. Shepherd asked that the radio call sign for the ISS be 'Alpha' instead of the more cumbersome 'International Space Station'. The Russians, led by Sergei Krikalev, initially objected, as they said that their space station *Mir* was the first space station, and so the ISS call sign should be 'Beta' or 'Mir2'. (There's always something to bicker over.) The name 'Alpha' won out.

From then on, the ISS grew and grew. Soyuz-U brought a docking compartment. The shuttles *Discovery*, *Atlantis* and *Endeavour* brought laboratory equipment and an airlock. Then the space shuttle *Columbia* disaster happened, stopping everything for two years. This accident happened on 1 February 2003 when the *Columbia* disintegrated during re-entry, resulting in the deaths of all seven crew members. Once the ISS programme restarted, more power generators were brought up, along with more pressurised modules and lots of solar arrays for power. In 2010 the Cupola was added, to give the astronauts great views and somewhere to relax. More modules are to be added for more space to carry out experiments. When it is finished the ISS will weigh 400 tonnes.

Inside, the ISS is split into two sections: the Russian Orbital Segment and the United States Orbital Segment. The names are to do with funding, however — anyone can stay in either segment. Both the Americans and the Russians have both guaranteed funding until 2024. There are no real guarantees, though (as with most science funding). Russia has said it wants to build another space station to replace it, but the US has yet to agree.

How do astronauts stay alive in the ISS? There are five things to consider: air, water, food, sanitation, and fire detection and suppression. The atmosphere is almost identical to that on Earth, with an air pressure like that at sea level. There is a chemical oxygen generator. The carbon dioxide breathed out by the astronauts is removed, as are various other waste products of human metabolism, such as methane from the astronauts' bowels (delightful) and ammonia from sweat. They are removed by activated charcoal filters.

Electrical power is provided by the aforementioned solar panels. These are a very distinctive feature of the ISS, looking like wings. Power is stored in huge nickel-hydrogen batteries, which have a 6.5-year lifetime. This year they are being replaced by lithium-ion batteries, which will last much longer. All of the equipment on board generates heat, and this has to be handled. Ammonia is pumped through pipes to collect the heat, which is passed into external radiators.

The ISS has elaborate radio telecommunication systems, which mainly use ultra-high frequency (UHF). It is in constant contact with Earth, most notably with Mission Control in Houston (where hopefully they won't hear that most famous of space phrases: 'Houston, we have a problem'). There are 100 commercially bought laptops on board. The heat they generate doesn't rise, but stagnates over the laptops and special forced ventilation is needed when they are being used. The astronauts can communicate via Wi-Fi with Earth. Try communicating via Wi-Fi in an aeroplane …

Astronauts spend up to six months on a mission. One cosmonaut, however, holds the record for the longest time in space. Sergei Krikalev, who was a member of the original crew, has spent 803 days, 9 hours and 39 minutes in space. He has been awarded the Order of Lenin, Hero of the Soviet Union, Hero of the Russian Federation and four NASA medals. Scott Kelly, meanwhile, holds the record for an American, at the rather risible 340 days. (Come on America! Make space great again …) Kelly is a big fan of the Irish

Antarctic explorer Ernest Shackleton, whose story often helped him on the
ISS, when he felt lonely or uncertain. In his memoir *Endurance: A Year in
Space, A Lifetime in Discovery* he describes looking down on the Earth and
being struck by one thought: 'every person who has ever lived or died', minus
the crew on the ISS, is down there[4].

Space tourists can also travel to the ISS provided they pass the medical
examination. Price per seat? Forty million dollars. But get in line as there is a
waiting list. And people who go resent being called space tourists. Everybody
hates a tourist. They are often scientists and participate in experiments.
Iranian-American Anousheh Ansari paid for herself, but did Russian and
European studies, as well as medicine and microbiology, during her 10-day stay.

Life on board begins with a wake-up call at 6 am. Following breakfast
(which hopefully doesn't involve an alien coming out of someone's stomach),
there is a planning meeting for the day ahead. The crew start work at around
8.10. They stop for specific exercises and then have a one-hour lunch break
from 13.05. The afternoon then involves more work and exercise. What is
called 'Pre-Sleep' activities then begin, which include dinner and another
crew conference. They turn in at 21.30.

The crew usually work a 10-hour day during the week, with five hours on
Saturdays. The rest of the time is for relaxation. The time on board is Greenwich
Mean Time (or as it's now called, Coordinated Universal Time, or, annoyingly,
UTC). Windows are covered at night to create darkness, because the ISS has 16
sunrises and sunsets per day. Each crew member has their own sleep module,
which is private and soundproofed. The visitors, in spite of spending all that
money, attach their sleeping bag to a space on the walls. Ryanair have allegedly
denied any involvement in this. It is possible to sleep floating freely through
the ISS but this is generally avoided, in case the sleeping person bumps into
equipment. Early missions discovered that ventilation was important, otherwise
astronauts woke up in a bubble of their own carbon dioxide.

What about food? It is brought vacuum-packed in sealed bags. Taste is lower
in zero gravity, and so more spices are added. Fresh fruit and vegetables are

occasionally delivered, which is a source of great excitement. The crew cook their own food. This means less argument, and gives them something to do. Any food that floats away must be caught, as it might clog up equipment.

Hygiene is tricky. There used to be showers but astronauts were only allowed to shower once a month, whether they needed it or not. This has been replaced with a water jet and wet wipes. The crew also have rinseless shampoo and edible toothpaste

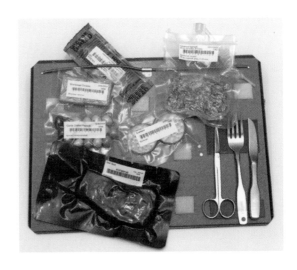

ASTRONAUTS MAINLY LIVE ON A DIET OF VACUUM-PACKED SPACE FOOD.

to save on water. There are two toilets, both designed by the Russians. Solid waste is stored for disposal, and urine is collected in anatomically appropriate funnels allowing men and women to pass urine. It is collected and recycled into drinking water.

The astronauts have to be careful about radiation exposure. Levels on board are about five times that which airline pilots are exposed to, and there is a risk of cancer and cataracts in the eye developing. The astronauts' immune systems are also somewhat compromised, further increasing the risk of infection and cancer. Shielding and special medicines help to ward off these potential problems. Whatever about these physical ailments, there is a real risk of psychosocial stress. Key issues include maintaining high performance under public scrutiny (if you have a major screw-up all Earthlings will find out) and isolation from peers and family members.

What is clear is the first three weeks are important — once they get through that, stress levels fall off. The astronauts also have access to a psychiatry support group, who help from the time of training all the way up to the end of the mission and beyond to post-mission acclimation. The counsellors involved get to know the astronauts and their families very well. They conduct a private video conference every two weeks when the astronauts are on the ISS. Leisure activities on the ISS are especially important for destressing. The future may involve artificial programmes that will provide cognitive behavioural therapy for astronauts on the ISS.

What kind of work happens up there? Just like sailors of yore scrubbing the decks and keeping things shipshape, maintenance is an important activity. Research also happens. One of the missions of the ISS is to prepare us for trips back to the moon or to Mars. Humans are therefore being tested in all kinds of ways in zero gravity. A lot of space medicine is happening up there. Several things happen to our bodies in zero gravity, including muscle-wasting, bone loss and fluids in our bodies behaving strangely. A recent study has shown that if humans are in zero gravity for six months, their bones will fracture when they land on a planet like Mars, or indeed come back to Earth. Astronauts therefore have to make sure their muscles and bones are subject to pressure by exercising regularly. In spite of this, astronauts still suffer when they return to Earth, reporting nausea, fever, rashes and aching joints, which take time to resolve.

Scientists are also testing how plants grow in zero gravity. They have found that crystals form in a strange way, which is proving useful for protein crystallography. To get the shape and structure of a protein, which can be useful say for finding drugs to interact with proteins that might have the makings of new medicines, crystals are needed. These are then shot with X-rays, which bounce off in ways that allow us to see the structure. Protein crystals are being grown on the ISS with this goal in mind. Scientists are also growing cells in space and scientist-come-astronaut Kate Rubins is the first person to sequence DNA in space.

The ISS also has an important educational role. Students on Earth can design experiments and can communicate with the astronauts via radio, videolink and email. The European Space Agency provides lots of free teaching material to use in classrooms. One interesting project organised from the ISS was to map exactly the path of Vostok 1, the mission that brought the first person into space in the form of Yuri Gagarin. Students could track the route and see what he saw. In May 2013, Commander Chris Hadfield played David Bowie's 'Space Oddity' on the ISS, and the film was released on YouTube[5]. It has garnered over 35 million views, and is the first ever music video shot in space.

It is also probably the most expensive video ever made. The total cost of the ISS is estimated to be $150 billion, with the US bearing the brunt of it (at $58 billion). You can calculate the cost per person on the ISS per day. This is $7.5 million. Let's say it took Chris Hadfield 30 minutes to make the video; that would mean it cost $625,000. Was it worth it? If the ISS means great science and world peace then yes, even if we had to watch Hadfield floating in a most peculiar way.

The cost of the ISS makes the Large Hadron Collider (LHC) seem cheap, coming in at a mere €7.5 billion. It is, however, the largest and most expensive single machine ever built[6]. In many ways a direct line can be drawn from Newcomen's steam engine to the LHC. Its job is to smash protons together. That is all it does. It is therefore called a particle collider. It was built by the European Organization for Nuclear Research (CERN) between 1998 and 2008[7]. It is a huge collaboration between 100 different countries, involving over 10,000 scientists and hundreds of universities. Who would have thought that such a thing could be built, by people who aren't that far removed from the humans who emerged from the plains of Africa. It involved (and involves) cooperation of a very high level. Humans have come together, not to hunt down a large animal and eat it, or to fight each other, but to discover the secrets of matter itself.

It is so big because it has to be. It comprises a tunnel 27 km in circumference beneath the French-Swiss border near Geneva. Its big success story thus far was to discover the Higgs boson, an elementary subatomic particle. And it is trying to find other particles, as well as answer big questions in physics. These include addressing why gravity is such a weak force, whether the proton is fundamentally stable and what the mass of a neutrino is. This is science at its most fundamental.

The LHC keeps breaking records. First, for the amount of energy in its beams of protons, which beat previous world records four-fold. Also for the data it collects. CERN of course is famous for the World Wide Web, which was invented by Tim Berners-Lee at CERN in 1989, who also invented the first ever website. Data has always been important for CERN, and the LHC generates tens of petabytes per year. A petabyte is one quadrillion bytes, or 10^{15} bytes (this number is 1 with 15 zeros after it). This amount of data is handled by 170 computing centres in 42 countries. An awful lot of bang for your buck.

So what is a hadron? The term refers to particles held together by what is called the 'strong force'. May the force indeed be with you. Atoms and molecules are held together by the so-called electromagnetic force. But particles like protons and neutrons are hadrons (which could almost be misspelt as hardon, given the level of excitement this all generates among physicists). The 'collider' part is obvious – it means it accelerates particles and then smashes them into each other to break them up. An early example of a collider was one used by Irish Nobel laureate Ernest Walton, who with John Cockcroft and Ernest Rutherford had a more primitive collider in the Cavendish Laboratory in Cambridge. They smashed together atoms of lithium, breaking them apart and making helium – the first time an atom had been split. Their original atom smasher is now in the reception of the LHC for all to see. It looks puny, but is a very important forerunner of the LHC.

Atom smashing is one thing, but proton smashing is quite another. The LHC is trying to address very fundamental questions in physics. The first one has been cracked. What gives elementary particles mass? Without mass, nothing would exist. It turns out the Higgs boson is a particle that gives everything mass. This was predicted by Peter Higgs and Satyendra Bose (after whom the boson was named) and is true. It's a great example of

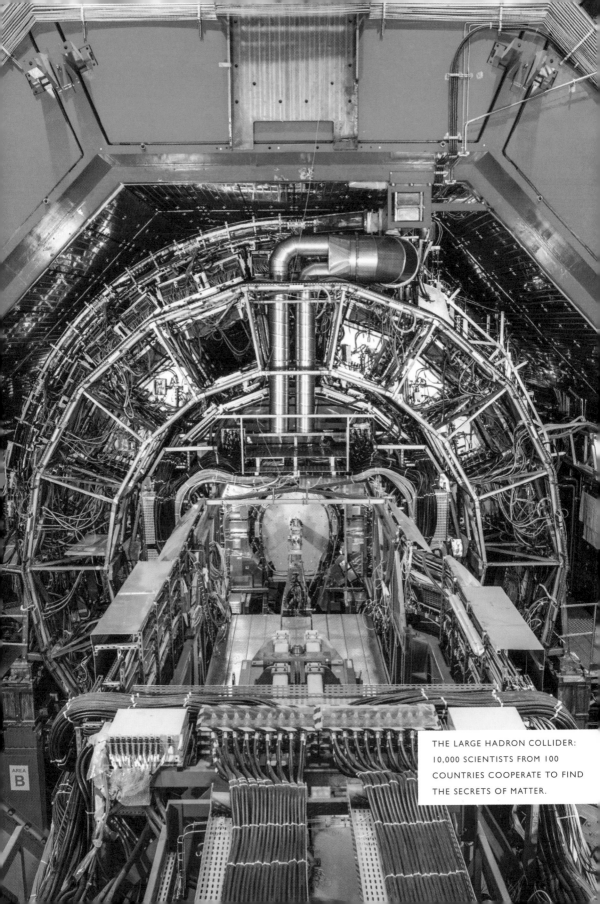

AREA
B

THE LARGE HADRON COLLIDER:
10,000 SCIENTISTS FROM 100
COUNTRIES COOPERATE TO FIND
THE SECRETS OF MATTER.

science at its best. It's an example of something that was predicted with very complex mathematics, and then was proved to be true using science.

Other ongoing questions include, Are there more dimensions (i.e. more than the four we know about – the three dimensions of space and the fourth being time)? What is the nature of dark matter? (This stuff makes up 27 per cent of the mass-energy of the universe and yet we don't know what it is.) Why is gravity so much weaker than other fundamental forces? What is the nature of the quark–gluon plasma, which was the type of matter that existed just after the Big Bang? (This is what the early universe might have been made of.) These are fundamental questions in physics, and the LHC is trying to answer them.

The LHC is one long circular tunnel. It has 1,232 'dipole magnets' to keep the beams on the straight and narrow, each of which weighs in at 27 tonnes, and another 392 magnets to keep the beams focused. It has a further 10,000 superconducting magnets, which drive the speed for the collisions. The magnets must be kept at a temperature of -271.25°C. This is achieved with superfluid helium-4. It makes the LHC the largest cryogenic facility in the world.

When it is up and running, protons can get around the 27 km in 90 millionths of a second. This is 0.999999999 times the speed of light (as in very very close to the speed of light, which Einstein predicts can't be reached by matter – or can it?). The numbers then get even more remarkable. When running the energy stored in the magnets equals 2,400 kg of TNT (one Tomahawk cruise missile, the standard atom bomb in the US army, has the equivalent of 500 kg of TNT, so five atom bomb equivalents are being stored in the magnets).

And in spite of spending €7.5 billion on it, there is thrift. It only runs in the summer, when electricity costs are cheaper. Also, as with all projects, there were cock-ups in its construction. Broken supports for magnets, the leakage of six tonnes of super-cooled liquid helium and faulty electrical connections (you've got to plug it in properly) have all occurred, and all led to delays but were overcome. And then the results started to come.

On 24 May 2011, the quark–gluon plasma was detected. This is the densest matter thought to exist outside black holes, and arose soon after the Big Bang. One gram of quark–gluon plasma has enough energy to power the whole world. Imagine if it could be captured? And then came the glorious day of 4 July 2012, when the Higgs boson was detected, providing us with an explanation of what gives matter mass. In the complex world of physics, this had to achieve a statistical significance of 5 sigma, and it did.

What about the dangers of these experiments? There was actually a real fear of the LHC becoming a doomsday machine. It might produce a black hole and suck all of the Earth into it, or produce dangerous particles which had been theorised called 'strangelets'. There was a fear that these strangelets would convert the entire Earth into a 'hot, large lump of strange matter'. Two safety reviews concluded that these were unlikely, since what is happening in the LHC actually happens naturally in the universe without hazardous consequences. What a relief … But this hasn't stopped the LHC from featuring in science fiction and even in the Dan Brown novel *Angels and Demons*, where the antimatter created by the LHC is used as a weapon against – guess where? The Vatican. Antimatter as Antichrist?

And the experiments continue. Upgrades are now needed if the LHC is to continue to make important discoveries. Scientists always want more. Upgrades are planned for 2018 and 2022, and the future experiments will continue to reveal the secrets of the matter that makes up our world. Who knows where the new knowledge might lead? One obvious output is perhaps safe energy for ever. When Faraday first demonstrated the mysterious force of electricity it had no application. He was asked by the then prime minister what it might be good for. He is said to have replied 'I don't know sir, but I am sure you will tax it.' Similarly, when nuclear physics began as a science, it wasn't that obvious that this would lead to the atomic bomb or nuclear fuel. As the physicist Richard Feynman has said, 'Physics research is like sex. Procreation may well be the result, but is not necessarily why we do it.'

REVEALING THE
SUBATOMIC WORLD BY
SMASHING PROTONS
TOGETHER.

The megamachines that are the ISS and the LHC are the culmination of the work of hundreds of thousands of people over thousands of years, building bit by bit on what has gone before. Both are propelled by the relentless and restless curiosity that drives the human race. When Neil Armstrong was the first human to walk on the moon, there were many many people behind him whose work allowed him to make that small step. All that maths, science and engineering. The engineering part can be traced back to that new noise down the mine near Dudley that was the Newcomen engine. Who knows what these two machines will continue to tell us? And who knows what marvellous new machines will be built? Let's hope they continue to typify the cooperative and peaceful nature of our species as we move towards the future.

CHAPTER 15

WILL WE STOP ALL DISEASES?

T HE FACEBOOK FOUNDER Mark Zuckerberg recently set up a foundation whose explicit aim is to find cures for all diseases by 2100[1]. Will this ambition ever be realised? Why do we get sick? Diseases have always plagued humankind. A disease is defined as a condition that impairs normal functioning and is typically manifested by distinguishing signs and symptoms. They stop us from leading full lives. They are very unequal in their distribution. Some of us get sick, some of us don't. This can be because we carry variants of genes that make us sick. Or it can be because our lifestyle makes us sick. Or perhaps it's a combination of both, which is often the case. Some people get sick because of poverty, or just because of bad luck.

Medicine provides us with wonderful treatments for many of the things that ail us, but many diseases are still hard to treat. We all know about the huge effort going on to find new treatments and we often read about 'breakthroughs'. But what do the prospects look like? Well, the signs are good. We now know more than ever about what goes wrong in the body when we become sick, in some cases right down to the molecules in our bodies that are causing mischief. The goal now is to stop it going wrong or correct it when it does.

The big killer before the discovery of antibiotics was infectious diseases. One idea is that once we stopped being nomadic, and began living in close

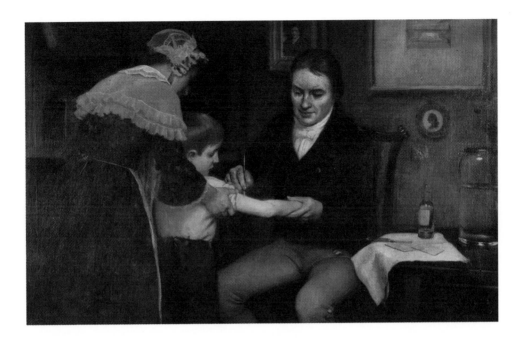

proximity, infections were more likely to spread among us. This might especially have been the case when we began living with our domesticated animals, as then their germs could spread to us (or vice versa), causing sickness[2]. The symptoms of

EDWARD JENNER (1749–1823) PERFORMING THE FIRST VACCINE ON JAMES PHIPPS TO PROTECT HIM FROM SMALLPOX.

infectious diseases are often triggered to allow the infectious agent, be it bacterial or viral, to spread. This is one reason why you cough and splutter when you have a cold. The virus makes you sneeze so that it can jump into someone else and breed there.

Three big breakthroughs limited the devastating effects of infectious diseases: clean water[3], vaccines[4] and antibiotics[5]. In the 19th century, engineers began to devise ways to provide clean water, including filtration methods. Edward Jenner gets the credit for discovering vaccination, when he noticed that milkmaids rarely got smallpox. He figured out (or more likely was told by a farmer neighbour called Benjamin Jesty) that this was because

ALEXANDER FLEMING (1881–1955)
WHO DISCOVERED PENICILLIN,
ULTIMATELY SAVING HUNDREDS OF
MILLIONS OF LIVES.

they already had the milder disease of cowpox[6]. This led Jenner to test cowpox on a young boy called James Phipps.

This was the scientific method in action: devise a hypothesis (in this case, that cowpox could protect against smallpox) then test the hypothesis (give someone cowpox and then smallpox and see if they are protected). He gave the boy cowpox and then tried to infect him with smallpox and hey presto he was protected. What had happened was that the boy's immune system had reacted to cowpox but had caused only a mild disease. Cowpox and smallpox viruses share many features, so when the boy was given smallpox, his immune system had been trained to recognise smallpox, and dealt with it effectively. It was something like a war, where the first encounter with the enemy is a bunch of old guys who are quickly eliminated. Then when the younger, fitter troops arrive in the same uniform they are recognised quickly and eliminated. This was a great advance, as smallpox was an often lethal virus that terrified everyone. Following on from Jenner, many other vaccines were developed using weakened versions of the pathogen you want to prevent, early examples being diphtheria and rabies. We now have vaccines for many diseases.

Antibiotics, on the other hand, kill bacteria on contact. Penicillin was the first of these to be characterised. It was discovered serendipitously (meaning he got lucky) by Alexander Fleming[7]. He noticed that a mould growing on a petri dish with a lawn of bacteria, killed the bacteria. The mould had actually come from a lab near the Fleming lab that was run by an Irish doctor called Charles La Touche. La Touche had been collecting cobwebs in the East End of London to explore if they caused asthma attacks. The cobwebs had captured the fungus penicillium, which makes penicillin to protect itself from bacteria. It was this that somehow blew out of La Touche's lab and into Fleming's, killing the bacteria. Fleming called it 'mould juice'. Antibiotics now save millions of lives every year, although there is a fear that bacteria will evolve a way around them.

We're also getting better at coming up with ways to beat viral infections, although some viruses remain a problem. Vaccines have been found for viruses such as those causing polio, but not against HIV, the virus that causes AIDS, nor for the virus that causes the liver disease hepatitis C. For these two viral diseases, though, there are drugs that target the virus itself, in a similar way to antibiotics targeting bacteria directly.

The fight against AIDS has been a particularly successful one. People with AIDS can now expect to live as long as people without it, which is a remarkable success given that it was a death sentence as recently as 20 years ago. HIV is a very cunning virus, as it infects T lymphocytes. These are the foot soldiers of our immune system, making HIV the enemy within. It eventually kills the T lymphocyte as it jumps from cell to cell. This is what causes the immunodeficiency, which in turn leads to all kinds of infections that will eventually kill the patient. Many die from severe pneumonia.

In 2016, 36.7 million people were estimated to have HIV, and 1 million people died. It probably began infecting humans when it jumped into a human from an ape or monkey (who don't get sick with HIV – they evolved to live with it). The AIDS epidemic in the US officially began on 5 June 1981, when the US Center for Disease Control reported an unusually high incidence of a fungus called *Pneumocystis jiroveci* in gay men. This was normally only seen in transplant patients who were immunosuppressed. The hunt was then on for what caused it, and in 1983 scientists at the Pasteur Institute in Paris identified HIV as the causative agent. Drug companies then began developing agents to stop the virus dividing, and this led to the discovery of antiretroviral therapies. HIV is a retrovirus – so-called because it has RNA instead of DNA in its genetic material, which is turned into DNA when inside the host T lymphocyte. In our own cells, DNA is turned into RNA.

The first drugs to be developed target the HIV enzyme that performs this reverse transcription — an enzyme called 'reverse transcriptase'. Three different reverse transcriptase inhibitors in a cocktail are especially effective. A recent study of 88,500 people with HIV from Europe and North America in 18 separate studies has shown that the projected age of death for a 20-year-old with HIV on antiretroviral therapy is now 78 years, which is similar to the general population[8]. This is a tremendous achievement with a disease that has killed so many.

And because of clean water, vaccines and antibiotics, we are now surviving a lot longer than we used to. Vaccines and antibiotics are widely considered the most important of all medical advances because of the numbers of lives they save. We might therefore survive infectious diseases, but we are at risk of many other diseases. Some estimates put the total number of diseases that afflict humanity at around 7,000. Many of these are rare. Some are caused by a genetic abnormality which can either arise spontaneously, or be passed from a parent to a child. An example is cystic fibrosis, where a gene for a protein in the lungs called CFTR is mutated. The job of CFTR is to regulate salt in the lungs. If it's broken the salt builds up, and this damages the lungs. This in turn promotes infections which cause a lot of the problems in cystic fibrosis.

But the big killers now are heart disease and cancer. The major form of heart disease, which is called atherosclerosis (meaning clogging of the arteries, which ultimately become blocked and stop blood flow to the heart in a heart attack), is caused by a number of risk factors, including smoking, stress and high levels of cholesterol. Cholesterol clogs arteries, causing the heart to stop because blood can't flow. Cholesterol-lowering drugs like statins are a major advance, as they lower cholesterol and so stop the clogging.

Cancer is caused by mutations in genes, but this time the mutations can be caused by environmental factors, like smoking or UV irradiation from the sun. A chemical reaction occurs, between noxious chemicals in cigarette smoke or by UV light in sun, and DNA. This alters the DNA such that the recipe for the protein to be made is altered. The new protein then causes cancer, by for example causing cells to grow out of control and form a tumour. The genes are usually for proteins that cause cell growth, and the mutant forms go out of control. Others are for proteins whose job it is to suppress tumours from growing (so-called tumour suppressor genes) and when they mutate, the tumour will grow. The tumour cells will spread in a process caused 'metastasis'. It is often where they lodge and grow (for example in the brain) that kills you.

Therapies to treat cancer involve poisons to kill the cancer cells (called chemotherapy), X-rays to burn it out or surgery to remove it. Doctors have increasingly been winning the war on cancer[9]. Today, 60 per cent of cancers are cured. Five-year survival rates of invasive cancers (the ones that really attack our bodies) have gone up from 45 per cent for patients diagnosed between 1994 and 1999 to 59 per cent for those diagnosed between 2006 and 2011. Currently, 81 per cent survive breast cancer and 91 per cent survive prostate cancer. This is because of earlier diagnosis. The sooner you can start treating cancer the better, as otherwise you are closing the stable door after the horse has bolted. But one breakthrough that is being hailed is that scientists have realised that in some situations your own immune system can kill the cancer cell[10]. It can recognise the mutated proteins in the cancer cell as foreign.

The job of the immune system it is to distinguish friend from foe, and a cancer cell is only sometimes seen as a foe. The problem is that cancer is cunning, sometimes called 'The Emperor of Maladies'. It has ways to switch off the immune attack against it. An important immune off-switch, also called a 'checkpoint', is PD1. The level of this protein increases on the tumour and then engages with a protein called PDL1 on immune cells, which are hitting off the tumour cells and trying to kill it. Once PDL1 is engaged by PD1, however, the immune cell is deactivated. It's somewhat like PD1 acting as a finger to flip the PDL1 switch, turning off all the lights in the immune cell. This led scientists to test checkpoint blockers, actually antibodies designed to stop the PD1 finger from touching the PDL1 off-switch, and so letting the immune cell do its job and kill the tumour cell. These new drugs have

THE EBERS PAPYRUS, AN EGYPTIAN
MEDICAL PAPYRUS DATING FROM
1550 BC. IT DESCRIBES THE USE OF
MARIJUANA AS A TREATMENT FOR EYE
INFLAMMATION AND HAEMORRHOIDS.

seen success where previously there was no treatment that would extend life, notably in the big killers of lung cancer and melanoma.

In melanoma the average survival time is around one year, but for some of those on anti-PD1 this has gone up to three years and counting. Some become disease-free. The prospect therefore of coming up with treatments for cancer that might actually cure the disease or at least slow it down is now a real prospect. PD1 is a brand new target which was gone after by scientists and has yielded a brand new medicine.

So we now have a reasonable idea of what causes the two big killers of heart disease and cancer. But there are many other diseases which afflict us for which there is no known cause. The next biggest group are the inflammatory diseases, which include diseases like rheumatoid arthritis, multiple sclerosis and inflammatory bowel disease. We also classify neurodegenerative diseases like Alzheimer's disease and Parkinson's disease as inflammatory, since in those diseases there is an inflammatory reaction in the brain to proteins being wrongly deposited there. In the case of Alzheimer's disease, two proteins, called beta-amyloid and tau, build up for some unknown reason. In the case of Parkinson's disease, a protein called alpha-synuclein builds up, again for an unknown reason.

What we do know is the immune system goes rogue in these inflammatory diseases, and starts to attack our own tissues. There are various anti-inflammatory medicines that can be used. Several of these originated in plants, as our ancient ancestors noticed that certain plant extracts could limit inflammation. Nearly all early medicines were derived from plants. Other primates had also noticed the beneficial effects of certain plants. When they have a worm infestation chimpanzees will eat certain plants, such as the *Aspilia mossambicensis*, which helps expel the worm[11].

Inflammation has always been easy to see. It meant you had an infection or an injury. The affected area becomes hot to touch, swollen, painful and red. So the ancients could see it and could rub in a plant or eat it to treat it. The first medicine that we know of ever to be depicted was a hieroglyph on the Ebers Papyrus (1550 BC)[12]. It was an anti-inflammatory plant that was used to treat eye inflammation and haemorrhoids in Ancient Egypt. And what was that plant? Marijuana. This is now known to have cannabinoids, active ingredients that suppress inflammation.

The first drug to be actually synthesised in a lab was aspirin, a derivative of salicylates which had been isolated from willow bark and had known anti-inflammatory properties. This was done by the German drug company Bayer, who at the same time made a derivative from morphine which they called heroin, because it made people feel like heroes. Bayer sold heroin for a number of years as a cough remedy, until they noticed that heroin had some rather perturbing other effects.

The main diseases of ageing are actually inflammatory diseases. In many ways, we caused these diseases, because humans who would otherwise be dead from infections now age. Being old looks like a disease: our eyes and ears don't work well, we have aches and pains, and we mightn't be able to lead as full a life as we used to. We don't know what causes these inflammatory diseases of ageing, other than to say that the inflammatory process goes out of kilter and starts to damage our tissues as we age. The pain, redness and swelling happen in whichever tissue might be affected — our joints in the case of arthritis, our digestive system in the case of inflammatory bowel disease and our central nervous system in the case of multiple sclerosis.

There have been advances in treatment, with new targets being found that are then turned off. A good example is a protein called TNF, which is made in inflamed tissues and promotes further inflammation and destruction. Drugs that target it are effective in diseases such as rheumatoid arthritis and Crohn's disease. These are very high-tech drugs, as they themselves are proteins (in the form of antibodies) that are engineered to act as sponges to mop up the TNF. This slows down disease progression and makes a big difference to patients, although the drugs do not cure them. For a cure we need to find out the underlying cause, which is likely to be a mix of genetic differences and environmental influence, perhaps even a virus yet to be discovered.

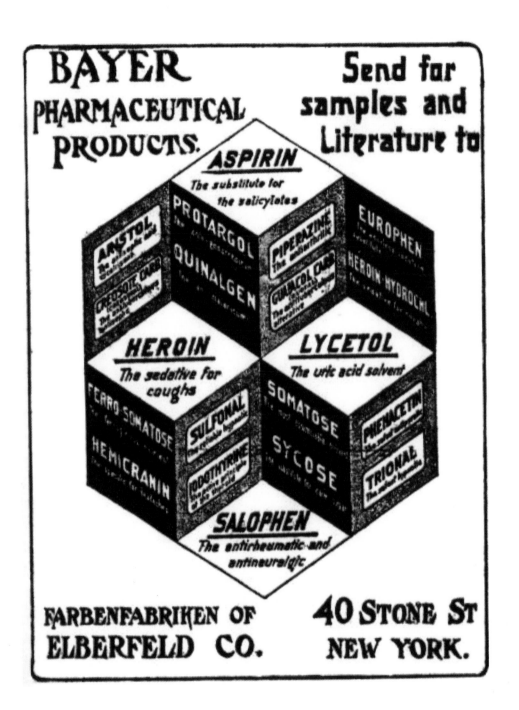

THE GERMAN PHARMACEUTICAL COMPANY BAYER MADE THE FIRST EVER SYNTHETIC MEDICINE, ASPIRIN. THEY ALSO MADE HEROIN AS A COUGH REMEDY WHICH WAS LATER WITHDRAWN BECAUSE OF ITS HIGHLY ADDICTIVE PROPERTIES.

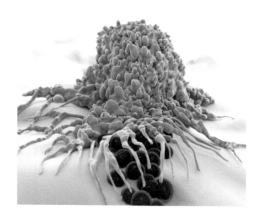

A MACROPHAGE ENGULFING BACTERIA. THESE CELLS DEFEND US BUT CAN ALSO DO MISCHIEF IN INFLAMMATORY DISEASES.

As our population ages, we will see more and more Alzheimer's disease and Parkinson's disease. Alzheimer's disease is an irreversible brain disease that slowly destroys memory and thinking skills. Symptoms usually begin to appear after the age of 60. It is named after Dr Alois Alzheimer, who examined the brain of a patient of his who had dementia and noticed clumps (now called amyloid plaques) and bundles of fibres in the hippocampus, the part of the brain most involved in memory. These clumps and fibres kill the nerve cells in the hippocampus, hence the memory loss.

Again it seems to involve the immune system, as immune cells try to clear these clumps, causing inflammation as a kind of collateral damage, killing the neurons in the process. Scientists have searched for genes that might be different in patients with Alzheimer's disease, and one called APOE-epsilon stands out. Carrying that gene increases the risk of the disease developing, and a recent study has shown that having this gene variant promotes the formation of the clumps and tangles. This might give rise to new drugs to target APOE-epsilon. Drugs that target the clumps and tangles themselves are also in development, although with only limited success so far.

Parkinson's disease is similar to Alzheimer's disease, but in this case the clumps are made of the protein alpha-synuclein. This is getting deposited in another part of the brain, called the substantia nigra. This part is involved in the control of movement, and so as the neurons die there movement is affected. Speech is also damaged, as the correct movements to form words are diminished. Treatment for Parkinson's is limited, and mainly involves trying to replace the neurotransmitter dopamine, which is made in the substantia nigra.

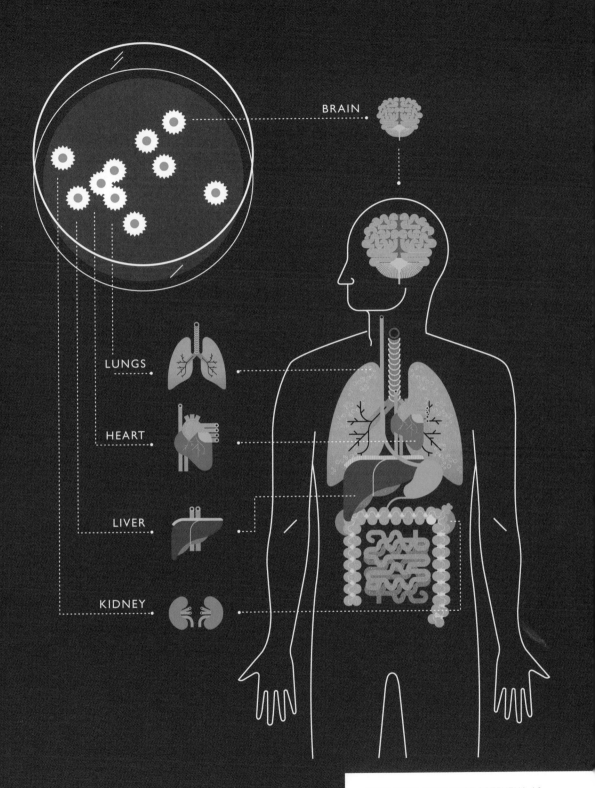

BRAIN

LUNGS

HEART

LIVER

KIDNEY

STEM CELLS HAVE HUGE POTENTIAL AS
THEY MIGHT ONE DAY BE USED TO GROW
DAMAGED ORGANS OR ORGANS THAT HAVE
BECOME WORN OUT BECAUSE OF AGE.

GERTRUDE ELION, WHO WON
THE NOBEL PRIZE WITH GEORGE
HITCHENS IN 1988 FOR THE
DISCOVERY OF MEDICINES FOR
GOUT, MALARIA AND HERPES.

But again there is good evidence that immune cell over-activation might be important, and so targeting the immune system and inflammatory process might give rise to therapeutics for Alzheimer's (for which current therapies are very limited) and Parkinson's disease. There is in fact a theme emerging of many inflammatory conditions, where an immune cell called the macrophage tries to clear the gunk that is being deposited as we age. The macrophage then gets very irritated and causes inflammation. Other examples include gout, which involves crystals of uric acid being deposited, atherosclerosis (the deposition of cholesterol crystals in the arterial wall) and type 2 diabetes (which involves a protein called IAPP being deposited). The macrophage tries to chew these things up, but a protein called NLRP3 senses them, and this triggers inflammation. Drugs that block NLRP3 are in development by a company I co-founded called Inflazome, along with other companies, and may prove useful in a whole host of diseases. NLRP3 was discovered by scientists interested in macrophages and the inflammatory process, and could turn out to be a very important discovery.

So what does the future hold? Medical research is a multibillion-euro activity going on all over the world. It's being carried out in universities, research institutes and pharmaceutical companies by scientists who are trying to make a difference. A real hero is Gertrude Elion. She shared the Nobel Prize in Physiology or Medicine in 1988 for discovering new medicines for diseases such as gout, malaria and herpes. She has said: 'When we began to see the results of our efforts in the form of new drugs which filled real medical needs and benefitted patients, our feeling of reward was immeasurable.'[15] The world spends more that $240 billion every year on biomedical research. This, however, is inclined to be skewed towards the diseases that afflict the Western world, such as heart disease and cancer, with infectious diseases such as malaria and TB (which have high mortality) being more neglected. This is partly commercial: pharmaceutical companies want to make profits, and these are driven by diseases that afflict more affluent countries. Sometimes a pharmaceutical company will give up on some diseases because they are deemed too difficult to crack, as happened recently with Pfizer announcing that they were halting internal work on diseases of the brain such as Alzheimer's disease.

Medical research begins with efforts to understand how living systems actually work, and from there moves on to figure out what happens when they are broken. The Medical Research Council in the UK funded the work that led to the discovery that DNA was a double helix which contained the information to make proteins. Changes in this information are the basis for genetic diseases. Genes could also be engineered to make important medicines like insulin for diabetes, so the Medical Research Council's money was very well spent. In general, scientists try to find a target to fire drugs at to treat diseases.

Many new medicines are in development, and there is great optimism. All that fundamental research is yielding new insights which will give rise to new medicines. We might have a situation where in the future, the main diseases that currently afflict us will be either prevented, slowed or cured. What might we then die of? Boredom? Will new diseases emerge or old ones come back to haunt us? We don't know. The recent emergence of the Ebola virus, which can now be vaccinated against, was a lesson in not being complacent. We must also be watchful for bacteria becoming resistant to antibiotics, returning us to the days of infectious diseases killing us by the millions – a frightening prospect.

We also have several brave new things to consider. One especially exciting area is technology to correct defective genes. This is a system that was

COMPANIES ARE OFFERING TO TAKE STEM
CELLS FROM YOUR BONE MARROW, STORE
THEM, AND THEN USE THEM IN YEARS TO
COME TO BUILD A NEW YOU.

originally described in bacteria, which chops up and manipulates foreign DNA in viruses. It is a key part of the bacterial immune system which fights viruses by targeting the virus's DNA. Scientists (notably Jennifer Doudna, Emanuelle Charpentier and Feng Zhang) then realised that this same machinery could be used to target any DNA, and even fix broken DNA as occurs in mutated genes. The technology is called CRISPR, and many labs are now testing it in different contexts[14]. It's been possible to correct a mutated gene that causes heart disease[15]. This correction was performed in a human fertilised egg, which means that if that egg were allowed to develop, the resulting human would now not get that particular form of heart disease. This holds great promise, as it might be possible to correct broken genes for many diseases, including diseases that cause blindness or muscle atrophy, and in fact a whole host of genetic diseases.

Stem cell research is another prominent area causing much excitement. We know that the fertilised egg contains all the information to make all the organs in your body. A Japanese scientist named Shinya Yamanaka found that putting in genes for four proteins, Oct3/4, Klf4, Sox2 and c-Myc, would reprogramme the cell and make it into what effectively is a fertilised egg[16]. This is called the 'OKSM protocol', which perhaps should stand for 'OK, So Make Me!'

These genes somehow wind the tape back for that cell (say a skin cell), and it effectively turns back into the fertilised egg. Remember, all the cells in our bodies have all the DNA you need to make a full human, since they are descended from that fertilised egg whose DNA just kept on getting copied. What makes each specialised cell type different is that some genes can be turned on and others off. So a skin cell makes proteins that say 'I'm a skin cell' and a liver cell makes proteins that say 'I'm a liver cell'. But if you put in OKSM, the skin cells revert back to being an undifferentiated stem cell. Almost back to the egg. It might then be possible to grow for yourself new nervous tissue that will repair a broken spinal cord, or a new kidney if yours have become damaged.

Companies are offering to take stem cells from your bone marrow, store them, and then use them in years to come to build a new you. A bit like replacing a part in a car engine, maybe we will be able to replace the parts that break or become old. Maybe we can defy ageing and live for ever. An important question though, is, How will we pay for all these new medicines? They are, and will be, expensive. The anti-cancer medicines that wake up our immune systems are currently costing up to €100,000 per patient per year in Ireland. Who will pay? Will governments cover the cost? Will we have a situation of inequality, where only the rich will be able to afford treatments, with the poor getting sick as they have always done? This is the case to some extent currently, especially with infectious diseases in Africa, which are treatable now, but where people can't get access to the medicines they so badly need.

Maybe the thing to do is to keep reminding people that, for most of us, there are three things needed to prevent diseases starting in the first place. We know that good diet, exercise and sleep will help ward off many of the diseases mentioned above. If we can correct the genes that might put us at risk of these, then the diseases may never start in the first place. Perhaps we should all follow what Jonathan Swift, the writer of *Gulliver's Travels*, wrote: the three best doctors are Dr Diet, Dr Quiet and Dr Merryman. Maybe laughter is the best medicine after all.

CHAPTER 16

WHY YOU SHOULDN'T WORRY ABOUT GETTING OLD

GROW OLD, I grow old / I shall wear the bottoms of my trousers rolled', as T.S. Eliot wrote in 'The Love Song of J. Alfred Prufrock', his musings on the human condition. We all grow old. Nearly all life on Earth grows old and dies. I say nearly all. Organisms like bacteria and yeast, which mainly live as single cells on their own, just divide and keep dividing, although there is some evidence that once they have undergone 40 or so budding events, a yeast cell doesn't divide any more, which means death[1].

That is a bit like us. Our cells keep dividing and then eventually stop. Cells in your gut, for instance, are replaced every two to four days[2]. But eventually you die. You might die in an accident, although even then your cells keep dividing in your bloodstream until they run out of food. Most of us die of diseases, and as we saw in the previous chapter many of us die of diseases of ageing. Our bodies eventually pack in, and perhaps an infection that we would normally fight kills us, or our hearts or brains eventually run down in a process called senescence. If you don't die an accidental death, or of some disease that strikes at any age like cancer, your body will age and die. We will look at death more closely in the next chapter. But what exactly is ageing?

We can start by looking at lifespan. The longest a human being has ever lived (that we know of) is Jeanne Calment of France (1875–1997), who lived to the age of 122 years, 164 days. Quite what her longevity was due to we don't know. She herself said: 'Always keep a smile. I attribute my long life to that. I believe I will die laughing. That's part of my program.' This is likely to be close to the absolute limit for humans. When we look at other creatures we see some striking results. Mice live an average of three years, cats for 12 years and dogs for up to 13 years. There is no accepted rhyme or reason to this. It was thought to be due to size – the bigger you are, the longer you live.

The creature on Earth thought to hold the record for having the longest lifespan is a type of creature called hydra, which is a small freshwater animal with tentacles; it can live for 1,400 years. In Ireland we can expect to live about 81.4 years on average (79.4 for males, 83.4 for females)[3]. We don't actually do too badly in Ireland compared to other countries. Japan

JEANNE CALMENT HAS THE LONGEST CONFIRMED HUMAN LIFESPAN, LIVING TO THE AGE OF 122 YEARS AND 164 DAYS.

tops the league table at 83.7 years. Ireland is number 19, just ahead of the UK, whose citizens have an average lifespan of 81.2 years. Sierra Leone isn't doing too well, with an average life span of 50.1 years, which is caused in part by diseases such as AIDS.

What determines how long a creature (including possibly us) lives might come down to number of heartbeats[4]. On average, humans have 2.21 billion heartbeats in their lifetime. Cats have 1.18 billion. The number of heartbeats has been shown to directly correlate with the number of years each organism lives. If you put the water flea *Daphnia* in a warmer environment, its heart rate goes up by 412 per cent, and it dies 77 per cent sooner. The number of heartbeats, though, stays the same, at 15,400,000. There are caveats, however, and ageing experts see it as a very rough rule of thumb. Birds and bats have much higher numbers of heartbeats than would be expected for their lifespan. However, the number of heartbeats in each species does seem to be finite. This kind of thing led astronaut Neil Armstrong to quip:

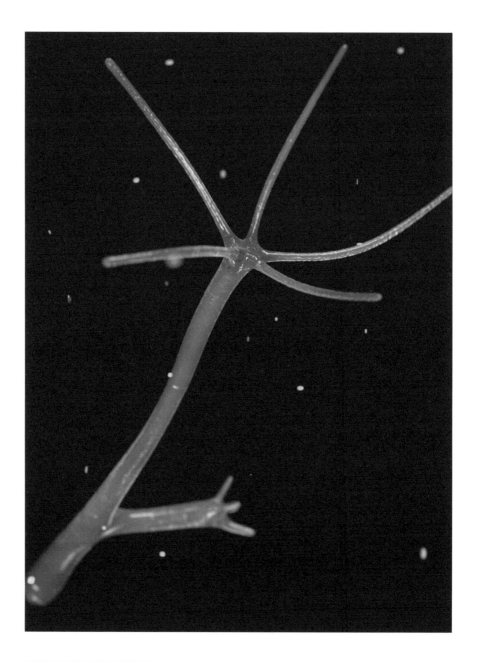

THE SEA CREATURE HYDRA
CAN LIVE FOR 1,400 YEARS.

'I believe every human has a finite number of heartbeats. I don't intend to waste any of mine.' It also might mean that if you exercise and increase your number of heartbeats per minute, it might actually shorten your life – which gives me the perfect justification to avoid exercise.

When it comes to the level of individual cells in your body, they divide a finite number of times and then stop. This was first studied in detail by a scientist named Leonard Hayflick, and the finite number of cell divisions for a given cell type is termed the 'Hayflick limit'[5]. This is the number of times each cell type can divide before it senesces. For foetal cells this is up to 60 times. Some cells never divide – they are known as end cells. The best example is neurons in your brain. This is why when you have a brain injury repair is defective because of the inherent reluctance of neurons to divide.

How does a cell know when it has reached its Hayflick limit? A striking discovery was made by Elizabeth Blackburn, Carol Greider and Jack Szostak, who noticed that at the end of our chromosomes there are repeats of nucleotides[6]. Remember, our chromosomes are made of DNA, which in turn is made of lots of nucleotides on a very long string, or in our case 23 pairs of strings, which make up our 23 chromosomes. Blackburn and colleagues noticed that there were lots of the same nucleotides at the ends of chromosomes – somewhat like lots of yellow coloured balls strung out at the end of a string of beads. These are called telomeres. They won the Nobel Prize for Physiology or Medicine in 2009 for this discovery.

Every time a cell divides, they are slightly shorter: the chromosome loses some beads. Finally they are so short that the cell senses this and stops dividing. It's like a counting mechanism in cells. Cancer cells, however, have the key feature of being immortal. They will keep on dividing and dividing, and will form a tumour (the name of which comes from the Latin for 'swollen' – like a lump). This is because they keep adding beads back on. The enzyme that does this is called telomerase, and is an interesting target being explored as a way to stop cancer cells from growing.

Quite how the Hayflick limit or telomere length relates to your final number being up (as in death) isn't known, but scientists feel there must be a connection. This is because eventually all the cells stop dividing and you die. It might be to do with stem cells. These cells are the ones that keep replenishing tissues as you age. They become, say, a gut cell, then undergo their number of divisions set by Hayflick and then die. When they stop getting replaced, that is a sign of ageing.

Attempts to further explain the mechanism of how we age have focused on two aspects. First, as with most things, variants in certain genes plays a role. We know this anecdotally, where longevity seems to run in families. There has been a problem pinpointing exactly what genes might be involved, however, as the second aspect, environmental factors, can play a confounding role. Your mother might bring you up in a certain way based on what she learnt from her own mother, and as a result both she and you live to a ripe old age.

But when it comes to the environment, one factor seems to play an especially important role, and that is what we eat. When you eat food, your body breaks it down and uses the products to help build more of you, and also to generate a molecule called ATP, which is the energy currency of all life. It is the battery that you use to fuel all the things in your body that need energy, be it muscle power, or blood flow or copying your DNA when a cell divides. There is a by-product from the production of ATP, though – a bit like the exhaust coming from a car engine when petrol is used.

That by-product is called 'reactive oxygen species', or ROS, and in the context of ageing it comes largely from mitochondria, the structures inside our cells that make ATP from food[7]. It's a highly reactive chemical (in fact bleach has a lot of ROS in it), and our bodies have ways to keep it under control. We make in our own cells, or take in as part of our diet, chemicals called antioxidants, which mop it up. But ROS is able to 'rust' our DNA – similar to air causing iron to rust. This damages the DNA in the long run, and some scientists are of the view that it is the rusting of DNA, meaning its gradual disintegration, that lies at the heart of ageing, although there are disagreements concerning this mechanism of ageing.

Gene variants that seem to promote old age make proteins that are good at detoxifying ROS, adding weight to the idea that it is what you eat that eventually kills you. These proteins act as supercharged antioxidants. It might be possible to counteract the damaging effect of ROS by eating certain foodstuffs rich in antioxidants, such as blueberries and broccoli[8]. There's not much we can do about food ultimately killing us, except not becoming obese and eating sparingly. In studies of people who have lived to be over 100, the main thing they shared was that they generally had small meals and they weren't obese.

Other studies have shown that if you exercise in your 50s you can prolong your life by 2.5 years. Marriage also promotes longevity by as much as seven years, probably because overall it decreases stress[9]. Getting divorced shortens life by three years on average. It's easy to see the health benefits of marriage. Your spouse provides support and often encourages you to develop good habits. However, there can be difficulties with cause and effect here. There is evidence that marriage enhances people's inherent higher odds of living a longer healthy life, whereas people with negative traits such as emotional instability already have lower odds of living a healthy life and are more prone to divorce. For some people, escaping a doomed marriage may provide a new lease of life, meaning that it will be longer and happier.

Work in animals has supported the idea of food being linked to ageing, especially studies in a microscopic worm called the nematode[10]. These creatures live on rotting mushrooms but people who study ageing love them. They live for a few weeks and so it's easy to see if they are living short or long lives. They are made of 1,096 cells in total (unlike our bodies, which have billions of cells), and these cells can all be followed. When I worked in Cambridge I met a scientist called John Sulston, and I asked him what he worked on. He told me he spent eight hours a day looking down a microscope counting and following the cells in a worm. I thought 'WTF?' He went on to win the Nobel Prize in 2002 for this ground-breaking work which provided huge insights

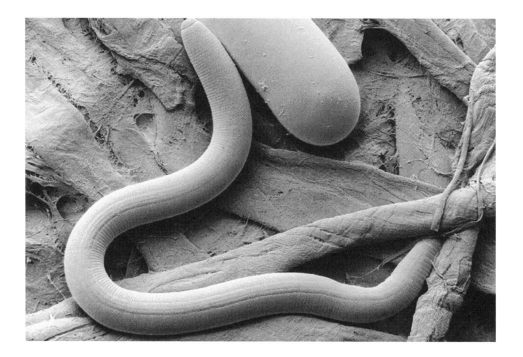

THE MICROSCOPIC WORM
THE NEMATODE CAN BE
MODIFIED TO LIVE TO FOUR
TIMES ITS NORMAL LIFE
SPAN. THE GENES THAT ARE
MODIFIED ARE INVOLVED IN
NUTRITION.

into how cells live and die. It's also easy to manipulate genes in nematodes and see what happens. When scientists mutated certain genes involved in nutrition in these little creatures, they extended their lives two-fold.

If that translated to humans, we would live to be over 200. The worms with the modified genes that prolonged their lives were most likely digesting their food more effectively – on a 'lean burn' mode in a sense, generating less ROS, and so less damage to DNA was occurring. We also have evidence in humans that DNA damage drives ageing. There is a disease called Werner's syndrome, or progeria, where people age much faster. People with this condition have a mutation in a gene for an enzyme that can repair damaged DNA, and so in these people, that damage builds up and promotes ageing. The normal enzyme repairs the damage to the DNA being caused by ROS, the by-product of nutrition.

So can we live longer if we watch what we eat? Well, that indeed is what the evidence seems to tell us. Overeating is bad. Certain diets seem especially good, notably the so-called Mediterranean diet, which consists of lots of fruit and vegetables, olive oil and seafood. Some exercise is also good but not too much. If you exercise hard you will generate more ROS. Light exercise gets the body to make chemicals that are beneficial in all kinds of ways, including for repairing damaged tissue.

THE ITALIAN TOWN OF ACCIAROLI HAS A REMARKABLE NUMBER OF CENTENARIANS. THEIR SECRET? LOTS OF EXERCISE AND EATING THE RIGHT DIET.

To get to the bottom of some of these things scientists often study populations where the people live much longer than the average. In the remote Italian town of Acciaroli[11], which was thought to have inspired Ernest Hemmingway's novel *The Old Man and the Sea*, around 300 people have lived to be 100 or more. These villagers are now being tormented by scientists trying to find out why, and may well have their lives shortened by all the attention. What is it about these people? They have very low rates of heart disease and Alzheimer's disease, both of which are diseases of ageing. The villagers have a classic Mediterranean diet, with lots of fish, olive oil and herbs such as rosemary. A natural chemical called carnosic acid occurs in rosemary, and this has been shown to improve memory in older people, and limit the damaging effects of ROS. The villagers also exercise more than average, living in a hilly region where they hike and hill walk as part of their day-to-day lives. As we have heard from time immemorial, the secret therefore seems to be to eat healthily and to take exercise. As the proverb says: 'You eat your own grave.'

Another interesting theory of ageing concerns the inflammatory process. As we saw in the last chapter, inflammation is an important part of our body's defences. If you have an infection, or if you sprain your ankle, inflammation is triggered, which means redness, soreness, swelling and the injured area becoming warm. The purpose of this is to repair the damage – most of these events are due to blood rushing in to bring in the immune system to defend us from the infection, but also to rebuild damaged tissue. This is a highly elaborate process that heals the body. However, it can go awry in a whole range of diseases, from arthritis (which is inflammation of the joints) to colitis (inflammation of the gut) to diseases that afflict the brain including multiple sclerosis and Alzheimer's disease.

There is a major effort to understand this process in order to devise new therapies for these very troubling diseases. Several of these diseases are diseases of ageing, and it is thought that the ageing process plays a role in their development. This gives rise to the term 'inflammaging', meaning inflammation as we age. ROS will provoke inflammation too. It is therefore possible that anti-inflammatory agents will limit ageing, and in fact a drug called rapamycin has been shown to do just that. This anti-inflammatory (among other things) drug extended life in mice by 20 per cent, which would mean an average extension to 96 years for humans[12].

It has also been shown that the hypothalamus in the brain is key to ageing because of an inflammatory factor there called NF-kappaB[13]. When this was blocked mice again lived 20 per cent longer. There is also a key driver of inflammation in macrophages in our blood called NLRP3 (see Chapter 15 for its role in disease), which is able to sense the build-up of damage as we age (say in the form of cholesterol in our blood vessels). Limiting NLRP3 in mice has been shown to slow down the ageing process[14]. Mice lacking it had fewer cataracts in their eyes, and less bone weakening. These results are remarkable, and bring us closer to new options for limiting the diseases of ageing.

There is a possibility that each country will find itself turning Japanese. By which I mean an ageing healthy population will be the norm. What has happened there has been remarkable. In 1950, 5 per cent of the Japanese population were over 65. This figure is now 50 per cent. There is a birth rate of 1.4 births per woman, which means the Japanese population is not replacing itself[15]. The Japanese are the first country where the sale of adult diapers has exceeded that of baby diapers. Playgrounds are being converted into exercise areas for the elderly. The reason for the longevity again appears to involve diet. The Japanese eat a lot of seafood and drink a lot fewer sugary drinks compared to Westerners. In Japan, obese people are a rarity, sumo wrestlers notwithstanding.

Given all this research the question is, Will we eventually discover the elixir of youth? We may be taking elixirs already, as drugs as common as low-dose aspirin (given to decrease the risk of heart attacks by thinning the blood) or metformin (which is used for type 2 diabetes) appear to prolong life somewhat[16], again most likely because they have anti-inflammatory properties. Metformin is in fact a fascinating drug. It was first synthesised in Trinity College Dublin by Emil Werner and James Bell, who made a derivative of a herbal agent from goat's rue, which had been used since antiquity for type 2 diabetes. This is a disease where your blood sugar stays high after a meal because of insulin insensitivity. In a study of 180,000 people in the UK there was a 15 per cent extension in lifespan for people on metformin. If we can find out exactly what it does, an even better form of metformin might emerge. We know again that it's tied into nutrition, as it can keep blood sugar low, and we also know that it has anti-inflammatory properties.

Another unlikely elixir that might prolong life is young blood[17]. In a rather unusual yet striking series of experiments, investigators noticed that if an old mouse was transfused with a young mouse's blood, the old mouse became healthier, his eyes cleared and his joints became more supple. The young blood had in fact rejuvenated the old mouse. This sounds a bit like Dracula feasting on the blood of the young. A factor called GDF11 is higher in young blood and declines as we age. When this factor was used in mice it had a similar effect. Quite how it works isn't clear but maybe it is the long-sought-for elixir – or maybe not, as there have been false dawns in this regard in the past.

YOUNG BLOOD HAS BEEN SHOWN
TO SLOW AGEING WHEN INJECTED
INTO OLD MICE. DOES THIS
EXPLAIN IMMORTALITY IN VAMPIRES?

Will all this research be worthwhile? It is still a fascinating philosoph-ical question, why we age – and, as we'll see in the next chapter, why and how we die. If we do find drugs to help us, it's unlikely that they will let us live beyond a certain finite span, which is probably around 120 years, unless we come up with ways to keep replacing our organs by growing them from stem cells in a dish and replacing our worn-out parts as we age. Instead we'll slow down the depredations of ageing, by limiting the disintegration that happens because of inflammaging. This should also include a lower incidence of dementia as we get older, since the ageing brain is more prone to diseases such as Alzheimer's disease. If we can somehow protect our brains by, say, keeping our minds active (which might bring benefits by increasing connections between brain cells, which in turn might mean that although people lose connections as they age they will have spare capacity), we will stave off dementia.

But maybe ageing isn't all bad. One thing that a series of studies has shown is that we peak at different things at different ages[18]. When you look back on your life, will you say that you loved being 24 or 47 or maybe 75? Scientists have been studying a wide range of both physical and mental traits to determine at what age we peak for each of them, and there have been some very interesting results. You are best able to learn a second language when you are seven or eight years of age. That seems to be when the mind is at its most receptive, probably because it's when we listen to the advice of our parents most acutely; otherwise we might get hurt in an accident, for example.

Mind you, it's also the age when we are highly susceptible to information, as the Jesuits spotted when they said 'Give me the boy at seven, and I will give you the man.' Try to learn a second language past 30 and it's much more difficult. Your brain-processing power, on the other hand (e.g. your ability to decode information and retain long strings of numbers), peaks at 18. This is good for when you are in university – your brain is most ready for the complexities of your degree. Your ability to remember unfamiliar names peaks at 22. This is possibly because you are now out in the wild, and you don't want to go offending the chief of another tribe by forgetting his name. Your status anxiety is therefore at its peak.

Men find women most attractive when the woman is 22. Women on the other hand tend to find men who are a year or two older than they are more attractive. (This could be nonsense as it was based on OKCupid's data pool, which may be unreliable overall, as the people on that dating site may not be the same as the general population.) Your muscle strength will peak at age 25. You will run your best marathon at age 28. And your bone mass will peak at age 30, because that is when you can retain the most calcium in your bones. If you are a chess player, you will peak at age 31. That finding came from a study of 96 grand masters.

According to a study of 10,000 people (which is a large number and therefore probably gave correct results), one's ability to understand someone else's emotional state peaks in your 40s and 50s. And then it gets better as you get older for certain things – your ability in arithmetic peaks at age 50, your vocabulary in your late 60s (so wait until then before you write your magnum opus). You feel much more comfortable in your own body in your 70s and, finally, and we all know this, you are at your wisest when you are over 70. This was a test where people were asked to judge someone else's point of view, consider possible outcomes in a given scenario and the ability to search for compromise. So it really is true that wisdom comes with age.

One striking result from several studies is that life satisfaction peaks at two ages: 23 and 69. This is the famous U-shaped curve, where you are happiest at 23 and then your happiness plummets, bottoming out at 50, and then climbing back up to peak again at 69[19]. This is independent of whether you have children or whether you are single or maybe even whether you support the Irish football team. It seems to be built into us for some unknown reason. Crucially, after 70 we rate our lives as being at least a seven out of ten. When we're younger we rate it lower. So, if you're feeling miserable with your life, wait. As a wise old man once said: 'At age 20 we worry about what others think of us. At age 40 we don't care what they think of us. And at age 60 we discover they haven't been thinking of us at all.' So it's well worth hanging on in there and ageing gracefully (and hopefully healthily), as things will only get better.

CHAPTER 17:

DON'T FEAR
THE REAPER:
DEATH AND
BEYOND

YOU ARE GOING TO DIE. Not a very cheerful prospect. But remember, science does not shirk from any topic. Every year, around 30,000 people die in Ireland[1]. This keeps the undertakers busy. They see a lot of dead people. Some die ahead of their natural lifespan because of an accident. Some make it to a ripe old age. We fill our lives with a busy schedule, but if you look at the calendar on your smartphone there will definitely be a date in the future on which you will die. Go on, scroll down through the dates into the future … you will pass a date on which you are going to die. The Grim Reaper just hasn't filled that date in yet.

What's interesting is that a child born in Ireland today can reasonably expect to live to be over 100. This is because of advances in modern medicine, with medicines like statins (which keep cholesterol in check in our bloodstream and therefore decrease the risk of heart attack), and hopefully better lifestyles (not smoking, eating less, exercising more and getting plenty of sleep) improving lifespan for all. However, around 20 per cent of people will die in a sudden or unexpected way – an accident or a stroke, perhaps. A further 20 per cent will die of cancer (although those numbers will improve, with new treatments continuing to emerge, as we saw in Chapter 14).

Those with cancer will stay relatively healthy until quite close to death, when there is usually a linear deterioration over a few weeks. The rest of us

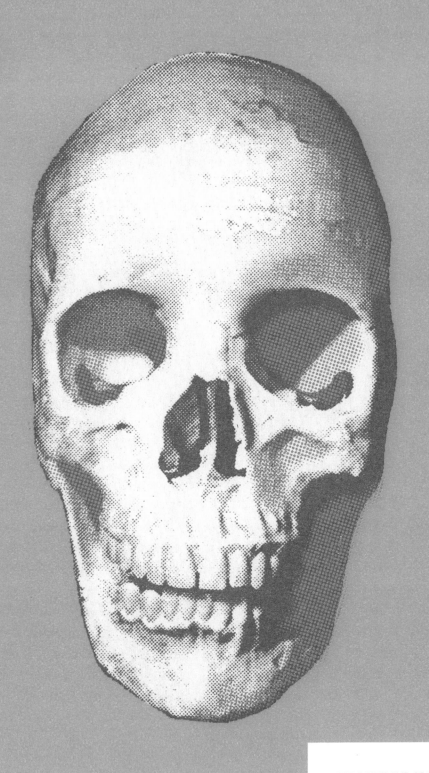

EAT, DRINK AND BE MERRY ...
FOR TOMORROW WE DIE

will undergo a slow deterioration as we age, suffering from various chronic medical problems such as heart or kidney failure, or dementia, buoyed by a range of medicines to keep us going longer[2]. By some estimates, more than 90 per cent of the medicines you will take will be taken in your last year of life. Your final months will be characterised by a series of relapses and remissions against a backdrop of slow deterioration in physical function. Pretty grim, huh? So eat, drink and be merry, for tomorrow (or whenever) we die.

One thing about death that has preoccupied people for hundreds of years is how we actually know someone is dead. It may seem obvious now, but in the past it wasn't (unless of course someone had their head chopped off). Say you lived a few hundred years ago and old Grandpa (who back then was probably 40 years of age) seemed to have croaked. You didn't call for a doctor, you called for the priest, who would make the determination of death. All the priest would have at his (never her) disposal would be outward signs of death. They might hold a mirror over Grandpa's mouth to see if it clouded over. Or a feather under his nose to see if it moved. In the 1700s enough was known about the human body to check for his heartbeat. The stethoscope, though, wasn't invented until 1816 by the French physician René Laennec. The binaural stethoscope (on which modern stethoscopes are based) was invented by Irish physician Arthur Leared. There was a rather gruesome procedure known as Balfour's test, where long thin needles were stuck into a person's heart and then left protruding with small flags attached. If the flags moved, the heart was beating and the person was deemed to be alive.

However, doctors began to realise that, although outwardly the person appeared to be dead (with no detectable heartbeat or breathing), they might in fact be still alive and perhaps might recover. This phenomenon led to people being buried alive, which wasn't especially unusual in the 19th century. Edgar Allan Poe (who according to John Lennon often got a kicking) made great mileage from such horror stories. To provide a safeguard, some coffins had a string from the inside up to the ground attached to a bell, which the unfortunate person could ring should they awake in their coffin – a dead (or actually live) ringer. Even today, doctors are cautious when pronouncing people dead under certain circumstances. When a patient is brought to a hospital comatose from, for example, attempted suicide or drowning, they may well have no signs of life. Their bodies, which will be cold to the touch, are usually warmed up first to check that they are actually dead, as signs of life might well return. The term 'warm and dead' is used for these unfortunate people.

Nowadays there are all kinds of ways to attempt to resuscitate someone, or keep them alive. A person can be hooked up to a ventilator, to maintain breathing and to keep blood circulating. There are a whole host of devices that can keep a person alive if you just measure their pulse as the indicator of being alive. But in the 1950s doctors recognised that people were being kept 'alive' by machines. The phrases 'persistent vegetative state' and 'irreversible coma' were invented to describe these people. They weren't coming back, because of brain damage that couldn't be repaired. We therefore now define death as being 'brain dead'.

A person who meets this whole-brain definition of death has lost the ability to breathe on their own. Breathing is essential to providing the oxygen your body needs to burn fuel in order to provide the necessary energy to keep the lights on. Simply put, dying starts when the body doesn't get enough oxygen to survive. Different cells in your body die at different speeds, however. If you cut yourself and your blood spills on the floor, that blood is full of white blood cells, which will continue to live for a few hours outside your body. The length of the dying process actually depends on which cells are deprived of oxygen.

The brain is especially greedy in this regard. It needs a lot of fuel to keep running. All those neurons crackling away burn 75 per cent of the glucose you consume, and need oxygen to do it. Any cut-off in oxygen to the brain (as happens in a massive stroke, which blocks the main blood vessel in the brain – the middle cerebral artery) will kill you within three to seven minutes. Cyanide kills in a similarly rapid fashion, because it directly interferes with the process of respiration (where oxygen is used to burn fuel to make the

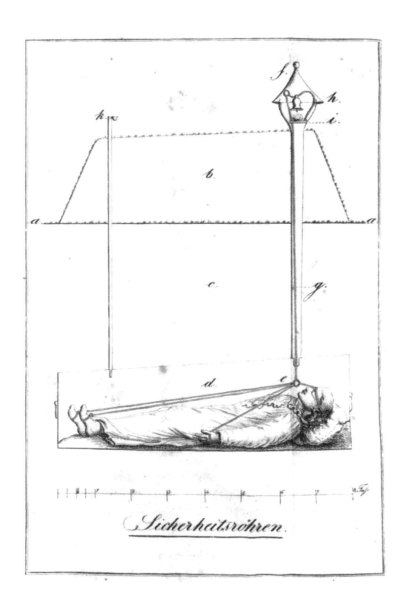

Sicherheitsröhren.

A COFFIN BELL – YOUR
SAFEGUARD AGAINST BEING
BURIED ALIVE.

energy currency of cells – ATP). Similarly, if you cut off the blood supply to the heart by blocking, say, the main coronary artery, death will happen relatively quickly, as the heart goes into spasm.

For most, though, these sudden deaths won't be the way you die. Your body's systems will simply break down with time, as we saw in the chapter on ageing. Like all machines, the component parts simply wear out. As death approaches, there will be some outward signs that these systems are slowly failing, and that the Grim Reaper is knocking on the door (or the banshee howling up on the roof). The person will sleep more to conserve whatever energy they have left, a bit like sleep mode on your computer. When energy reserves are very low, you won't have the energy to eat and drink. Swallowing will become difficult and your mouth will become very dry. Any pain you might feel can usually be managed by a doctor. Many people in fact shuffle off this mortal coil blissed out on a morphine-type sedative, falling almost literally into the arms of Morpheus. Not a bad way to go.

When someone is dying, that brings us into the realm of palliative care. The goal of palliative care is to improve a person's comfort and quality of life rather than trying to extend it per se. This can be a challenge for the medical professional, who will sometimes try their best to extend life. This is an important area, since, as the writer Cicely Saunders has said, 'How we die remains in the memory of those who live on.'

One disconcerting aspect of dying which grieving relatives might hear is known as the 'death rattle'. This happens when fluid builds up in the lungs, and the resulting congestion makes a noise as the person breathes their last breaths. Then, your heart stops, and that's that. All those heartbeats, which began in your mother's womb when you were developing, not stopping year after year after year, totalling on average over 2 billion – a remarkable piece of bioengineering, but like all good things, it has to come to an end.

One thing we don't know is what exactly a dying person is feeling. However, some people have come back from death's door and reported a feeling of peace and well-being[3]. These are called near-death experiences (or NDEs in the trade), and there is a remarkable commonality in what people report. Some report an out-of-body experience, a feeling of floating above their own body. Some report seeing a bright light and moving towards it. Some even say they see dead relatives beckoning them. These things are remarkably common across all cultures.

One explanation for the bright light is the last firing of the optic nerves. The most likely explanation for the other responses is brain changes, which lead to hallucination. They may be caused by the body making its own endorphins, the natural painkillers, released normally when we are in pain, or after strenuous exercise. They will act as a sedative to ease pain, and may give rise to a dream-like state. Others of course interpret these things in a spiritual way. The process lets others know that death is nothing to be frightened of. And indeed so it seems. People close to death in general are not anxious about dying, perhaps because endorphins start to kick in as the death process begins.

Eventually, a point of no return is reached, which is termed 'biological death'. After your heart stops beating, the brain cells will begin to die because of a lack of oxygen. Once this happens, any resuscitation is impossible. Death can play one last trick, though. The Lazarus sign refers to a rare spinal reflex that can happen in the newly deceased. Neurons in the spinal cord are not yet dead and trigger a reflex. The person's arms rise up and cross over each other on their chest before falling back down. This dramatic event is sure to make the medical team or unfortunate relatives jump.

Once death has occurred, what you think has happened to the essence of the person who has died will depend on your religious or cultural beliefs. The loss of a loved one might mean people are comforted by the notion of seeing that person again in some kind of afterlife. But without doubt, death fascinates us all. A scientific question that has come to the fore of late is, Can you predict at what age you might die? Governments and actuaries in insurance companies like to do these kinds of calculations, as they allow them to figure out how much to charge to cover pensions, and how much healthcare people might need as they grow old.

There are online questionnaires you can fill in for which you provide information on your weight, bad habits, family history of illness and the like, and they will spit out a possible date when you might expect to die. Then there is the 'Death Clock', which predicts the chances of a healthy person dying from any medical condition in the next five years[4]. I just did it on myself and it told me that I will die when I'm 78 years, three months and 14 days of age. It has given me 219,012 hours, 17 minutes and 21 seconds to live, and it's counting down; I must mark the date in my diary immediately: 1 October 2042 – gulp!

Scientists were surprised to find that an easy blood test was able to predict if a person was likely to die even if they were not ill[5]. Levels of four specific factors in the blood taken together gave a measure of how 'frail' you might be. If these so-called biomarkers were sufficiently different from the average, the person was five times more likely to die within five years. What was interesting was these markers gave an indication of dying not from something specific like heart disease, but instead were signs of general well-being. Biomarkers include things like cholesterol levels, which will give a prediction of your chance of having a heart attack.

But these biomarkers were different, and comprised four biochemicals: albumin, alpha-1-acid glycoprotein, citrate and the size of very low-density lipoproteins, particles that occur in the blood. Blood was taken from 17,000 generally healthy people, and more than 100 biomarkers were examined. These four were the ones that gave the best association with likelihood of dying – 684 people died, and it was in these people that the four biomarkers were most out of kilter. One in five people with the highest level died within one year.

This study was actually an excellent example of science in action. The findings were first made in 9,842 people in Estonia, but the scientists didn't quite believe the result, and so examined another 7,503 people in Finland and got the same trend. The effect therefore was reproducible and likely to be universal. When a discovery is made it must be reproduced to ensure it's accurate. The analysis of these four biomarkers might become a widely used test, which might predict people at a higher risk of dying and so might need medical intervention.

Ethics comes into play, however. Remember, these are generally healthy people. Would the scientists have to tell the people that they are at a high risk of dying within a year? Would the people want to know? How would it affect their behaviour? Would they immediately draw up a bucket list, leave their families and go on a hedonistic trip around the world? Who knows? Maybe we all need a licence to enjoy the time we have on Earth, and maybe a test like this might help us, but remember, it only gives our *risk* of dying, not absolute certainty. And some will have elevated biomarkers and not die.

So once you're dead what happens next? Well, it's about to get much more gruesome, so those of a fragile disposition might make sure the lights are on, and that you have a stiff drink in hand. But again, as scientists we shirk at nothing. Once you are dead, the second law of thermodynamics kicks in. This law says that things will always become more random, or to put it more scientifically, everything tends towards an increase in entropy. In this case, the body decomposes[6]. It breaks down into its component parts (which in that state will have increased entropy – a bit like a gas with the molecules all moving randomly).

One definition of life is 'a defiance of entropy': your body maintains itself in a highly ordered state (as in all your structures – bones, organs and tissues – are intact when you're alive, via the input of energy in the form of the food you eat). Once that energy drains away, the second law does its remorseless job and you start to decay. How long that takes will depend on where your body is. If you are refrigerated everything is slowed down, since molecules move much more slowly when they are cold. Decay will take some time to happen, as we know when we put meat in the fridge. If you are encased in a lead-lined coffin, it can take decades to completely decompose. But if left out in the open or buried in soil, the body will disappear in a few months.

Let's look at the sequence of events. These have been mapped out by forensic scientists who try and establish time of death. Within minutes of death, carbon dioxide starts to build up in your bloodstream. This is because you normally breathe this out – it's part of the exhaust that comes off from the burning of food in your body, to release energy. This gas, however, is quite toxic to cells, which start to burst open. Cells have proteins in them that digest things (for example the food they eat), and so these get to work on digesting you. Your tissues begin to get chewed up from within.

After 30 minutes or so, your blood (which has stopped circulating because your heart is no longer beating) will start to pool at the lowest point. This can mean a corpse can turn black on its underside because of the pooled blood, while the rest of the body goes very pale. Calcium begins to leach out of your muscle cells, and this means they contract. This is called rigor mortis – a well-known stiffening of the body. A dear friend of mine who himself has sadly passed, Stephen Connelly, used to refer to an erection as a 'Rigorous Mortimer', but this is something quite different.

The next big event is your guts burst, again because of a gaseous build-up. This releases all the billions of bacteria from your gut, which help with more digestion but also give rise to the unpleasant odour of a rotting corpse. The bacteria also produce gases that bloat the body and build up over the course of about two weeks. This is when drowned people surface and get washed ashore.

Gradually more bacteria move in, as do a whole host of creatures. The first insects to arrive are flies, including houseflies. Different species of flies arrive at different times, and this is highly informative for the forensic pathologist. There is in fact a specialism within forensics – forensic entomology[7] – that studies this aspect: which insects appear on a corpse when, and which maggots grow first. This is a wonderful topic to discuss at a dinner party. Some flies prefer a body that is much riper than others. Beetles tend to arrive latest to the party, as they prefer a well-decomposed body. The flies lay eggs and maggots will soon appear to give rise to more flies, and so the cycle continues.

Eventually, after a period of months (or years, depending on the climate and where the body is), all that is left is bones. Even the collagen in the bones, which is especially tough, will be broken down. No creatures can digest bone, which is a hard, calcium-based mineral. Sometimes, though, the bones will crumble and turn to dust and be blown away. Your body has now been fully

recycled and gone back to the stardust whence it came. In the immortal words of David Bowie: ashes to ashes, funk to funky.

Estimating the time of death is actually a very precise science. The first thing that is done is to see if the dead person is wearing a watch to see if it's stopped because of being broken. Pretty obvious, huh? There are in fact three times of death: the biological time of death (which is when the person actually died), the estimated time of death (which should be the same as the biological time of death but might be slightly off) and finally the legal time of death, which is entered on your death certificate. This is when the body was discovered or pronounced dead by another individual. One method that is used to estimate the time of death is to measure the body temperature. When you're alive, your core body temperature is 37.5 °C. After death your body will cool by 1.5 °C per hour until you reach room temperature.

Another method that is used is called LABRADOR[8], which stands for 'Lightweight Analyser for Buried Remains and Decomposition Odour Recognition'. It's a cutesy name (that must have taken some time to come up

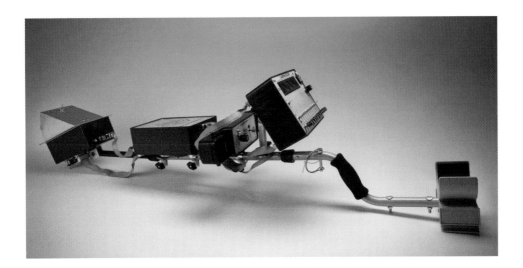

with) for a rather unpleasant device that 'sniffs' the various chemicals released by decaying bodies. The odours come from chemicals being released by different species of bacteria. Like insects, different species arrive at different times, and this

EVERY HOME SHOULD HAVE A LIGHTWEIGHT ANALYSER FOR BURIED REMAINS AND DECOMPOSITION ODOUR RECOGNITION – OR LABRADOR FOR SHORT. IT DETECTS THE VARIOUS CHEMICALS RELEASED BY DECAYING BODIES TO CALCULATE TIME OF DEATH.

means different odours being produced. This study is carried out at what can only be described as possibly the most gruesome place for science – the Human Decomposition Research Laboratory in Huntsville, Texas. This site contains donated cadavers which are left to decompose at various locations on the seven-acre site. The scientists found that specific populations of 'decomposer' bacteria, microbes on the skin of the corpses but also in the soil under them, gave an accurate prediction of time of death. One fascinating finding was that the microbial composition of the soil under the body changes dramatically, acting as a signature that a dead body was there. This could prove that a body has been moved after death, which might become relevant in murder trials.

Finally, to further emphasise what a hot topic of research this is, a recent breakthrough that might provide a very accurate time of death is to measure the expression of genes. Surprisingly, even though you're dead, some of your cells are still alive and are making proteins – some of their genes are still active[9]. This was first shown in mice and zebra fish, but also probably occurs in humans. They measured mRNA (the first product of a gene, which then becomes a protein) in brain and liver samples from mice and zebra fish up to four days after death.

As expected, many mRNAs are decreased as a cell switches off. However, mRNA for 548 zebra fish genes and 515 mouse genes saw one or more peaks of activity after death. This means that the cells had sufficient energy to crank out at least some proteins. What was especially interesting was that some genes 'woke up' after death. These were genes previously seen in the foetus, which was a surprise. Almost as if there was a rebirth after death. Some of the genes are associated with growth and repair. It looks as if the body is trying to defy death. It wants to go back to being a foetus with its whole life ahead of it, or repair the damage that has happened and restore the body back to normal.

It could also be that these genes are normally kept in check by genes that are being turned off after the death of the cell. Whatever the reason, because these genes are switched on and off at specific times, it might be possible to time death very precisely based on gene expression changes. It might even be possible to get the time of death down to a level of accuracy that is in the order of minutes. What is intriguing here is that we have life in the face of death.

And so your life is top and tailed – your birth cert recording when you were born, and your death cert recording when you died, perhaps to the very minute. With your life, with all its ups and downs and ins and outs, in between those two dates. Food for worms at last. Make of this what you will.

CHAPTER 18

DEFYING

DEATH

O N THE OTHER HAND – you're very rich and you don't want to die. You want to live for ever. Life is good and you still have things you want to do. You want to keep having fun. But sadly immortality is still not possible. One prominent person in the Middle East claimed to have come back from the dead 2,000 years ago, but that looks like something of a one-off. So you settle for second best. You have your body or maybe your head frozen. And you leave instructions that you are to be thawed out when the time comes that the disease you died from has been eradicated. This is the world of cryonics – the science of freezing human bodies to thaw them out in the future and jumpstart them when the time is right.

Cryonics (from the Greek 'kryos', meaning 'cold') is defined as the low-temperature preservation (usually at a very cold -196°C) of people who cannot be kept alive using the medical interventions that we have today. The hope is that resuscitation and restoration back to normal might be possible at some point in the future. In a notable recent case, a 14-year-old girl dying of cancer in the UK asked to be cryonically frozen[1]. Her father refused and her mother agreed, so the matter was brought before the unfortunate High Court Judge Mr Justice Peter Jackson, who had to decide what to do. He ruled that the mother's opinion should prevail, and the girl is now cryonically

preserved in a facility in the US, dead, but floating in a tank of liquid nitrogen. Waiting (even though she's dead) for a cure that might come, when she might be

A MEDIEVAL DEPICTION OF A RICH MAN DYING.

awakened like Sleeping Beauty and brought to full health. Only it won't be Prince Charming waking her, but the Cryonics Institute in the US. I wonder whether the scientific equivalent of the seven dwarves will be there when she wakes up – meaning scientists in different specialisms. She herself pleaded with the judge, writing, 'I think being cryopreserved gives me a chance to be cured and woken up, even in hundreds of years. I don't want to be buried underground.' The case was the first of its kind, and yet again illustrates that you never know what might come up before a judge.

Cryonics is not part of regular medical practice, and is looked upon with scepticism by the medical community. This is because cryopreservation is

CRYONICS: DR JAMES
BEDFORD IS PREPARED FOR
CRYOPRESERVATION.

currently not reversible, and it's not known whether it ever will be. However, it is a very active area of science, with several laboratories experimenting with the freezing of various animals and, more importantly, organs for transplantation. If it were possible to freeze, say, a kidney for use in a transplantation, this might increase the chances of the transplantation working. Often, transplanted organs are rejected because they have been kept too long outside the body. They effectively go off. Cooling fluids are sometimes used, but if the organ were to be frozen fresh from the donor, it might fare better when thawed than an organ kept above freezing for hours on end, where the cells become damaged.

Legally the procedure can only begin after someone is certified as dead. There is now a standard series of things that are done to cryopreserve a body. The first person ever to be cryopreserved was Dr James Bedford in 1967. Since then, there are estimates that around 250 people have been cryopreserved in the US[2], with another 1,500 having it in their wills. Freezing needs to be carried out as soon as possible after death to limit the damaging effects that occur following death (described in the previous chapter)[3]. The first thing that happens is the body is cooled in an ice bath. Sometimes cardiopulmonary resuscitation is carried out (which can include the shocking of the heart to keep it beating) to limit brain damage.

The procedure at this stage almost resembles the kind of things happening in *Frankenstein*, the story of how electricity was used to bring the unintended monster back to life. Flashes of lightning, very very frightening, and an awful lot of shouting, with the head bolted onto the body. Not that any of these things happen in the high-tech world of cryonics, but you get the idea. That book, written by Mary Shelley, was inspired by the experiments of Luigi Galvani in Italy, who made muscles twitch after death by applying an electrical current.

That kind of thing blew people's minds in the 19th century, making a dead man's limb twitch as if by magic (since nobody knew what electricity was). Even today this might be considered slightly odd, though we now know that the electrical current causes nerves to discharge, which in turn makes the muscle contract. It can be done on a dead person up until the stiffening of muscles (rigor mortis) occurs (or, as is always said, 'sets in').

The next step is to drain the body of all its fluids, and to replace those fluids with an anti-freeze based on glycerol, which stops ice crystals forming when the deep freeze begins. This is important because ice crystals can damage the delicate structures in the body, such as the many tiny blood vessels that course through our bodies. The body is then packed in ice and transported to a cryonic facility, either in the US or Russia, depending on who you're paying. The 14-year-old girl's body was taken to a US facility. Once it arrives the body is put in a special arctic sleeping bag and then cooled to -110°C over several hours using nitrogen gas. This is a very low temperature.

Over the course of the next two weeks, the body is then progressively cooled down to -196°C. Very, very cold indeed. Then the spooky thing happens. The body is suspended in a big vat of liquid nitrogen, bobbing away like a cork. It is then transferred to the 'patient care bay', where it will be kept until either the money runs out or the relevant technology is found to bring the body back to life in full health, emerging like Lazarus from the tomb. A cheaper option is neurocryopreservation, which involves preserving the head only. There has been a strong rumour that Walt Disney's head is frozen in a cryonics facility in the US, although this has been hotly denied.

You might be wondering at this stage how much all this costs. The cost of cryonically preserving the 14-year-old girl was £37,000, although this only covered the cryonic process of freezing. The costs include having medical personnel on standby for the moment of death, the cryonic process (which is called vitrification, because the body effectively becomes glass-like and could actually shatter), and the setting up of a trust fund to pay for the upkeep (which means the cost of the facility and the electricity bills to keep everything cool, with the occasional top-up of liquid nitrogen). In the US, the costs can vary from a cheaper option of $28,000 to the deluxe option of $200,000.

One company stores multiple bodies in the same dewar (as the big jar that the bodies are kept in is called). All of those corks bobbing together. At least it's sociable. This is a cheaper option, costing as little as $12,000. There was a major setback in the 1970s, however, when a company in California ran out of money and began stuffing too many bodies into containers. Two of the containers broke and nine bodies decomposed. Not a great result.

One company charges €75,000 for head-only cryopreservation. About one-third of this goes to the medical team who are on standby, and who then remove the head and preserve it. One-third goes into a fund for future revival and the rest goes into the trust to generate the income to top up the liquid nitrogen. There are a total of three cryonics facilities in the US and one in Russia. The British court which arbitrated on the 14-year-old girl calculated a total cost of £43,000, although it must be said that this is probably literally the tip of the iceberg.

So the question is, how likely is it that cryonics will work? Well, experiments have been done on animals as large as dogs and monkeys. There are claims that these animals have been resuscitated after being frozen to just below zero, with their blood being replaced with anti-freeze and then given rapid transfusions. This might be something like what happens when someone has had a heart attack and appears to be dead. They can be resuscitated by cardiopulmonary resuscitation. One company claims to have frozen a rabbit kidney to -135°C and brought it back for a successful transplantation[4]. This provides hope that the technology might work for preserving organs for transplantation. A company in California recently reported that it has frozen a rabbit's brain and recovered it back to a 'near perfect' state, meaning they could restore electrical activity. What the rabbit's thoughts might have been after this process we'll never know, but this procedure brings a whole new meaning to the term 'brain freeze'. The same company are now testing pigs' brains.

The science of cryopreservation (which is actually what was being carried out on the rabbit kidney and brain) is more reputable than cryonics. Many labs will freeze cells to thaw out for experiments later. And sperm and eggs can be frozen and thawed for use in in vitro fertilisation. It was thought that

water inside cells would freeze and burst the cells open during thawing but this is not what happens. Instead the water outside the cells freezes, and the cells themselves actually become dehydrated and squashed. Cryoprotectants like glycerol prevent this happening.

The difficulties of thawing a whole animal have been known for decades, however. Crystals form in tissues and damage them or stop communication between cells needed for organs to work properly. Cryoprotectants stop ice crystals forming and allow for cooling and solidification of the tissues. This is the process of vitrification[5]. The problem is that large tissues can crack during cooling, so that when they are subsequently thawed out, major damage has occurred. A piece of brain or liver might fall off. One issue is that death of the tissue will definitely occur during vitrification, meaning life might never be restored.

Another problem applies specifically to the brain, where different parts appear to need freezing at different rates, otherwise damage occurs to a part being treated the same as another part. This is never done, either during whole body or head cryopreservation, giving rise to much scepticism in the cryopreservation community. They might well bring back your liver from the frozen wasteland of a liquid nitrogen dewar, but they won't bring back the brain.

Then there is the question of how revival might work. This will require a lot of repair and restoration. A lot of face cream and Botox. A lack of oxygen is seen as a major cause of damage, so this would somehow have to be reversed. The cryoprotectant itself might be toxic, the organs might fracture and of course the cause of death would have to be reversed. People have a blind faith that all these problems will be solved in the future, or at least they are sold on the idea.

One company has an interesting selling point, which says that the cryonics procedures are getting better, and so as we get closer to the time when revival is possible, the most recent bodies preserved will be the ones most likely to be revived. Scientists will learn from these people, and then work backwards to the ones preserved the longest time ago, which will be more difficult to work on, increasing the chances of success with the expertise that will have been learnt. Would you trust that kind of sales patter? What would it take to make you believe?

To improve the chances of revival, scientists are studying what we can learn from nature about cryopreservation. It turns out there is a lot of research happening. Many creatures are able to survive prolonged periods of time below zero. Many of these make their own cryopreserving chemicals, including special proteins, compounds called polyols (a type of alcohol) and even lots of glucose can help. Plants are especially good at surviving very low temperatures. Tardigrades are tiny micro-animals that are resilient to extreme conditions, including temperatures as low as -272°C, which is close to absolute zero.

They've even survived being in outer space. Three species of bacteria, with the catchy names *Carnobacterium pleistocenium*, *Chryseobacterium greenlandensis* and *Herminiimonas glaciei*, have been revived after surviving thousands of years locked in ice. The red flat bark beetle has been shown to survive after being frozen to below -150°C. The fungus gnat *Exechia nugatoria* can be frozen to -50°C using the clever trick of only having ice crystals form in its body, and not its head. The scientists who devote themselves to the study of the fungus gnat deserve a special shout-out.

But there are two stars of the world of freezing animals and their restoration back to life[6]. The wood frog *Rana sylvatica* will freeze in the winter, with 45 per cent of its body turning to ice. Ice crystals form beneath its skin and become dispersed in its muscles. Amazingly, it stops breathing, its heartbeat ceases and blood flow halts. It makes special proteins and lots of glucose to preserve its tissues during this process. These prevent its vital organs from freezing. It can survive for up to 11 days at -4°C, which is no mean feat. The other star of the world of frozen creatures is the arctic ground squirrel, which is especially interesting as it's a mammal and so is warm-blooded unlike the wood frog[7]. This animal can survive temperatures as low as -2.9°C for three weeks at a time, although its head is kept at zero or slightly above. Scientists studying these animals hope to learn biochemical tricks that may be useful for organ preservation or, who knows, for cryonics itself.

Although cryonics seems to be a long way off from being fully realised, this hasn't stopped people saying they plan to have it done to them. Timothy Leary, the countercultural icon of the 1960s, publicly declared that he would be cryonically preserved, but disappointingly he changed his mind just before his death. We'd love to see him bobbing up and down. Perhaps he thought it would be too cool. Larry King and Britney Spears have both expressed an interest in it, although time will tell whether they follow through. For the moment, therefore, cryonics is a limited option for defying death.

Are there other options? Well, yes. It might be possible to keep replacing your organs once they pack in[8]. The science of stem cells has advanced greatly in the past ten years, as we saw in Chapter 15. This promises to be the answer to many medical issues, including repairing damaged spinal cords with freshly grown neurons. It effectively involves taking some cells from your body and then reprogramming them back into being like the fertilised

egg. There are companies exploring this technology, or technologies like it. They claim that they can take some of your cells, store them, and then when you're older, grow you a new liver or a kidney. These will be good as new, and can be used to replace the old ones in your body. Your immune system won't reject them because they are you, and so won't be seen as foreign. We therefore might see a scenario where you will order up spare parts, just like you would for your car.

THE ARCTIC GROUND SQUIRREL CAN SURVIVE FOR WEEKS AT SUB-ZERO TEMPERATURES ALTHOUGH IT KEEPS ITS HEAD AT SLIGHTLY ABOVE FREEZING TO AVOID BRAIN FREEZE.

The brain, though, might be tricky, as brain transplants have yet to be mastered, and may never be. But other scientists are speculating that it might one day be possible to upload the information in your brain into a supercomputer and that might then take charge, running all those fresh organs that are grown in the lab. Or perhaps operate an avatar. This seems like science fiction, right? A world where when we age, we simply replace old organs

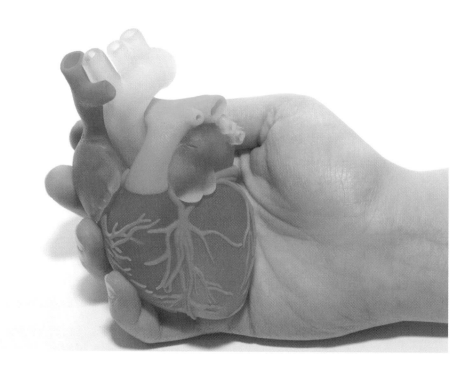

with new ones and hook our bodies up to a supercomputer. Immortality at last! But will it be fun? Will it be alive? Will the new you be a different person? At this stage we don't know, but it's intriguing to speculate and perhaps write a script for a Hollywood movie. Ultimately, though, we have to confront the reality that we can't cheat death. Or if we do, the resulting person will not be you, it will someone with a different personality or disposition and organs that haven't lived the life you've lived.

Spending years floating in liquid nitrogen or being made of organs grown in a lab are not ideal prospects for many of us. Perhaps it's best to grow old gracefully and die at a venerable age, having passed on your wisdom to the next generation, as we saw in Chapter 16. We need to make room for them anyway, and give them a chance during their lifespan on Earth. Anything else is narcissistic and greedy. Who would want to live for ever anyway? Apart from that guy born 2,000 years ago …

CHAPTER 19

WILL
WE BECOME
EXTINCT?

THE END IS NIGH. In most major cities, people walk around with placards calling upon us to repent. There are earthquakes, hurricanes, biblical predictions, fire-and-fury pronouncements from presidents and dictators. But when will the end come for us, as it most certainly will? It might be millions of years away, when our sun gets even hotter, or it might be some nasty germ that will wipe us all out. But one thing is for sure – there will be a time on Earth when we humans are no longer here.

Life on Earth is actually quite a fragile thing[1]. At least five times in history it nearly became extinct. Climate change, a meteorite strike, a gamma-ray burst from a distant star, all nearly did for life on Earth. Scientists call these 'extinction events', also known as 'mass extinctions' or a 'biotic crisis', 'biotic' being another word for life. Such an event is defined as a sharp and relatively rapid change in the diversity or abundance of life on Earth. But what are these extinction events that happened in Earth's history?

The first big one happened around 2.45 billion years ago. It's called the Great Oxygenation Event, and it happened because oxygen built up in the atmosphere. Oxygen is actually a very toxic molecule, as it can react with other chemicals and oxidise them. A good example is iron, which when oxidised becomes rust, which is less stable than iron. Oxidation usually means that something is broken down. Biological molecules like DNA and proteins are very prone to oxidation, so our cells have all kinds of ways to detoxify oxygen. We use oxygen to break down food, which is one way to keep oxygen under control. And our cells are packed full of molecules called antioxidants that keep it at bay.

So why did oxygen build up? Organisms called cyanobacteria evolved which could perform a marvellous trick, perhaps the greatest trick of all in biology. They could take carbon dioxide from the air and, using the energy in sunlight, combine it with water to make more of themselves – they could make carbohydrates. The evolution of cyanobacteria meant that life on Earth plugged into the cosmos. Imagine, air and water to make plants (which is what cyanobacteria are). This process is termed 'photosynthesis'. And a by-product from this chemical reaction is oxygen.

Normally oxygen would be captured by iron or other dissolved chemicals, but it is thought that this became saturated, releasing oxygen into the atmosphere. This can be detected in rocks from that time. The oxygen was toxic to other organisms, which died off in their droves. The cyanobacteria themselves evolved protective measures, and other organisms called aerobic bacteria could also use the oxygen, most probably to get the most from food by oxidation.

And so life persisted on Earth, but in different forms than before. There was an adaptation to the new oxygen-rich conditions. It was a bit like being at a party, and someone turns the music up loud. Lots of people leave and only those with earplugs stay behind, procreate and give rise to more people with earphones. In this case, the loud music was oxygen.

These events had a very important role in the evolution of life on Earth. Some of the aerobic bacteria went inside an anaerobic bacterium (one that couldn't use oxygen) and formed a special symbiotic relationship, as we saw in Chapter 1. This is called endosymbiosis, and was especially promulgated by the American biologist Lynn Margulis. Those aerobic bacteria subsequently became what we now know as mitochondria. Most of the oxygen consumption in our cells occurs in the mitochondria, which use oxygen to burn food and make the energy molecule ATP. These mitochondria are a relic of the early aerobic bacteria that could handle oxygen.

It's spooky to think that every cell in your body has the descendant of a bacteria lurking there, using oxygen. At some point the cyanobacteria also went inside the new cells with the aerobic bacterium inside. They went on to form what we now call 'chloroplasts'. This is what makes a plant. So the increase in oxygen, as well as causing the first great extinction on Earth, was the driving force that led to plant and animal cells evolving, since all plant cells have chloroplasts and mitochondria, and all animal cells have mitochondria. So the almost complete destruction of life on Earth had the fortunate spin-off of driving evolution forward all the way to us.

The reason this was so important was that it gave the ability to make the energy molecule ATP by using oxygen, which is what happens in mitochondria. This was a very effective way to make ATP, which provided the energy to feed the evolution of multicellular life. To evolve, an organism with lots of different cell types appears to have needed an effective way to make ATP, which was what the mitochondria did. Those multicellular organisms eventually evolved into us. As Nick Lane put it in his book *The Vital Question*, 'the role of energy in Darwin has been neglected for too long'[2].

The next big extinction, which happened 450–550 million years ago, goes by the catchy name the Ordovician-Silurian extinction event, during which up to 70 per cent of all life on Earth became extinct. Then there was the late Devonian extinction, between 375 and 360 million years ago, when again around 70 per cent of species became extinct. That one seemed to go on for 20 million years, with what are called 'extinction pulses' occurring in that period. Then there came the daddy of them all – the Permian-Triassic extinction event, which killed 96 per cent of marine life and 70 per cent of land species, including most insect species. The insects are especially noteworthy, as they are thought to be very robust, notoriously predicted to be able to survive a nuclear holocaust. But the Permian-Triassic extinction event nearly did for them.

Then, 201 million years ago, the Triassic-Jurassic extinction event occurred, and 75 per cent of species were wiped out. This included many species of amphibians, and the view is that this left the stage clear for the dinosaurs to evolve, as they were left with little competition. And so the age of dinosaurs begins. However, Mother Nature had it in for the dinosaurs too, because 66 million years ago they were all wiped out[3]. They must have gotten too cocky. This is the Cretaceous-Paleogene extinction event. Overall, 75 per cent of all species became extinct. All non-bird-like dinosaurs became extinct (the birds we see today are descended from dinosaurs), and the way was clear for mammals and birds to evolve. It's a bit like if you hack away in a dense forest, the way is cleared for new plants to grow.

To summarise – a whole lot of extinctions going on. And an important consequence of the extinctions was that one species' crisis is another species' opportunity. For example, without oxygen building up, we would never have evolved, and without the dinosaurs being wiped out the jungle would have been too crowded for us to make our way in the world.

The cause of the Great Oxygen Event extinction is clear-cut: the evolution of organisms that could perform photosynthesis leading to oxygen building up. What was the cause of the other extinction events? The one that killed off the dinosaurs is perhaps the best known. It is now thought that it involved a large asteroid striking Earth just off the coast of the Yucatán peninsula in Mexico. The evidence for this is the presence of a large crater, and also a layer of iridium all over the world from that time, which came from dust thrown up by the asteroid that then settled back on Earth. The impact raised so much dust, both asteroid- and Earth-derived, that it blocked out the sun. It was like someone putting the lights out.

This meant that many plants could no longer photosynthesise, and so they died. This in turn led to the collapse of the food chain. It is also thought that sulphur-rich rocks were broken up, producing poisonous acid rain which further damaged the food chain. So in effect, Earth became dark and a hard rain fell, killing many plants. Clearly the big dinosaurs were especially suscep-

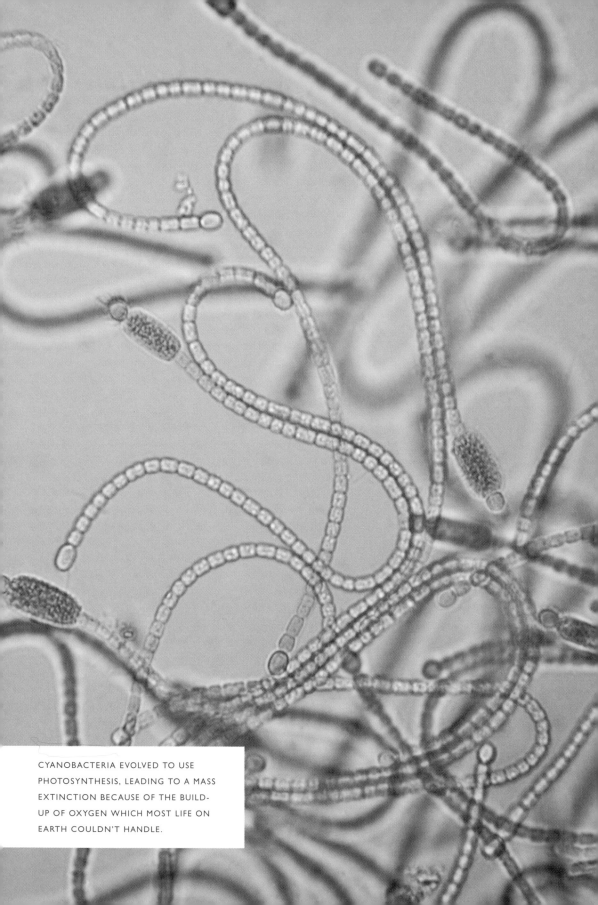

CYANOBACTERIA EVOLVED TO USE
PHOTOSYNTHESIS, LEADING TO A MASS
EXTINCTION BECAUSE OF THE BUILD-
UP OF OXYGEN WHICH MOST LIFE ON
EARTH COULDN'T HANDLE.

tible. Our ancestors (which were a small, shrew-like creature) could scavenge and survive. There were no humans around at the time of the dinosaurs, unlike what has been depicted in movies and cartoons.

Two of the extinctions – Ordivician and Late Devonian – are thought to have been caused by global cooling[4]. This made the Earth a dry place, as water got trapped in ice and snow. Plants became extinct because of the cold temperatures and dryness, again breaking the food chain. The Permian extinction is thought to have been caused by the opposite: global warming. This is something that is worrying us now, but back in the Permian era it was devastating. The Earth became much wetter and many plants got wiped out because they couldn't tolerate the warmer climate.

Another consequence of global warming is the release of the greenhouse gas methane. This gas can be trapped in a type of chemical called a clathrate. Once the Earth's temperature started to rise, these clathrates released methane, which then accelerated global warming even more. This is known as the 'clathrate gun hypothesis', since the release of methane is thought to be like a gun going off. What might have caused global cooling or warming isn't fully known, but it could have been due to changes in the power of the sun, which is known to fluctuate. Life on Earth has such a dependency on the sun that it's not surprising that great extinctions happen when the sun changes. This sets up a feed-forward loop which reaches some kind of maximum and then begins to relent, restoring things to some kind of normality.

Other events are also thought to have contributed to some of the mass extinctions. Oceanic overturn may have played a part in the late Devonian extinction event[5]. A good example of an oceanic overturn is when a so-called thermohaline circulation is disrupted. This kind of circulation is driven by deep water having more salt, as it doesn't evaporate as much. If it overturns, the circulation will stop and more importantly oxygen-poor water from the deep moves to the top, killing a lot of life as it does so. Disruption can happen when too much fresh water (say, from glaciers melting) goes into the sea. The Gulf Stream is an example of an ocean current being driven by thermohaline circulation. If it were to overturn,

the climate of Ireland would change radically, as the Gulf Stream keeps our climate temperate (meaning constant drizzle). This allows certain plants and animals to thrive, and so if it stopped there would be extinctions in Ireland.

If a nearby nova or supernova were to give off a gamma-ray burst (which they are inclined to do), this could have a devastating effect. If it happens from a nova 6,000 light years away (which is not that far away on a cosmic scale, although it sounds like a lot) it would strip away the Earth's ozone layer. This would leave life on Earth vulnerable to UV irradiation, which would be devastating. This is thought to have contributed to the Ordivician extinction event[6]. A zapping from a distant star might kill up to 70 per cent of life on Earth, then, including us. It would probably look spectacular, though.

So asteroids, gamma-ray bursts, the Earth heating up too much or cooling down too much, or the oceans going topsy-turvy have all nearly wiped out

PACIFIC
OCEAN

WARM SURFACE FLOW

COOL SUBSURFACE FLOW

OCEAN CURRENTS ARE CRITICAL FOR
MAINTAINING DIFFERENT CLIMATES.
IF THEY SHOULD STOP BECAUSE OF
CLIMATE CHANGE, THIS COULD SPELL
THE END FOR MANY SPECIES.

life on Earth. This begs the question, what are the chances of these things happening again? The chance of an asteroid hitting us or a gamma-ray burst are thought to be very, very small. They are random, once-in-a-blue-moon events, although you never know.

The eventual warming and expanding of the sun, combined with the eventual drop in atmospheric carbon dioxide, could cause the biggest mass extinction event in Earth's history and would spell the end of all life. As the sun expands (which will happen millions of years from now), it will boil away the oceans, increase the breakdown of rocks from weathering (which has the effect of lowering carbon dioxide) and kill plant life on Earth, since plants need carbon dioxide and water. With all photosynthetic life now gone, all aerobic life (which needs oxygen from the plants) will also die off. This will leave behind the ancestors of the first cells on Earth, which are anaerobic bacteria. These too will eventually die out, from the heat of the sun. Life on Earth will have been burnt away. Life's journey will then be complete, starting with the first cell 4.2 billion years ago, going through all the trouble of evolving all those millions of species including us, only to end up back where it all started, with a single-celled anaerobic prokaryote, which itself will die. Cheery, isn't it?

Those events, though, are very much in the future. Humans will in all likelihood have evolved into some other kind of species, which we may not even recognise. Predictions as to what we might evolve into include less muscle mass (since machines will do all the heavy lifting), weaker eyes (since visual aids will be commonly used) and perhaps less body hair. Maybe our genes will carry on in some other species, as we saw with the Neanderthals, some of whose genes continue in us. Our genes may end up in some strange human/computer hybrid, in the form of a cyborg, who may live on another planet.

There is still the possibility that, instead of an asteroid wiping us out, or the sun eventually killing us, other more immediate things might kill us off. This is known as anthropogenic extinction, or extinction caused by humans. What might the risks be of that? Nuclear annihilation has always hung over

AN ARTIST'S IMPRESSION OF A GAMMA-RAY BURST. ONE SUCH BURST IS THOUGHT TO HAVE WIPED OUT 70% OF LIFE ON EARTH IN THE ORDIVICIAN EXTINCTION EVENT.

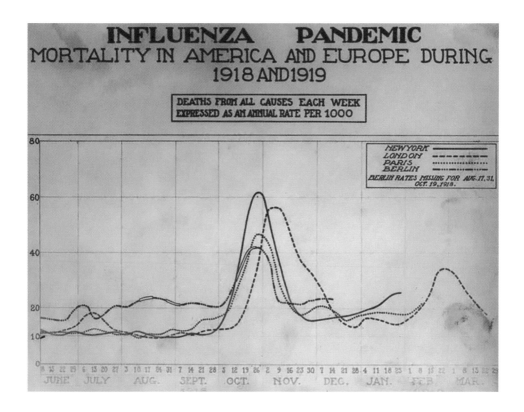

THE 1918 SPANISH FLU KILLED MORE PEOPLE THAN WORLD WAR I.

us. A hypothetical World War III could kill us all off. Surely we wouldn't be that stupid, though. Right?

A more likely event (although still unlikely) is some kind of pandemic involving a virus, or maybe even an antibiotic-resistant bacteria. This has happened before, with the 1918 Spanish flu killing more people than World War I. A deadly pandemic restricted to humans would burn itself out, and isolated human populations would be OK. However, if other species were infected it might eventually spread to even the remote humans. Population decline due to a preference to have fewer children is another possibility, and some scientists have predicted that by the year 3000 we will have become extinct because of that. This seems unlikely, though, as some humans are bound to buck the trend and have plenty of children.

Human-driven damage to our habitat might also badly affect us. Greenhouse gases in our atmosphere not only cause global warming but can also damage our health by affecting our breathing. If that were to get more severe, it could decrease the Earth's population. Overpopulation may get there first, though. No other large vertebrate has expanded as quickly as us. The Earth's population was 1 billion in 1800 and is now at 7 billion and rising. One prediction, by the famous Swedish statistician Hans Rosling, was that we will top out at 12 billion and then either start to die off because of not enough resources, or self-correct by a decrease in birth rate.

Beyond these possibilities we enter the world of science fiction. There is a fear that we might create a superintelligent entity (or entities in the form of thousands of nanobots) that will take over the Earth and annihilate us. Or that in the course of high-energy physics experiments we'll create a 'micro black hole' that will suck up the entire Earth. This was actually a fear during experiments into atom smashing at the Large Hadron Collider. Colliding protons at close to the speed of light in particular was somewhat feared, as it might have created a black hole. It didn't.

All of these kinds of fears have given rise to big business in the US. Some people are getting ready for the coming apocalypse. Recent earthquakes or extreme weather have heightened people's fears, and they are stocking up on freeze-dried foods, gas masks and other survival equipment. You can buy a $500 CBRN suit (which will protect against chemical, biological, radiological and nuclear attack) and a $200 gas mask. Every time Kim Jong-un implies that a nuclear bomb might be launched, sales of survival equipment go up. Maybe he has shares in the companies involved. I wonder does it ever occur to these people what kind of world they will enter after the apocalypse? Not a pleasant one I should think.

So where does that leave us? Well, our extinction as a species is likely to be a very long way off, so far off that we will no longer be *Homo sapiens*, but will have evolved into some other species. So we needn't worry too much.

THE GREAT IRISH ELK (WHICH IS NEITHER GREAT, NOR IRISH, NOR AN ELK) BECAME EXTINCT 10,000 YEARS AGO, WIPED OUT BY HUMANS DIRECTLY FROM OVER-HUNTING OR INDIRECTLY FROM ENVIRONMENTAL CHANGE.

What should worry us though is not about us at all. Scientists think that we are now in the middle of the sixth great extinction event, which has been dubbed the 'Holocene extinction'[7]. The trouble with this one is we are causing it. Since 1900, extinctions of animals or plants on Earth have been at over 1,000 times the background rate. This is a shocking number. Effectively human activities have been causing many plant and animal species to become extinct.

Apart from human-made climate change, we have also been over-hunting, over-fishing and introducing invasive species which then cause mayhem and destruction of habitats, all of which are combining to cause mass carnage. Well-known examples include the dodo, which we drove to extinction. We also got rid of the great Irish elk and the mammoth, again most likely from over-hunting them. Half of all animals that lived on Earth are now extinct. It may well be that when species become extinct, it gives rise to new species emerging, but that doesn't take away from the fact that we are destroying many species.

Do we not owe it to our fellow life forms, who are our cousins in DNA, to keep them alive so that they can evolve and thrive? Furthermore, the complex web of life on Earth means that if it becomes disturbed, knock-on consequences will inevitably follow, including possibly our own extinction. And all because of our vanity and incompetence. So instead of being afraid, being very afraid, we should be very ashamed.

CHAPTER 20

THINGS WILL
ONLY GET
BETTER

WHAT DOES THE FUTURE hold for *Homo sapiens*? Well, in spite of all the glass-half-empty people, the naysayers, the pessimists, the negative people, all this science and technology is actually making the world a better place overall for humans, and will continue to do so. In spite of what it looks like, with war and famine and crime, things are actually as good as they have ever been for humanity, at least since we invented agriculture. There is good evidence that agriculture was actually the cause of much misery and inequality in the world. The workers had to toil in the fields for The Man, who could lord it over them and make them slaves. Agriculture gave rise to inequality and overcrowding, which in turn bred infectious diseases.

For much of the history of humankind a tiny minority held most of the wealth and set up a system to keep the peasants under control. Barring the occasional revolution which shook things up for a while, humans returned to a situation where some humans were more equal than others. But now, perhaps we see the beginnings of an actual Brave New World, where at last, largely through science and technology, we will be free again.

Am I talking nonsense? Why should the world owe us a comfortable living? Won't there always be the unlucky ones, the ones who perhaps are born with the wrong set of genes in the wrong place or at the wrong time?

Or who through bad luck end up doing less well than others? Well, no. The signs for humanity as a whole look good'. There is a lot less poverty in the world, especially since World War II ended. There are far fewer children dying, there is more democracy than ever, more education and less death in wars. This is on a global scale, taking the population of the Earth as a whole. There will be pockets of awfulness mainly because of what are technically known as 'assholes' running things, but when looked at globally, it looks like things are good and will only get better.

First let's look at poverty. Extreme poverty is at the moment defined as living on less than $1.90 a day. Poverty measurement also takes into account non-monetary income, and is corrected for different price levels in different countries and adjusted for inflation over time. If we go back to the 1820s, only a tiny minority had a high standard of living. These were the ones living in the castles, who had armies to protect them. The vast majority lived in extreme poverty, literally living from hand to mouth, dying in their droves of malnutrition and infections.

Since 1820, the percentage of extremely poor people has fallen steadily. In 1950, 75 per cent of people in the world lived in extreme poverty. In 1981 it was 44 per cent. The most recent figures show that it is now 10 per cent. This still means that an awful lot of people are living in poverty in terms of numbers, given population growth, but the percentage has gone down substantially. Why did the situation improve? Industrialisation. This increased productivity and gave people a greater share of the wealth. And the people who built the technology – the makers of the machines – got really rich and became fat cats.

But the tide lifted all boats. People became ever more productive, and their incomes rose. This is perhaps the greatest achievement for humankind in our history. A whopping 90 per cent of the Earth's population now do not live in extreme poverty. What makes it all the more amazing is the rise in the population of the Earth, which has grown sevenfold over the last 200 years. In spite of this, we managed to lift more and more people out of extreme poverty. Increased productivity meant more goods and services, better food, better clothes and better housing and sanitation. Lifting people out of poverty also meant better health and better prospects. Subsistence farmers don't have much time to teach their children things other than farming. And so education improved as well.

That brings us to the second aspect where there has been remarkable progress: literacy. In the past again, only a tiny proportion could read and write – 1,500 years ago that was restricted to the clergy (hence the word 'clerk'), who learnt to read because of the Bible, or to civil servants who served the king. They were mainly tax collectors. Reading must have been seen as an odd thing to do. The Irish monks who created the Book of Kells saw writing as a sacred act. Writing down a prayer or the story of Jesus was seen as remarkable. It did things to your mind. The idle rich could read and write too. They could lounge around in Greece thinking deep, meaningful thoughts. In 1820 only one in ten was literate. In 1930, it was one-third, and today 85 per cent of the world's population can read and write. Again, this is a remarkable achievement. And if you're young, chances are its above 85 per cent, as most of the illiterate population are old. Put another way, in 1800 there were 120 million people who could read and write. Now there are 6.2 billion. And tragically they're all on Facebook.

The statistics in relation to health are also striking. In 1800, 43 per cent of babies died before the age of five. Think about that. If a mother had two babies, one was likely to die before reaching five. This seems like an awful waste but for biology it doesn't matter a damn – as long as some babies survive to have more babies. In 1915, the average life expectancy was 35. To live into your 40s was to become a wise old man. Remember, Leopold Bloom in *Ulysses* was 38, and his wife Molly was 33, and they felt themselves to be middle-aged. Nowadays the average life expectancy in Ireland is 78.3 for a man and 82.7 for a woman.

This isn't only down to new medicines. A big factor was improved housing and sanitation. Poor sanitation leads to more infectious diseases. It happened

THE INVENTION OF THE PRINTING PRESS
BROUGHT HUGE ADVANCES IN KNOWLEDGE
DISSEMINATION AND LEARNING.

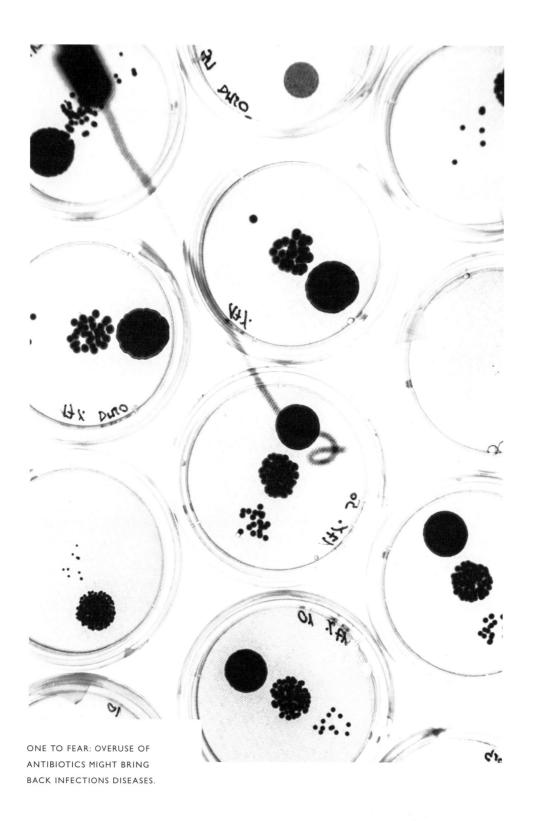

ONE TO FEAR: OVERUSE OF
ANTIBIOTICS MIGHT BRING
BACK INFECTIONS DISEASES.

because of the switch from us being nomads to being settled farmers, and leaving our refuse all around us. Better housing and sanitation improved our chances against infectious agents, which were the main cause of death.

Better food also made our immune systems stronger to fight the infection. Science and medicine of course mattered as well. Science became a profession because of increased productivity again, allowing for a better education system. These educated scientists were then ready to make scientific breakthroughs. Perhaps one of the most important was the so-called germ theory of disease propounded by Robert Koch and others. The idea that microscopic creatures were causing diseases like TB that destroyed the lungs seemed preposterous. But it meant that something simple like doctors washing their hands when switching from a post-mortem to delivering a baby made all the difference. A big reason for infant mortality was dirty doctors.

The germ theory was the basis for the discovery of antibiotics and also vaccines. This in turn gave rise to public health – monitoring and treating the health of the public. This is especially important for vaccines, where everybody being vaccinated benefits everybody else because of so-called herd immunity. A certain percentage of the herd has to be vaccinated to outdo the germ. It has insufficient hosts to hide in and so dies out.

In 2015 childhood mortality worldwide was down to 4.3 per cent – 10 times lower than 200 years earlier. As we saw in Chapter 14, vaccines have made a huge contribution to human health. Polio has almost been eliminated from Earth. Smallpox, the scourge of the Dark Ages, is now gone completely. Without a global programme of vaccination, around 4 million cases of measles occurred in the US each year. After the anti-measles vaccine was introduced in 1963 measles was almost eliminated, with only 667 cases reported in 2014, for example[2]. Again, a quite remarkable statistic.

The second-greatest contribution is antibiotics. Without them, people would continue to die of infectious diseases, which would return as the commonest cause of death (as opposed to cancer and heart disease, which together hold the current title). Surgery could not be performed without them, because of the risk of life-threatening infections in wounds. This is why we greatly fear antibiotic resistance. If bacteria evolve to resist bacteria, as is actually happening, the world will be a very different place, and the successes seen in human health will be severely reduced, back to the era before antibiotics. Let's hope we can use our ingenuity to outwit the bugs, otherwise they will kill us. I can hear them. They're laughing at us now.

The decrease in infant and overall mortality with less poverty is the main reason for population growth. The Chinese of course had a problem with overpopulation, and so introduced the one-child policy. This was a very sensible thing to do to try to limit the population, which was felt to be growing at too fast a rate, although it did create problems such as forced abortions. But it reflected the increased fertility in China because of better income and health, a worldwide phenomenon. Some estimates have fertility in the pre-modern era (meaning before the Industrial Revolution) as high – five or six children per woman.

What kept the population down, however, was the rate at which children and babies died. Population growth happens because of high fertility and low mortality. A strange and somewhat counterintuitive consequence of decreased infant mortality is a decrease in the birth rate. It looks like once women realise that the chances of their baby dying has decreased, they choose to have fewer children. This has been shown to be the case in country after country over the past 200 years.

As a result population growth comes to an end, which is increasingly the case on Earth. This is called the 'demographic transition'. The numbers are interesting. In those countries that industrialised first (e.g. the UK) it took 95 years for fertility to decline from above six children per woman to under three. Other countries that have industrialised more recently had an even faster demographic transition. South Korea went from six babies per mother to fewer than three in just 18 years. In Iran it was even faster: the demographic transition happened in only 10 years. Overall though, the global population has increased four-fold during the 20th century.

In this century this will be much less. A doubling of the population by 2100 will be viewed as being remarkable. The current projections are that the Earth's population will stop growing around 2075, and will then start to decline. It may go back up again in the future as women decide to have more babies in an underpopulated world. One thing is clear, though; the more educated a woman is the fewer children she will have. Education would appear to broaden horizons and decrease the rate of babies being born. It could be that education delays the time for when a woman will have a baby, and some women leave it too late, as their fertility has then declined. Whatever way you look at it, women were freed from the relentless treadmill of having babies and then watching half of them die. That is real progress.

MALALA YOUSAFZAI, AN ADVOCATE FOR EDUCATION. LITERACY USED TO BE THE PRESERVE OF RICH MEN. NOWADAYS 85% OF THE WORLD'S POPULATION ARE LITERATE, A PARTICULAR ADVANCE BEING AMONG WOMEN.

Education is of course the key to all the progress that has been made. It is straightforward to project the future of education. A literate young woman today will be a literate old woman in 2080. A secondary school student will become a university student in the future. Education is self-sustaining, and the good news is that more and more of the world's population are getting educated. This trains the minds of our children, drawing out what they're good at, and then they grow up and make their difference, in an autocatalytic manner. Money spent on education is never wasted.

Current projections have, by 2100, 7 billion people on Earth who will have received an education at least up to second level. Again, this is a huge achievement for Planet Earth. The value of education has of course been recognised for centuries. As the astronaut John Glenn said, 'Everywhere

NO MORE WAR? MY FATHER, KEVIN O'NEILL (LEFT) IN THE WESTERN DESERT, NORTH AFRICA IN 1942. HE DROVE A SHERMAN TANK WITH THE BRITISH EIGHTH ARMY AT THE BATTLE OF EL ALAMEIN IN WORLD WAR II.

that Americans spread off the Eastern seaboard, heading west across the country, they put up the schoolhouse first, hired a schoolteacher and put all the kids in school.' Without education we don't have the scientists, engineers, businesspeople and doctors who make a difference to our society. Education could be seen as the most important thing to get right, for the lives of people on Earth to continue to improve. This is why teachers are so important – they open the mystic portal for the student to go through. Education unleashes talents and capabilities. So stand up, teachers – you are the most important of people.

That brings us to the final thing that has shown remarkable improvement: peace (not war)[3]. I once met a pedagogist – an expert on education. She said to me that one of the purposes of a university education is to make people reasonable. Being able to debate with people is critically important to stop wars. More people are living in peace than ever before. We have really Given Peace a Chance.

In the 1980s, military experts, the ones who study war (and peace) as a process, noticed something astonishing. What had been the greatest cause of death (outside infection) – war among great powers and developed states – had effectively stopped. Sabre-rattling had happened from time to time of course (for example the Cuban Missile Crisis between the USSR and the USA), and the nuclear threat was there (and is still there) but no major armed conflicts have happened in some time. This became known as the 'long peace', and it has held for over 40 years. The per-capita death rate (which those who study war use as a key quantitative indicator) fell more than tenfold from its peak in World War II to the Korean War, and then dropped even more precipitously, falling an additional hundredfold. Other data show steep drops in genocides and other mass killings. Of course, when we hear about a mass killing we are horrified. They still happen, but a lot less frequently, and let's hope the downward trend continues.

So as a species more of us are more prosperous than ever before, and we're living longer, healthier lives. More of us are well educated. And we're not being drawn into needless wars, the purposes of which are often impossible to interpret. So why is it that most people think things have got worse and will continue to do so, in spite of the evidence staring them in the face? Recent studies have shown that only 10 per cent of Swedes think things will get better. The number was 6 per cent in the USA (the Trump effect?) and 4 per cent in Germany (the Angela effect?).

Psychologists call this phenomenon 'cognitive dissonance', where what you see (e.g. a death on TV) points to one thing, but the data doesn't agree (e.g. lots of people still being alive). Most people assess the world from Facebook or Twitter. As long as they see that violence hasn't vanished, that there are still explosions and wars going on, they will have a pessimistic outlook. This is in spite of the fact that the vast majority of people aren't subjected to these events. One problem is that no one wants to report on peace. George Mitchell, Bill Clinton's special envoy to Northern Ireland during the Troubles, said he longed for the day when the assembly in Stormont would be debating sheep quotas. No one would report on that. They want more bang for their buck.

Perhaps this is a safety mechanism. We are drawn to the more pessimistic position to protect ourselves. To be prepared for the worst-case scenario. To batten down the hatches against the storm that might come. Only by gathering the data (a very important role for all scientists), systematically analysing it and plotting the data over time do we get the accurate picture.

Life for us therefore began as a single cell around 4.2 billion years ago. Evolution then played out according to Darwin's law of natural selection.

LIVE LONG, MY FELLOW
HUMAN BEINGS, AND PROSPER.

Life then became a fight. Cells and organisms were in a competition with rivals for resources, to allow for yet more evolution. All of it random, to get to us: hairless, bipedal apes. A chance in a million or more for us to arise. It could all have been so different. Our ancestors could have become extinct in one of the great extinction events. The dinosaurs could have survived to rule the roost, leaving little room for us.

As a species, we're curious, so we discover all kinds of interesting things. But life was brutish for the vast majority for a very long time. Poverty, infant mortality, oppression, wars, all put upon us for reasons that were never fully explained. And then, things begin to get better. Educated scientists and engineers come along to help. Engineers come up with sanitation strategies. Scientists discover drugs to kill bacteria. Things then improve and improve, and the trajectory says up, up, up. What will continue to improve? Will there be more and more people out of poverty and well above the poverty line? Will we prevent or cure diseases that still afflict us, especially in the developing world? Will the world become more equal? Will robotics and artificial intelligence make a huge difference to our lives? We control our environment like no other species before. As long as we stop making a hames of it by threatening the water or food supply, or continue to destroy our environment, we should be fine.

Every single human being on Earth has a right to continue to reap the benefits of all the science that's been done in their name and for future generations. It's been done out of curiosity. It's been done to make things better, either through enlightenment or for practical benefits. It's been done to enhance the lives of people. Scientists continue to go boldly, where no one has gone before. Live long, my fellow human beings … and prosper.

ENDNOTES

CHAPTER 1

1 Dalrymple, G.B. (2001). The age of the Earth in the twentieth century: a problem (mostly) solved. Special Publications, *Geological Society of London* 190(1): 205–221

2 Dodd, M.S. et al. (2017). Evidence for early life in Earth's oldest hydrothermal vent precipitates. *Nature* 543: 60–64. doi:10.1038/nature21377

3 Gould, S. J. (1993). *Fall in the House of Ussher*. In Eight Little Piggies (Penguin Books)

4 John Joly, 1857–1933. (1934). *Obituary Notices of Fellows of the Royal Society,* 1(3), 259–286.

5 Service, R.F. (2015). Origin of life puzzle cracked. *Science* 347, 1298–1299

6 Bell, E.A. et al. (2015). Potentially biogenic carbon preserved in a 4.1 billion-year-old zircon. *Proc. Natl Acad. Sci.* USA 912: 14518–14521

7 Y.M Bar-On, Y.M., Phillips, R. and Milo, R. (2018) The biomass distribution on Earth.*Proc Natl Acad Sci USA* doi: 10.1073/pnas.1711842115

8 Miller, S.L. (1953). Production of amino acids under possible primitive Earth conditions. Science 117 (3046): 528. doi:10.1126/science.117.3046.528

9 Patel, B.H. et al. (2015). Common origins of RNA, protein and lipid precursors in cyanosulfidic protometabolism. *Nat. Chem.* 7: 301–307

10 Margulis, L. (1998). *The Symbiotic Planet: A New Look at Evolution.* London: Weidenfeld & Nicolson; Choi, C.Q. (2017). How Did Multicellular Life Evolve? NASA. Available at: https://astrobiology. nasa.gov/news/how-did-multicellular-life-evolve/

11 Lane, N. (2015). *The Vital Question.* London: Profile Books

12 Altwegg, K. et al. (2016). Prebiotic chemicals – amino acid and phosphorus in the coma of comet 67P/Churyumov-Gerasimenko. *Science Advances* 2, no. 5, e1600285

CHAPTER 2

1 Diamond, Jared (1991). *The Third Chimpanzee: The Evolution and Future of the Human Animal.* London: Hutchinson Radius

2 Thompson, J.D., Higgins, D.G. and Gibson, T.J. (1994). CLUSTAL W: improving the sensitivity of progressive multiple sequence alignment through sequence weighting, position-specific gap penalties and weight matrix choice. *Nucleic Acids Research* 22(22): 4673–4680

3 Britten, R.J. (2002). Divergence between samples of chimpanzee and human DNA sequences in 5 per cent counting indels. *Proceedings of the National Academy of Sciences* 99, 13633–13635

4 Diogo, R., Molnar, J. L. and Wood, B. (2017) Bonobo anatomy reveals stasis and mosaicism in chimpanzee evolution, and supports bonobos as the most appropriate extant model for the common ancestor of chimpanzees and humans. *Scientific Reports* 7: 608

5 Harari, Y. (2014). *Sapiens: A Brief History of Humankind.* New York: Harper

6 Klein, R. (1995). Anatomy, behavior, and modern human origins. *Journal of World Prehistory* 9(2): 167–198

7 Dhillon, P. (2006). Humans, A migration out of Africa? *The Naked Scientist.* Available at: https://www.thenakedscientists.com/articles/features/humans-migration-out-africa

8 Elliott, M. (2017). Inequality has deep roots in Eurasia. *Nature* 551, 573–574

9 Gibbons, J. (2014). Why did Neanderthals go extinct? *Smithsonian Insider.* Available at: https://insider.si.edu/2015/08/why-did-neanderthals-go-extinct

10 Gibbons, Ann (2017). Neanderthals mated early with modern humans. Science 356, 14; Sankararaman, S. et al (2014). The genomic landscape of Neanderthal ancestry in present-day humans. *Nature* 507, 354–357; Vernot, B. and Akey, J.M. (2014). Resurrecting surviving Neanderthal lineages from modern human genomes. *Science* 343, 1017–1021

11 Sankararaman, S., et al. (2016). The combined landscape of Denisovan and Neanderthal ancestry in present-day humans. *Current Biology* 26 (9): 1241–1247

12 Diamond, J. (1999). *Guns, Germs, and Steel: The Fates of Human Societies.* New York: W.W. Norton & Company

CHAPTER 3

1 Joel, S., Eastwick, P.W. and Finkel, E.J. (2017). Is romantic desire predictable? Machine learning applied to initial romantic attraction. *Psychological Science* 28, 1478–1489

2 Anders, S. et al. (2016). Neural mechanisms of interpersonal attraction. *Proceedings of the National Academy of Sciences* Apr 2016, 201516191

3 Singh, D. and Bronstad, P.M. (22 April 2001). Female body odour is a potential cue to ovulation. *Proceedings of the Royal Society B.* 268(1469): 797–801

4 Burriss, R. (2015). The face of fertility – why do men find women who are near ovulation more attractive? *The Independent.* Available at: www. independent.co.uk/life-style/health-and-families/features/the-face-of-fertility-why-do-men-find-women-who-are-near-ovulation-more-attractive-10359906.html

5   Haselton, M. et al. (2007). Ovulation and human female ornamentation: Near ovulation, women dress to impress. *Hormones and Behavior* 51, 41–45.

6   Niesta Kayser, D., Agthe, M. and Maner, J. K. (2016). Strategic sexual signals: Women's display versus avoidance of the color red depends on the attractiveness of an anticipated interaction partner. *PLoS One*, 11(3), e0148501

7   Thornhill, R. and Gangestad, S.W. (1999). The scent of symmetry: A human sex pheromone that signals fitness? *Evolution and Human Behaviour* 20(3): 175–201

8   Thornhill, R., Gangestad, S. and Comer, R. (1995). Human female orgasm and mate fluctuating asymmetry. *Animal Behaviour* 50, 1601–1615

9   Jasienska, G. et al. (2006). Symmetrical women have higher potential fertility. *Evolution and Human Behaviour* 390–400

10   Ferdenzi, C. et al. (2011). Digit ratio (2D:4D) predicts facial, but not voice or body odour, attractiveness in men. *Proceedings of the Royal Society B: Biological Sciences* 278(1724), 3551–3557.

11   Price, M. (2017). Study finds some significant differences in brains of men and women. *Science.* Available at: http://www.sciencemag.org/news/2017/04/study-finds-some-significant-differences-brains-men-and-women

12   Fujita, M. et al. (2012). In poor families, mothers' milk is richer for daughters than sons: A test of Trivers–Willard hypothesis in agropastoral settlements in Northern Kenya. *Am. J. Phys. Anthropol,* 149: 52–59

13   Feinberg, D.R, et al. (2006). Menstrual cycle, trait estrogen level, and masculinity preferences in the human voice. *Hormones and Behavior* 49(2): 215–222; Gangestad, S.W, Thornhill, R. and Garver-Apgar, C.E. (2005). Women's sexual interests across the ovulatory cycle depend on primary partner developmental instability. *Proceedings of the Royal Society B: Biological Sciences* 272 (1576): 2023–2027

14   Wedekind, C. et al (1995). MHC-dependent mate preferences in humans. *Proceedings of the Royal Society B* 260(1359): 245–249

15   Alvergne, A. et al. (2010). Does the contraceptive pill alter mate choice in humans? *Trends in Ecol Evol* 25: 171–179

16   Ronay, R. and von Hippel, W. (2010). The presence of an attractive woman elevates testosterone and physical risk taking in young men. Social Psychological and Personality Science 1(1): 57–64

17   Zhang, Y., Zheng, M. and Wang, X. (2016). Effects of facial attractiveness on personality stimuli in an implicit priming task: an ERP study. *Neurological Research* 38(8): 685–691

18   Singh, D. et al. (2010). Cross-cultural consensus for waist–hip ratio and women's attractiveness. Evolution and Human Behavior 31(3): 176–81; Hughes, S.M. and Gallup, G.R. (2003). Sex differences in morphological predictors of sexual behavior: Shoulder to hip and waist to hip ratios. *Evolution and Human Behavior* 24 (3), 173–178.

19   Maratzitti, D. and Canale, D. (2004). Hormonal changes when falling in love. *Psychoneuroendocrinology* 29, 931–936

20   Song, H. et al. (2015). Love-related changes in the brain: a resting-state functional magnetic resonance imaging study. *Front Hum. Neurosci.* 13(9): 71

21   Lee, H.J. et al. (2009). Oxytocin: the great facilitator of life. *Progress in Neurobiology* 88(2): 127–151

22   Wang, H. et al. (2013). Histone deacetylase inhibitors facilitate partner preference formation in female prairie voles. *Nat. Neurosci.* 16(7): 919–24

23   Dolder, P. et al. (2016). Acute emotional and social cognitive effects of beer. *European Neuropsychopharmacology* 26, S678

24   Haase, C.M. et al. (2013). The 5-HTTLPR polymorphism in the serotonin transporter gene moderates the association between emotional behavior and changes in marital satisfaction over time. *Emotion* 13(6): 1068–1079

CHAPTER 4

1   Knight, S. (2015). Everything you always wanted to know about panda sex (but were afraid to ask). *The Guardian.* Available at: https://www.theguardian.com/world/2015/aug/25/everything-about-panda-sex-edinburgh-zoo-long-read

2   Blocker, W. (2016). The journey from egg to embryo. *OnHealth.* Available at: https://www.onhealth.com/content/1/conception_pregnancy

3   Ikawa, M. et al. (2010). Fertilization: a sperm's journey to and interaction with the oocyte. J. *Clin. Invest.* 120, 984–994

4   Inoue, N., et al. (2005). The immunoglobulin superfamily protein Izumo is required for sperm to fuse with eggs. *Nature* 434, 234–238

5   Bianchi, E. et al. (2014). Juno is the egg Izumo receptor and is essential for mammalian fertilization. *Nature* 508, 483–487

6   Argo, J. (2007). Chronic disease and early exposure to air-borne mixtures: Exposure assessment. *Environ. Sci. Technol.* 15:41(20): 7185–7191

7   Fukuda, M. et al. (2014) Climate change is associated with male:female ratios of fetal deaths and newborn infants in Japan. *Fertility and Sterility* 102(5) 1364–1370.e2

8   Levine, H. et al. (2017). Temporal trends in sperm count: A systematic review and meta-regression analysis. *Hum Reprod Update* 23(6): 646–659

9   Reece, R. (2018). 10 ways he can have better baby-making sperm. *Parents*. Available at: www.parents.com/getting-pregnant/trying-to-conceive/tips/better-babymaking-sperm-healthy

10 Zhou, Q. et al. (2016). Complete meiosis from embryonic stem cell-derived germ cells in vitro. *Cell Stem Cell* 18(3): 330–340

CHAPTER 5

1   Shakeshaft, N.G. et al. (2013). Strong genetic influence on a UK nationwide test of educational achievement at the end of compulsory education at age 16. *PLoS One* 8(12): e80341

2   Turkheimer, E. (1991). Individual and group differences in adoption studies of IQ. *Psychological Bulletin* 110(3), 392–405

3   Kan, K-J. et al. (2013). On the nature and nurture of intelligence and specific cognitive abilities: The more heritable, the more culture dependent. *Psychological Science* 24(12): 2420–2428

4   Freitag, C.M. (2007). The genetics of autistic disorders and its clinical relevance: A review of the literature. *Mol. Psychiatry* 12(1): 2–22

5   Rettew, D.C. and Hudziak, J.J. (2009). Genetics of ADHD, in Brown, T.E. (ed) *ADHD Comorbidities: Handbook for ADHD Complications in Children and Adults*. Washington, DC: American Psychiatric Publishing

6   Kaufman, S.B. (2009). The truth about the 'Termites'. *Psychology Today*. Available at: https://www.psychologytoday.com/blog/beautiful-minds/200909/the-truth-about-the-termites

7   Biedinger, N. (2011). The influence of education and home environment on the cognitive outcomes of preschool children. *Germany Child Development Research Volume*, Article ID 916303

8   Moffitt, T.E. et al. (2011). A gradient of childhood self-control predicts health, wealth, and public safety. *Proc. Natl Acad. Sci.* 108, 2693–2698

9   Mischel, W., Shoda, Y. and Rodriguzez, M.L. (1989). Delay of gratification in children. *Science* 244: 933–938

10 Torrance, E. P. (1993). The beyonders in a thirty year longitudinal study of creative achievement. *Roeper Review: A Journal on Gifted Education* 15(3): 131–135

CHAPTER 6

1   Williams, R. (2014). Facebook's 71 gender options come to UK users. *The Telegraph*. Available at: www.telegraph.co.uk/technology/facebook/10930654/Facebooks-71-gender-options-come-to-UK-users.html

2   Miss Tiffany Universe. Available at: www.misstiffanyuniverse.com

3   Stein, M.T., Zucker, K.J. and Dixon, S.D. (1997). Gender Identity, *The Nurse Practitioner* 22(12): 104

4   Berta, P. et al. (1990). Genetic evidence equating SRY and the testis-determining factor. *Nature* 348 (6300): 448–450

5   Bermon, S and Garner, P. (2017). Serum androgen levels and their relation to performance in track and field: Mass spectrometry results from 2127 observations in male and female elite athletes. *British Journal of Sports Medicine* 51(17): 1309–1314

6   Park, D., et al. (2010). Male-like sexual behavior of female mouse lacking fucose mutarotase. *BMC Genetics* 11(1)

7   Långström, N., et al. (2010). Genetic and environmental effects on same-sex sexual behavior: a population study of twins in Sweden. *Arch. Sex. Behav.* 39(1): 75–80

8   Hamer, D.H., et al. (1999). Genetics and male sexual orientation. *Science.* 285(5429): 803

9   Ngun, T.C. and Vilain, E. (2014). The biological basis of human sexual orientation: Is there a role for epigenetics? *Advances in Genetics* 86: 167–184

10 Zietsch, B. et al. (2008). Genetic factors predisposing to homosexuality may increase mating success in heterosexuals. *Evolution and Human Behavior* 29(6): 424–433

11 Vasey, P. (2010). Study reveals potential evolutionary role for same-sex attraction. *Psychological Science*. Available at: www.psychologicalscience.org/news/releases/study-reveals-potential-evolutionary-role-for-same-sex-attraction.html

12 Barber, N. (2010) The secret of creativity: an oblique perspective. Why immigrants and gays are so creative. *Psychology Today*. Available at: https://www.psychologytoday.com/us/blog/the-human-beast/201009/the-secret-creativity-oblique-perspective

13 Bogaert, A.F. and Skorska, M. (2011). Sexual orientation, fraternal birth order, and the maternal immune hypothesis: A review. *Frontiers in neuroendocrinology* 32(2): 247–254

CHAPTER 7

1   Richards, J. (2014). Is the world becoming less religious and more secular? *Quora*. Available at: https://www.quora.com/Is-the-world-becoming-less-religious-and-more-secular

2   Singer, M. (2016). The mystery of the minimal cell, Craig Venter's new synthetic life form. *Wired*. Available at: https://www.wired.com/2016/03/mystery-minimal-cell-craig-venters-new-synthetic-life-form

3   Atran, S. and Norenzayan, A. (2004). Religion's evolutionary landscape: Counterintuition, commitment, compassion, communion. *Behavioral and Brain Sciences* 27 (6): 713–30

4   Shermer, M. (2004). *The Science of Good and Evil.* New York: Holt

5   McKee, M. (2005). Genes contribute to religious inclination. *New Scientist.* Available at: https://www.newscientist.com/article/dn7147-genes-con-tribute-to-religious-inclination

6   Hol-Lunstad, J and Smith, T.B. (2016). Loneliness and social isolation as risk factors for CVD: Implications for evidence-based patient care and scientific enquiry. Heart 102(13): 987–989.

7   Bartholomew, R. (2017). Why are females prone to mass hysteria? *Psychology Today.* Available at: https://www.psychologytoday.com/us/blog/its-catching/201703/why-are-females-prone-mass-hysteria

8   Paxman, J. (2017). Jeremy Paxman on the Church of England's fight to survive. *Financial Times.* Available at: https://www.ft.com/content/fced3f20-9294-11e7-a9e6-11d2f0ebb7f0

9   Ecklund, E. H. (2010) *Science vs. Religion: What Scientists Really Think.* New York: Oxford University Press

10   LaFrance, M., Hecht, M.A. and Paluck, E.L. (2003). The contingent smile: A meta-analysis of sex differences in smiling. *Psychol. Bull.* Mar. 129(2): 305–334

11   Barker E. (2014) Science of Sexy: 5 things that can make you irresistible. *Time.* Available at: http://time.com/2859728/science-of-sexy-5-things-that-can-make-you-irresistible

12   Liana, S.E., Hone, H., William and Lieberman, D. (2015). Sex differences in preferences for humor: A replication, modification. *Evol. Psychol.* 13(1): 167–181

13   Mitchell, C.V. (2016). Male humor versus female humor – it's no April fool's joke. *Huffington Post.* Available at: https://www.huffingtonpost.com/carol-vallone-mitchell/male-humor-versus-fe-male-_b_9558646.html

14   Hall, J.A. (2017). Humor in romantic relationships: A meta-analysis. *Personal Relationships,* 24(2): 306–322

15   Ishiyama, S. and Brecht, M. (2016). Neural correlates of ticklishness in the rat somatosensory cortex. *Science* 354(6313): 757–760

CHAPTER 8

1   Bennett, M.P., Zeller, J.M., Rosenberg, L. and Mc-Cann, J. (2003). The effect of mirthful laughter on stress and natural killer cell activity. *Altern. Ther. Health Med.* Mar.–Apr. 9(2): 38–45

2   Rosenkranz, M.A. et. al. (2003). Affective style and in vivo immune response: Neurobehavioral mechanisms. *Proc Natl Acad Sci USA* 100, 11148–11152

3   Laughing 100 times is equivalent to 15 minutes of exercise on a stationary bicycle (2016). *The Fact Speak.* Available at: www.thefactspeak.com/laughing-100-times-equivalent-exercise

4   Hayashi, T. and Murakami, K. (2009). The effects of laughter on post-prandial glucose levels and gene expression in type 2 diabetic patients. *Life Sci.* 31:85(5–6): 185–187

5   Gendry, S. (2016). Social benefits of laughter, improves cooperation, communication, romance. *Laughter Online University.* Available at: www.laughteronlineuniversity.com/social-bene-fits-laughter

6   Provine, Robert. (2000). *Laughter: A Scientific Investigation.* New York: Penguin

7   Joseph, J. (2008). World's oldest joke traced back to 1900 BC. *Reuters.* Available at: https://www.reu-ters.com/article/us-joke-odd-worlds-oldest-joke-traced-back-to-1900-bc-idUSKUA14785120080801

8   Dickerson, K. (2015). Here's the funniest joke in the world. *Business Insider.* Available at: www.uk.businessinsider.com/heres-the-funniest-joke-in-the-world-2015-9?r=US&IR=T

9   Freud, Sigmund (1905). *Jokes and Their Relation to the Unconscious.* Vienna: Franz Deuticke

CHAPTER 9

1   Higham, T. et al. (2012). Testing models for the beginnings of the Aurignacian and the advent of figurative art and music: The radiocarbon chronology of Geißenklösterle. *J. Hum. Evol.* 62(6): 664–676

2   Donovan, L. (2016). Do dogs like listening to music? *American Kennel Club.* Available at: www.akc.org/content/news/articles/do-dogs-like-listening-to-music

3   Snowdon, C.T., Teie, D. and Savage, M. (2015). Cats prefer species-appropriate music. *Applied Animal Behavior Science* 166, 106–111

4   Pearce, J.M.S. (2005). Selected observations on amusia. *European Neurology* 54(3): 145–148

5   Peretz, I., Cummings, S. and Dube, M.P. (2007). The genetics of congenital amusia (tone deafness): A family-aggregation study. *American Journal of Human Genetics* 81(3): 582–588

6   Loui, P., Alsop, D. and Schlaug, S. (2009). Tone deafness: A new disconnection syndrome? *Journal of Neuroscience* 29 (33): 10215–10220

7   Masataka, N. and Perlovsky, L. (2013). Cognitive interference can be mitigated by consonant music and facilitated by dissonant music. *Sci. Rep.* 3:2028; Perlovsky, L. (2015). Origin of music and embodied cognition. *Front Psychol.* 28:6: 538; Perlovsky, L. et al. (2013). Mozart effect, cognitive dissonance, and the pleasure of music. *Behav. Brain Res.* 244: 9–14

8   Perlovsky, L. (2015). How music helps resolve our deepest inner conflicts. *The Conversation.* Availa-

ble at: https://theconversation.com/how-music-helps-resolve-our-deepest-inner-conflicts-38531

9   Bowling, D.L. et al. (2010) Major and minor music compared to excited and subdued speech. *J. Acoust Soc. Am.* 127, 491–503

10 Balkwill, L.L. and Thompson, W.F. (1999). A cross-cultural investigation of perception of emotion in music: Psychophysical and cultural cues. *Music Percept.* 17, 43–64

11 McDermott, Josh H. et al. (2016) Indifference to dissonance in native Amazonians reveals cultural variation in music perception. *Nature* 535, 547–550

12 Charnetski, C.J., Brennan, F.X. and Harrison, J.F. (1998). Effect of music and auditory stimuli on secretory immunoglobulin A (IgA). *Percept. Mot. Skills* 87(3): 1163–1170

13 Wachi, M., et al. (2007). Recreational music-making modulates natural killer cell activity, cytokines, and mood states in corporate employees. *Med. Sci. Monit.* 13(2): CR57–1170

14 Keeler, J.R. et al. (2015). The neurochemistry and social flow of singing: bonding and oxytocin. *Front Hum. Neurosci.* 23(9): 518; Moss, H., Lynch, J. and O'Donoghue, J. (2017). Exploring the perceived health benefits of singing in a choir: An international cross-sectional mixed-methods study. *Perspect. Public Health.* Nov. 1:1757913917739652

15 Yelbay Yilmaz, Y. (2011). The Mozart effect in the foreign language classroom – a study on the effect of music in learning vocabulary in a foreign language. *International Journal on New Trends in Education and Their Implications* 2, 88.

16 Bones, O. and Plack, C.J. (2015). Losing the music: Aging affects the perception and subcortical neural representation of musical harmony. *J. Neurosci.* 35(9): 4071–4080

17 Gullick, J.G., Kwan, X.X. (2015). Patient-directed music therapy reduces anxiety and sedation exposure in mechanically-ventilated patients: A research critique. *Aust. Crit. Care.* 28(2): 103–105

18 Brand, D. (2015). Calming music can relax patients and staff in the operating theatre. *Nurs. Stand.* 29(51): 30

CHAPTER 10

1   Maquet, Pierre A.A. et al. (2005). Brain Imaging on Passing to Sleep. In Parmeggiani and Velluti (eds) *The Physiologic Nature of Sleep.* London: Imperial College Press

2   Siegel, J.M. (2005). Clues to the functions of mammalian sleep. *Nature* 437(7063): 1264–1271

3   Cespuglio, R., Colas, D. and Gautier-Sauvigné, S. (2005). Energy Processes Underlying the Sleep Wake Cycle. In Parmeggiani and Velluti (eds) *The Physiologic Nature of Sleep.* London: Imperial College Press

4   Xie, L. et al (2013). Sleep drives metabolite clearance from the adult brain. *Science* 342(6156): 373–377.

5   Naska, A. et al. (2007). Siesta in healthy adults and coronary mortality in the general population. *Archives of Internal Medicine* 167(3): 296–301

6   How much sleep do we really need? (2018). *Sleep Foundation.* Available at: https://sleepfoundation.org/how-sleep-works/how-much-sleep-do-we-really-need

7   Liu, Y. et al. (2013) Sleep duration and chronic diseases among US adults age 45 years and older: Evidence from the 2010 behavioral risk factor surveillance system. *Sleep* 36(10), 1421–1427

8   Swanson, C.M. et al. (2017). Bone turnover markers after sleep restriction and circadian disruption: A mechanism for sleep-related bone loss in humans. *J. Clin. Endocrinol. Metab* 102(10): 3722–3730

9   International Bedroom Poll (2013). *Sleep Foundation.* Available at: https://sleepfoundation.org/sites/default/files/RPT495a.pdf

10 Walch, O.J, Cochran, A. and Forger D.B (2016). A global quantification of 'normal' sleep schedules using smartphone data. *Science Advances* 2(5)

11 Vitaterna, M.S., Takahashi, J.S. and Turek, F.W. (2001). Overview of circadian rhythms. *Alcohol Research and Health* 25(2): 85–93

12 Bass, Joseph (2012). Circadian topology of metabolism. *Nature* 491 (7424): 348–356

13 Toh, K.L. et al. (2001). An hPer2 phosphorylation site mutation in familial advanced sleep phase syndrome. *Science* 291, 1040–1043

14 Jaffe, E. (2015) Morning people vs. night owls: 9 insights backed by science. *Co.Design.* Available at: www.fastcodesign.com/3046391/morning-people-vs-night-people-9-insights-backed-by-science

15 Man, K., Loudon, A. and Chawla, A. (2016). Immunity around the clock. *Science* 354(6315): 999–1003

16 He, Ying et al (2009). The transcriptional repressor DEC2 regulates sleep length in mammals. *Science* 325(5942): 866–870

CHAPTER 11

1   Cullen, P. (2016). Ireland's obesity rate among world's worst. *Irish Times.* Available at: https://www.irishtimes.com/news/health/ireland-s-obesity-rate-among-world-s-worst-1.2594266

2   Ramos-Lobo, A.M., Donato, J. (2017). The role of leptin in health and disease. *Temperature* 26:4(3): 258–291

3   Bouret, S.G. (2017). Development of Hypothalamic Circuits That Control Food Intake and Energy Balance. In Harris, R.B.S. (ed.) *Appetite and Food Intake: Central Control.* 2nd edition. Oxford Taylor & Francis; Zanchi, D. et al. (2017). The impact of

gut hormones on the neural circuit of appetite and satiety: A systematic review. *Neurosci. Biobehav. Rev.* 80: 457–475

4   Søberg, S. et al. (2017). FGF21 is a sugar-induced hormone associated with sweet intake and preference in humans. *Cell Metabolism* 25, 1045–1053

5   Obert, J. et al. (2017). Popular weight loss strategies: A review of four weight loss techniques. *Curr. Gastroenterol. Rep.* 19(12): 61

6   Fleming, A. (2015). Pregnancy food: What you eat can affect your child for life. *The Guardian.* Available at: https://www.theguardian.com/lifeandstyle/2015/jun/15/pregnancy-food-af-fect-child-eating-healthily-obesity

7   Stewart, P.C. and Goss, E. (2013). Plate shape and colour interact to influence taste and quality judgments. *Flavour* 2:27

8   Singh, S.B. et al. (1997). High altitude effects on human taste intensity and hedonics. *Aviat. Space Environ. Med.* 68(12): 1123–1128

9   Heid, M. (2016). You asked: Should I be nervous about lab-grown meat? *Time.* Available at: www.time.com/4490128/artificial-meat-protein

10 Loizos, C. (2017). Impossible Foods just raised $75 million for its plant-based burgers. *TechCrunch.* Available at: https://techcrunch.com/2017/08/01/impossible-foods-just-raised-75-million-for-its-plant-based-burgers/

11 Oaklander, M. (2013). 11 most fraudulent foods. *Prevention.* Available at: https://www.prevention.com/food/healthy-eating-tips/food-fraud-11-most-common-cases

12 Ní Aodha, G. (2017). How did Ireland's horsemeat scandal spark a Europe-wide investigation? *TheJournal.ie.* Available at: www.thejournal.ie/horsemeat-scandal-explainer-3499580-Jul2017/

CHAPTER 12

1   Ma, H. et al. (2017). Correction of a pathogenic gene mutation in human embryos. *Nature* 548, 413–419

2   Servick, K. (2017) CRISPR slices virus genes out of pigs, but will it make organ transplants to humans safer? *Science.* Available at: www.sciencemag.org/news/2017/08/crispr-slices-virus-genes-out-pigs-will-it-make-organ-transplants-humans-safer

3   Chen, R. et al. (2016). Analysis of 589,306 genomes identifies individuals resilient to severe Mendelian childhood diseases. *Nature Biotechnology* 34, 531–538

4   Naranbhai, V. and Carrington, M. (2017). Host genetic variation and HIV disease: from mapping to mechanism. *Immunogenetics.* 69(8-9): 489–498

5   Klein, G. (2016). Toward a genetics of cancer resistance. *Proc. Natl Acad. Sci. USA* 106, 859–867

6   Hough, A. (2010) Britain's 'oldest smoker' dies after puffing on cigarettes for 95 years. *The Telegraph.* Available at: www.telegraph.co.uk/news/health/news/7941676/Britains-oldest-smoker-dies-after-puffing-on-cigarettes-for-95-years.html

7   Galbraith, A. (2016). Can genetics explain the success of East African distance runners? *The Conversation.* Available at: www.theconversation.com/can-genetics-explain-the-success-of-east-afri-can-distance-runners-62586

8   Yamamoto, H. et al. (2011). NCoR1 is a conserved physiological modulator of muscle mass and oxidative function. *Cell.* 147(4): 827–39

9   Ahlstrom, D. (2016) The science behind superheroes' powers. *Irish Times.* Available at: https://www.irishtimes.com/news/science/the-sci-ence-behind-superheroes-powers-1.2619521

CHAPTER 13

1   Aberystwyth and Cambridge universities – Robot ferments fresh findings. (2009). *Times Higher Education.* Available at: https://www.timeshigher-education.com/news/aberystwyth-and-cam-bridge-universities-robot-ferments-fresh-find-ings/406064.article

2   Extance, A. (2015). Robot scientist discovers potential malaria drug. *Scientific American.* Available at: https://www.scientificamerican.com/article/robot-scientist-discovers-potential-malaria-drug/

3   Makary, M.A. and Daniel, M. (2016). Medical error – the third leading cause of death in the US. *BMJ* 353:i2139

4   Cunninghan, S.A. et al. (2008). Doctors' strikes and mortality: A review. *Soc. Sci. Med.* 67(11): 1784–1788

5   Muro, M. and Andes, S. (2015). Robots seem to be improving productivity, not costing jobs. *Harvard Business Review.* Available at: https://hbr.org/2015/06/robots-seem-to-be-improving-pro-ductivity-not-costing-jobs

6   Palermo, E. (2014). Robot 'army' can swarm into 3D formations. *Life Science.* Available at: https://www.livescience.com/47359-robot-swarms-build-structures.html

7   Ohnsman, A. (2017) At $1.1 billion Google's self-driving car moonshot looks like a bargain. *Forbes.* Available at: https://www.forbes.com/sites/alanohnsman/2017/09/15/at-1-1-billion-googles-self-driving-car-moonshot-looks-like-a-bargain/#a05ff4f57bbf

8   Frey, F. (2017) 25 shocking predictions about the coming driverless car era in the U.S. *Futurist Speaker.* Available at: www.futuristspeaker.com/job-opportunities/25-shocking-predictions-about-the-coming-driverless-car-era-in-the-u-s/

9   'Google founder defends accident records of self-driving cars. (2015) *Associated Press*. Available at: www.latimes.com/business/la-fi-google-cars-20150603-story.html

10   Moral Machine. Available at: www.moralmachine.mit.edu

CHAPTER 14

1   Harari, Y. (2014). *Sapiens: A Brief History of Humankind*. New York: Harper

2   What is the International Space Station? (2001). *NASA*. Available at: https://www.nasa.gov/audience/forstudents/k-4/stories/nasa-knows/what-is-the-iss-k4.html; How could the Large Hadron Collider unlock other dimensions? (2017). *Wired*. Available at: www.wired.co.uk/article/large-hadron-collider-explained

3   Payette, J. (2012). Research and diplomacy 350 kilometers above the earth: lessons from the international space station. *Science & Diplomacy* 1(4)

4   Kelly, S. (2017). *Endurance: A Year in Space, A Lifetime of Discovery*. New York: Doubleday

5   Astronaut bids farewell with Bowie cover version (2013) *BBC*. Available at: http://www.bbc.com/news/av/science-environment-22506395/astronaut-bids-farewell-with-bowie-cover-version

6   The Large Hadron Collider. *CERN*. https://home.cern/topics/large-hadron-collider

7   Highfield, R. (2008). Large Hadron Collider: Thirteen ways to change the world. *The Daily Telegraph*. Available at: https://www.telegraph.co.uk/news/science/large-hadron-collider/3351899/Large-Hadron-Collider-thirteen-ways-to-change-the-world.html

CHAPTER 15

1   Chan Zuckerberg Foundation. Available at: https://chanzuckerberg.com

2   Barberis, I. et al. (2017). The history of tuberculosis: From the first historical records to the isolation of Koch's bacillus. *J. Prev. Med. Hyg.* 58(1): E9–E12

3   History of drinking water treatment. *Centre for Disease Control*. Available at: https://www.cdc.gov/healthywater/drinking/history.html

4   Hajj Hussein, I. et al. (2015). Vaccines through centuries: major cornerstones of global health. *Front Public Health* 3:269

5   Sinicki, A. (2018) Top 10 greatest medical discoveries of all time. *Health Guidance*. Available at: www.healthguidance.org/entry/16851/1/top-10-greatest-medical-discoveries-of-all-time.html

6   Hammarsten, J.F. et al. (1979). Who discovered smallpox vaccination? Edward Jenner or Benjamin Jesty? *Transactions of the American Clinical and Climatological Association*. 90: 44–55

7   Lobanovska, M. and Pilla, G. (2017). Penicillin's discovery and antibiotic resistance: Lessons for the future? *Yale J. Biol. Med.* 90(1): 135–145; Ban, T.A. (2006). The role of serendipity in drug discovery. *Dialogues Clin. Neurosci.* 8(3): 335–44

8   HIV/AIDS. *World Health Organisation*. Available at: www.who.int/gho/hiv/en; Trickey, A. et. al. (2017). Survival of HIV-positive patients starting antiretroviral therapy between 1996 and 2013: A collaborative analysis of cohort studies. *Lancet* 4, No. 8, e349–e356; Mandal, A. (2014). History of AIDS. *News Medical*. Available at: https://www.news-medical.net/health/History-of-AIDS.aspx

9   Cullen, P. (2014) Cancer survival rates higher than ever, says report. *Irish Times*. Available at: https://www.irishtimes.com/news/health/cancer-survival-rates-higher-than-ever-says-report-1.2041527; Cancer survival statistics. *Cancer Research UK*. Available at: www.cancerresearchuk.org/health-professional/cancer-statistics/survival

10   Sukari, A. et al. (2016). Cancer immunology and immunotherapy. *Anticancer Res.* 36(11): 5593–5606; Edwards, E. (2017). Hundreds of cancer patients may benefit from breakthrough drug. *Irish Times*. Available at: https://www.irishtimes.com/news/health/hundreds-of-cancer-patients-may-benefit-from-breakthrough-drug-1.3248595

11   Sarusi, D. (2017) 10 things chimpanzees eat. *Jane Goodall Institute*. Available at: https://janegoodall.ca/our-stories/10-things-chimpanzees-eat/

12   Ebbell, B. and Banov, L. (1937). *The Papyrus Ebers: The greatest Egyptian medical document*. Copenhagen: Levin & Munksgaard.

13   Gertrude B. Elion – Biographical. Nobelprize.org. Available at: https://www.nobelprize.org/nobel_prizes/medicine/laureates/1988/elion-bio.html

14   Redman, M. et al. (2016) What is CRISPR/Cas9? *Archives of Disease in Childhood. Education and Practise edition*, 101, 213–215

15   Hong, Ma et. al. (2017). Correction of a pathogenic gene mutation in human embryos. *Nature* 548, 413–419

16   Liu, X et al. (2008) Yamanaka factors critically regulate the developmental signalling network in mouse embryonic stem cells. *Cell Res* 18, 1177–1189

CHAPTER 16

1   Longo, V.D. et al. (2012). Replicative and chronological aging in saccharomyces cerevisiae. *Cell. Metabolism* 16, 18–31

2   How quickly do different cells in the body replace themselves? *Cell Biology by the Numbers*. Available at: www.book.bionumbers.org/how-quickly-do-different-cells-in-the-body-replace-themselves

3   List of countries by life expectancy. *Wikipedia.* Available at: https://en.wikipedia.org/wiki/List_of_countries_by_life_expectancy

4   Chan, C. (2013). How many heartbeats does each species get in a lifetime? *Gizmodo.* Available at: https://gizmodo.com/5982977/how-many-heartbeats-does-each-species-get-in-a-lifetime

5   Watts, G. (2011). Leonard Hayflick and the limits of ageing. *The Lancet.* 377 (9783): 2075

6   Shay, J.W. (2017). Telomeres and aging. *Curr. Opin. Cell. Biol.* 52: 1–7

7   Miranda-Vizuete, A. and Veal, E.A. (2017). *Caenorhabditis elegans* as a model for understanding ROS function in physiology and disease. *Redox. Biol.* 11: 708–714; Williams, M.E. (2016). Oxygen and aging. *Psychology Today.* Available at: https://www.psychologytoday.com/blog/the-art-and-science-aging-well/201609/oxygen-and-aging; Srivastava, S. (2017). The mitochondrial basis of aging and age-related disorders. *Genes* (Basel) 8(12). pii: E398

8   Pasternak, H. and Moser, L. (2010). *The 5-Factor World Diet.* New York: Ballantine Books

9   Gallacher, D. and Gallacher, J. (2011) Are relationships good for your health? *Student BMJ* 19

10 Tissenbaum H.A. (2015) Using *C.elegans* for aging research. *Invertebr Reprod Dev* 59: 59–63

11 Cockburn, H. (2016). Scientists find 'key to longevity' in Italian village. *The Independent.* Available at: www.independent.co.uk/life-style/health-and-families/health-news/scientists-key-to-longevity-italy-acciaroli-centenarian-mediterranean-diet-a7230956.html

12 Harrison, D.E. et al. (2009) Rapamycin fed late in life extends lifespan in genetically heterogenous mice. *Nature* 460, 392–395

13 Zhang, G. et al. (2013). Hypothalamic programming of systemic ageing involving IKK-ß, NF-KB and GnRH. *Nature* 497(7448): 211–216

14 Youm, Y.H. et al. (2013). Canonical Nlrp3 inflammasome links systemic low-grade inflammation to functional decline in aging. *Cell. Metab.* 18(4): 519–32

15 Web Clock of Child Population in Japan. Available at: http://mega.econ.tohoku.ac.jp/Children/index_en_2015.jsp

16 Dronsfield, A. and Ellis, P. (2011) Drug discovery: Metformin and the control of diabetes. *Royal Society of Chemistry.* Available at: www.rsc.org/images/eic_nov2011_metformin_tcm18-210010.pdf; Bannister, C.A. et al. (2014). Can people with type 2 diabetes live longer than those without? *Diabetes Obes. Metab.* 16(11): 1165–1173

17 Conese, M. et al. (2017). The fountain of youth: a tale of parabiosis, stem cells, and rejuvenation. *Open Med.* (Wars), 28(12): 376–383

18 Weller, C. (2017) Here are the ages you peak at everything throughout life. *Business Insider.* Available at: www.businessinsider.fr/us/best-age-for-everything-2017-3/

19 Stone, A.A. et al. (2010). A snapshot of the age distribution of psychological well-being in the United States. *Proc. Natl Acad. Sci. USA* 107(22): 9985–9990

CHAPTER 17

1   Jordan, A. (2018). Death and disease in Ireland: We reveal the nation's top 10 killer illnesses. *Irish Mirror.* Available at: www.irishmirror.ie/news/irish-news/health-news/death-disease-ireland-reveal-nations-5494134

2   Emonds, M. (2009) How Dying Works. *How Stuff Works.* Available at: https://health.howstuffworks.com/diseases-conditions/death-dying/dying3.htm

3   Sleutjes, A. et al. (2014). Almost 40 years investigating near-death experiences: an overview of mainstream scientific journals. *J. Nerv. Ment. Dis.* 202: 833–836

4   Death Clock. Available at: www.death-clock.org

5   Fischer, K. et al. (2014). Biomarker profiling by nuclear magnetic resonance spectroscopy for the prediction of all-cause mortality: An observational study of 17,345 persons. *PLoS Med.* 11(2):e1001606

6   Janaway, R.C., Percival, S.L. and Wilson, A.S. (2009). Decomposition of Human Remains. In Percival, S.L. (ed.), *Microbiology and Aging.* New York: Springer, pp. 13–334

7   Villet, M.H., Amendt, J. (2011). Advances in Entomological Methods for Estimating Time of Death. In Turk, E.E. (ed.), *Forensic Pathology Reviews.* New York: Springer, pp. 213–238

8   Page, D. (2010). LABRADOR: New alpha dog in human remains detection? *Forensic.* Available at: https://www.forensicmag.com/article/2010/06/labrador-new-alpha-dog-human-remains-detection

9   Pozhitkov, A.E. et al. (2017). Tracing the dynamics of gene transcripts after organismal death. *Open Biol.* 7(1): 160267

CHAPTER 18

1   Rayner, G. (2011). Girl, 14, who died of cancer cryogenically frozen after telling judge she wanted to be brought back to life 'in hundreds of years'. *The Telegraph.* Available at: www.telegraph.co.uk/news/2016/11/18/cancer-girl-14-is-cryogenically-frozen-after-telling-judge-she-w/

2   Varmon, V. (2013) How many people are currently estimated to be cryogenically frozen? *Quora.* Available at: www.quora.com/How-many-people-are-currently-estimated-to-be-cryogenically-frozen

3   Guide to cryonics procedures. *Cryonics Institute.* Available at: www.cryonics.org/ci-landing/guide-to-cryonics-procedures/

4   Thomson, H. (2016). Frozen rabbit kidneys could solve organ shortage for transplants. *New Scientist.* Available at: www.newscientist.com/article/2081623-frozen-rabbit-kidneys-could-solve-organ-shortage-for-transplants

5   Fahy, G.M. (2009). Physical and biological aspects of renal vitrification. *Organogenesis.* 5(3): 167–175

6   Storey, K.B. (1990). Life in a frozen state: Adaptive strategies for natural freeze tolerance in amphibians and reptiles. *Am. J. Physiol.* 258(3 Pt 2): R559–68

7   Williams, C.T., Barnes, B.M. and Buck, C.L. (2016). Integrating physiology, behavior, and energetics: Biologging in a free-living arctic hibernator. *Comp. Biochem. Physiol. A. Mol. Integr. Physiol.* 202: 53–62

8   Kulcenty, K. et al. (2015). Molecular mechanisms of induced pluripotency. *Contemp. Oncol.* (Pozn). 19(1A): A22–9

CHAPTER 19

1   Dunhill, A. (2017). Five mass extinctions – and what we can learn from them about the planet today. *The Conversation.* Available at: https://theconversation.com/five-mass-extinctions-and-what-we-can-learn-from-them-about-the-planet-today-79971

2   Lane, N. (2016). *The Vital Question: Why is Life the Way it is?* (paperback ed.). London: Profile Books

3   Dinosaur Extinction. *National Geographic.* Available at: www.nationalgeographic.com/science/prehistoric-world/dinosaur-extinction

4   Mayhew, P.J., Jenkins, G.B. and Benton, T.G. (2008). A long-term association between global temperature and biodiversity, origination and extinction in the fossil record. *Proceedings of the Royal Society B: Biological Sciences.* 275 (1630): 47–53

5   Wilde, P. and Berry, W.B.N. (1984). Destabilization of the oceanic density structure and its significance to marine 'extinction' events. *Palaeogeography, Palaeoclimatology, Palaeoecology,* 48(2–4): 143–162

6   Podsiadlowski, Ph. et al. (2004). The rates of hypernovae and gamma-ray bursts: Implications for their progenitors. *Astrophysical Journal Letters* 607: L17; Benitez, N. et al. (2002). Evidence for nearby supernova explosions. *Phys. Rev. Lett.* 88(8): 081101

7   Ceballos, G., Ehrlich, P.R. and Dirzo, R. (2017). Biological annihilation via the ongoing sixth mass extinction signaled by vertebrate population losses and declines. *Proc. Natl Acad. Sci. USA* 25, 114(30): E6089–E6096

CHAPTER 20

1   Roser, M. (2016) Proof that life is getting better for humanity, in 5 charts. *Vox.* Available at: https://www.vox.com/the-big-idea/2016/12/23/14062168/history-global-conditions-charts-life-span-poverty; Burkeman, O. (2017). Is the world really better than ever? *The Guardian.* Available at: https://www.theguardian.com/news/2017/jul/28/is-the-world-really-better-than-ever-the-new-optimists

2   Goodson, J.L. and Seward, J.F. (2015). Measles 50 years after use of measles vaccine. *Infect. Dis. Clin. North Am.* Dec. 29(4): 725–743

3   Saperstein, A.M. (1991). The 'Long Peace' – result of a bipolar competitive world? *Journal of Conflict Resolution* March 35(1): 68–79

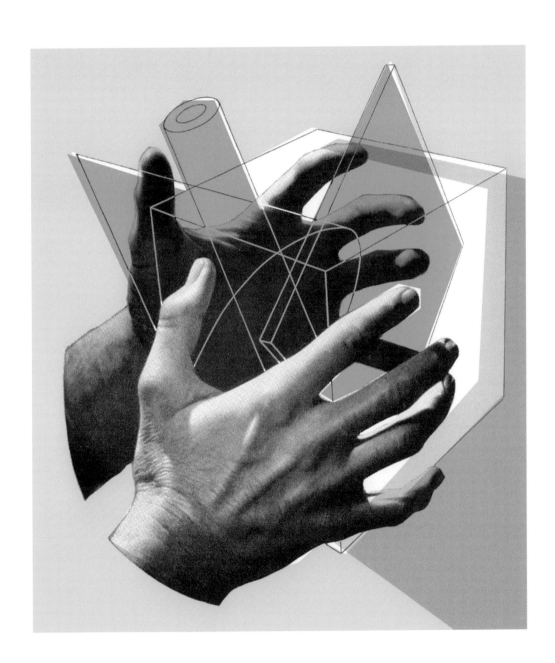